GARDENERS' QUESTIONS ANSWERED

NATIONAL GARDENING ASSOCIATION

GARDENERS' QUESTIONS ANSWERED

Expert advice and practical solutions for all your gardening problems

by the

National Gardening ASSOCIATION

with Dr. Stefan Buczacki

Villard Books   New York   1987

Conceived, edited and
designed by
Marshall Editions Limited
170 Piccadilly
London W1V 9DD

Editor: Gwen Rigby

Designer: Simon Blacker / Elgin Press

Research: Jazz Wilson

Research and writing: Andrea Chesman
                         Eve Pranis

Technical review: Don Ballin
                     Leonard Perry
                     Barbara Hughey

Production: Janice Storr

**Library of Congress Cataloging-in-Publication
Data**

Gardeners' questions answered.

   Includes index.
   1. Gardening.   2. Gardening—Great Britain.
I. National Gardening Association (U.S.)
SB453.G2775 1987   635   86-15759

ISBN 0-394-55843-X

Originated by
Reprocolor Llovet, S.A., Barcelona, Spain

Typeset by
MS Filmsetting Limited, Frome, Somerset, U.K.

Printed and bound by
Graficas Estella, S.A.,
Estella, Spain

D.L. NA-1446-1986

First American Edition

Contents

Introduction

Gardening is the number one outdoor leisure activity in the U.S. with, in 1985, over 84 percent of households involved in at least one form of gardening activity. This is the finding of the National Gardening Association, a national member-supported non-profit organization whose goal is to help people become successful gardeners. NGA responds in many ways to the need for gardening information, services and publications. Our monthly magazine, *National GARDENING*, addresses gardening problems with proven solutions from members across the country, and our skilled staff provides all members with a fulltime Gardening Answer Service. We publish many comprehensive books with information for both home and community gardeners.

The questions in this book reflect a broad range of commonly asked and increasingly popular questions about a diversity of gardening and landscaping activities. As we are well aware here at NGA, there is no one correct way to garden, and our answers are drawn on the varied experience of our own members, our horticultural staff and many experts. We have tried to provide you, the gardener, with an understanding of the "why" in addition to the "how" of each answer so that you can understand the reasoning or pros and cons behind various solutions. Cross references are provided for related questions and illustrations are included which either support points made in the text or cover additional information. Since garden catalogs and nurseries use both common and Latin botanical names for plants, we have included both, where appropriate.

One of the most controversial aspects of gardening relates to the use of synthetic chemical pesticides and herbicides. We advocate the use of "non-chemical" solutions to a problem whenever possible since they disrupt the ecological balance least. We do, however, refer to using "approved" pesticides or herbicides when necessary. Since regulations vary among states and recommended products change rapidly, we prefer not to make specific recommendations. We strongly recommend that you check with your county Extension office regarding approved products and that you carefully read and follow all manufacturer's instructions before using them.

We have designed this book to be a useful resource for gardeners in all parts of the country. Since there is such a diversity of climatic zones in the U.S., we have indicated hardiness zones for many specific plants. Hardiness zones are described and a hardiness zone map is provided in Chapter 1.

If you would like to learn more about the National Gardening Association, refer to page 153 in this book.

Happy gardening!

CHARLES SCOTT,
NGA President

SOILS, FERTILIZERS AND CLIMATE

The basic ingredients
of gardening

How much do I need to know about the type of soil I have in my garden?

The best way to learn about your soil is to work with it. But once you understand the properties of the basic categories of soil, determined by particle size — clay, silt, and sand — and the role organic matter plays, you will have a good basis for making decisions about improving your soil.

Soils are a blend of living, once-living, and never-living components. The living organisms include plants and animals, ranging from relatively enormous mammals (moles, for instance), to microscopic (eel-worms and algae, for example) and submicroscopic organisms that perform most of the chemical processes taking place in the soil.

The once-living component of the soil is humus — the remains, mostly of plants, that are broken down into their chemical constituents by the living micro-organisms. The never-living bulk of the soil is the mineral matter, derived from the breakdown of the underlying original rock. As rocks are weathered and broken down, the surface layers of the soil are affected by environmental conditions, such as wind and water, which can move them considerable distances. That's why the soil in your garden may differ drastically from the soil in a neighboring garden.

Variations in soil texture are important to gardeners since the relative proportions of different sized particles

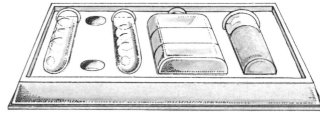

Soil testing kits generally contain some chemicals, containers for soil and a chart. To find the pH level, take a number of soil samples at a 6-in depth from various parts of the garden; mix the soil and chemicals as directed and match the color of the solutions with the chart.

LEVELS OF LIME REQUIRED BY SOIL TYPES

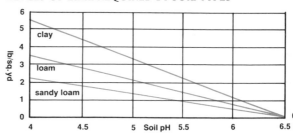

Most crops prefer soil with a pH of around 6.5; the pH can be raised by adding lime in the approximate amounts shown in the diagram, *above*.

See also:
Saline soil/clay soil pp12, 13
Soil preparation for planting:
bulbs p67;
lawns pp98–9;
trees p109

What exactly is topsoil?

Should I buy some to improve

my garden?

Topsoil is the upper layer of soil in which plants grow. Beneath it is a region known as subsoil, made of the less well-weathered parts of the underlying rock. Generally, subsoil lacks any humus content. The relative depths of topsoil and subsoil vary greatly from site to site, depending on how easily the underlying rock breaks down, on the factors that influence this breakdown, and the extent to which mineral matter has been added to or removed from the site, by wind and water for example.

Sometimes you will see topsoil advertised for sale, especially by builders who have removed it from a development site. Topsoil is rarely sold cheaply, and there is no guarantee as to the type or quality of the soil. Along with the topsoil, you may have to buy fertilizers and add organic matter to improve it. But if you have an eroded site, buying topsoil may represent the best, and certainly the quickest, way to produce a few small beds for growing plants satisfactorily.

Topsoil is generally sold by the cubic yard. This weighs between 1¼ and 1½ tons. If you want 12 inches of soil, a cubic yard will cover only 27 square feet.

can dramatically influence the amount of water, air, and nutrients that a soil can hold (see illustration). Almost all soils contain a combination of particle sizes. The "perfect" garden soil is called loam, and it, too, contains a mixture of the three.

You can get a good idea of the texture of your soil by an easy test. Shake up a soil sample with water in a tall glass container and allow it to settle out. The relative amounts of clay (at the top of the sediment), sand (at the bottom), and humus (mostly floating) will slowly become apparent.

Although you can't greatly influence the mineral content of your garden soil, you can increase the organic matter content by using bulky organic fertilizers (farmyard manure, for example) and growing green manure crops. If you have sandy soil, you will find that adding organic matter will increase the ability of the soil to retain water and nutrients. If you have clay soil, you will find that adding organic matter improves drainage and aeration.

What about pH? This is a measure of the acidity or alkalinity of the soil on a scale of 1 to 14. Values below 7 are acid and above 7 are alkaline. Garden soils rarely have pH values that lie below 4.5 (very acid) or rise above 8 (very alkaline).

It is important to provide your garden plants with a good pH range because some nutrients will become unavailable at extremes of pH. Also, some elements (aluminum, for example) can become toxic at certain pH levels. And soil bacteria function best in a certain range.

Most garden plants, and certainly most fruit and vegetables, prefer a pH just on the acid side of neutral (about 6.5), although a few lime-tolerant species prefer it slightly higher, and a fairly large group of attractive oranamentals (including rhododendrons and azaleas) prefers it more acid.

It is easy to test the pH of garden soil with a kit. If you find your soil is too acidic, you can add lime to raise the pH. You can lower the pH of alkaline soils by adding sulfur or, to a lesser extent, acidic organic matter such as peat moss (see page 16).

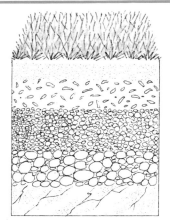

Several layers of increasingly degraded material lie between the topsoil and the bedrock. The best way to find out the composition of the soil in your garden is to dig a steep-sided hole about 3ft deep. This will reveal the various strata, show how deep the topsoil is and also how well the soil retains moisture.

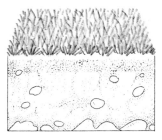

The Ideal soil for gardening is referred to as loam. It contains a mixture of sand, silt, clay and humus. The darker the soil, the more humus it contains, the richer and warmer it is, and the easier it is to work.

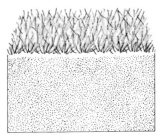

Sandy soils are light and well-drained but cannot hold onto water or nutrients well. Their ability to do this can be improved by incorporating quantities of organic matter.

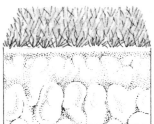

The fine particles that make up a clay soil stick together when wet and cause it to become waterlogged. Although rich in nutrients, clay must be lightened and aerated by the addition of organic matter and by digging and turning.

What is the best way to make compost from garden waste?

There are all sorts of ways to make compost. One common method is to create a 5-foot by 5-foot or larger pile of grass clippings, leaves, plant residues, kitchen scraps, and like material. The minimum size is needed to ensure the proper heating of the composting materials.

Most gardeners prefer to confine the compost to a bin — you can easily build or buy one. Efficient bins come in various styles, including wooden frames, interlocking branches, bricks, wire fencing, even plastic barrels. The best bins provide good ventilation, with no base or lid.

We don't recommend painting preservatives on your wooden bins. Chemicals toxic to plants and people may leach from the wood into your soil. Use hardwoods or pressure-treated wood instead or a copper napthenate type preservative which is generally considered safe with most types of soil and plant.

Whether you make a free-standing pile or use a bin, you should build the compost pile in a way that provides the ideal environment for the microorganisms in the soil that will decompose the organic matter. This ideal environment contains the proper proportions of carbon and nitrogen necessary for the microorganisms and allows for plenty of air circulation.

For good air circulation, start with a 5-inch to 6-inch layer of coarse matter, such as hay. Follow this with a layer of nonwoody organic material — garden wastes, kitchen scraps, grass clippings. Try to strike a balance between easily decomposed materials, such as grass, and coarser materials, such as hay. Shredded materials will decompose faster than coarser ones.

Avoid animal remains and diseased plants. Although the heat of a good pile can kill off garden diseases and weed seeds, it is best to avoid using plants affected with persistent diseases, such as clubroot. If possible, avoid throwing in the roots of perennial weeds, such as quackgrass, since they may survive the experience.

To assure adequate nitrogen for decomposition, include a small layer of manure, cottonseed meal, or other high-nitrogen material. Top that layer with some garden soil to add the necessary microorganisms for initiating the composting process. A dusting of lime can keep the pH at a level most suitable for microorganisms.

Repeat the layers until the pile is about 5 foot tall. Then make sure it is well watered (moist but not soaking) and keep it that way. If the weather is cool, or there isn't much sun, you can cover the pile with black plastic to increase the heat. Occasionally turning the pile will speed up the composting process.

Compost may be finished anywhere after several weeks to a year, depending on the weather, how frequently it was turned, and the size of the materials that went into it. Finished compost that has had ideal conditions generally will smell sweet, look uniformly dark and crumbly, and the center of the pile will no longer be hot.

Some gardeners prefer a method known as sheet composting; they simply spread their garden waste on the soil and turn it under, where it eventually composts.

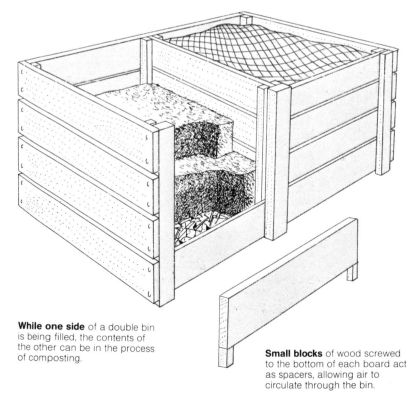

While one side of a double bin is being filled, the contents of the other can be in the process of composting.

Small blocks of wood screwed to the bottom of each board act as spacers, allowing air to circulate through the bin.

Ready-made compost bins of various sizes and shapes are ideal for the small garden with little waste.

See also:
Leaf mold p14
Potting mixes p15
Woodchips on path p28
Starting seedlings pp43, 142

 ## Can I use my compost to prepare potting mixes for seedlings?

If garden compost is well made, it shouldn't contain any pests or diseases, so it should be safe to incorporate it into your potting mix. But you can't be absolutely certain that every contaminating organism has been killed in the composting process and that it will not proliferate in the warm, moist conditions that are needed to germinate seeds.

To be perfectly safe, if you do want to use compost for starting seedlings, you will want to pasteurize the compost first. This can be done in small doses in a regular oven — though the heating soil will smell rather unpleasant. The heat will kill the harmful, but not most beneficial, organisms. Heat small amounts of the compost in an oven at 200 degrees F. for 30 minutes. Then mix the compost with other materials to form a balanced potting mix. You may want to pass the compost through a sieve or screen first to remove any coarse particles.

On the other hand, sterile potting soil mixes are relatively inexpensive and readily available. Certainly they can save you the trouble of pasteurizing the compost. And there are many other more valuable uses for your compost in the garden, such as using it in the soil mix for large potted plants, where the economy of using homemade compost makes particular sense.

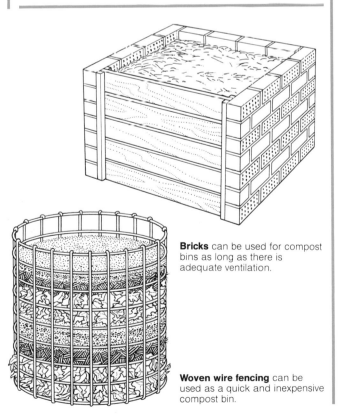

Bricks can be used for compost bins as long as there is adequate ventilation.

Woven wire fencing can be used as a quick and inexpensive compost bin.

 ## How does the fertilizer value of compost compare with that of animal manure?

There is little difference between well-made compost and well-rotted animal manure. Both contain approximately 0.5 percent of the major plant nutrients: nitrogen, phosphorus, and potassium, as well as many important trace elements — but relatively little when compared to concentrated commercial fertilizers. Their special value is as soil conditioners.

In most gardens, the amount of compost that can be made each season, is inadequate for all purposes. As a soil amendment, some supplement will be needed in the form of animal manure or other fertilizer.

 ## Can I add woody materials to my compost pile?

Adding some woody materials is fine, provided they are shredded first. There are some hand-operated shredders you can use, but they require a lot of hard work — especially if you are working with large amounts. There are also a number of power shredders on the market. They do a good job and are easy to operate, but they are expensive to buy. Remember, it's important to keep a good balance of woody and more easily decomposed materials, so don't overdo it!

 ## Does the presence of earthworms indicate good soil conditions?

Yes. Earthworms are fairly sensitive to soil conditions. They do best in well-drained soils with abundant organic matter as a food source. They are susceptible to drought, cold, waterlogging, and extremes of pH.

Earthworms improve soil conditions by mixing surface organic matter with underlying soil, improving aeration, improving water movement, and breaking down organic matter in their gut. Additionally, some theories suggest that this action increases the availability of nutrients from the organic matter.

11

Do organic and inorganic fertilizers perform differently in the soil?

Yes, but the difference arises mainly from the different forms in which the fertilizers are available.

Inorganic fertilizers are synthetically produced as liquids, wettable powders, granules, or pellets. These fertilizers are easily analyzed and we know exactly how much of which nutrients is available. Their nutrients tend to be immediately available to plants, an advantage where there is an immediate need to correct a nutrient imbalance. The disadvantage is that the nutrients are used up more quickly (unless you are using a slow-release formula), so more frequent applications are needed. Additionally, the nutrients in these are more easily lost through leaching. Inorganic fertilizers are generally more concentrated than organic fertilizers, so care must be taken not to overfertilize, which could harm the plants.

Organic fertilizers can come as bulky (raw) organic matter, (mineral) rock powders, dried granules, or liquids. Because they depend on soil microorganisms to break them down and make their nutrients more available, most organic fertilizers release their nutrients more slowly and steadily to plants. The disadvantage is that organic fertilizers cannot always act quickly enough, especially when the soil is cold and microbes are less active.

Another important difference between the two is that many forms of organic fertilizers work as soil conditioners and can help to improve the structure of the soil as well as to add nutrients.

Some people feel that, since plants take up chemicals in simple forms, the nature of the original source — organic or inorganic — is of little importance. However, there are theories to suggest that plants can absorb complex organic molecules, such as vitamins and antibiotics, and therefore benefit more from the use of organic fertilizers.

This remains a controversial issue — it's up to you to experiment and choose the best fertilizer for use in your garden.

What special problems exist on saline soils?

All soils normally contain salts. But in saline soils, soluble salts accumulate in the soil and cause movement of water out of the plant cells, which causes them to shrink and collapse. Plants growing on saline soils will be stunted, often with much darker green foilage.

Saline soils are found primarily in arid and semiarid climates where there is not enough rainfall to leach salts down through the soil, so they accumulate in the growing zone. Water also evaporates very quickly in such climates, which worsens the problem.

The most common way to deal with saline soils is to leach, or flush, the soils to carry dissolved salts through the root zones and below them.

If you have saline soils, it is a good idea to build garden beds with furrows in between the beds. Set the plants close to the edge of the beds. Water that is flushed through the furrows whenever it rains or when you irrigate will carry salts down through the root zones to below the center of the bed.

Mulching the plants to prevent rapid evaporation of water will also lessen the accumulation of salts.

Some vegetable crops, such as beets, kale, asparagus, and spinach, as well as many ornamentals, such as oleander, have a fairly high salt tolerance and can do well in saline soils.

One method of planting in a saline soil involves the use of raised planting beds and furrows. The crops are planted near the edges of the beds and, as the furrows are irrigated, salts are washed down through the root zone and accumulate below the center of the ridge, away from the roots.

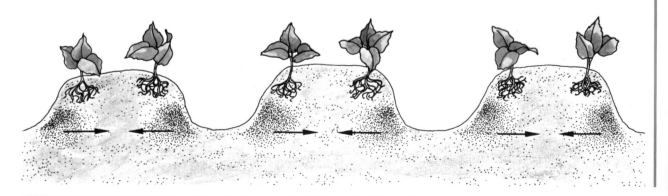

See also:
Compost making p10
Compost and manure as soil
    conditioners p11
Peat moss as a soil improver p15
Raised beds for better drainage p120

What are some ways to improve a heavy clay soil?

In clay soils, fine particles of mineral matter pack down very closely and prevent the free movement of water and air through the soil. As a result, water accumulates and doesn't drain, the soil remains cold, and there is little oxygen available for plant roots.

You can improve the structure of clay soils by several different methods, depending on the size of the area you are working to improve.

On a small scale, the best way to improve clay soil is to incorporate large quantities of organic matter while simultaneously working the soil with a spading fork to break up soil clods. It matters very little what form the organic matter takes — peat, farmyard manure, and compost are all effective — the choice really depends on local availability and cost. Whatever the material you use, dig it in as thoroughly and deeply as possible. The consolation for all that work is that when the exercise is done, you will also have improved the fertility of the soil.

Growing green manure crops with penetrating root systems, such as clover and alfalfa, can improve the structure of clay soils over time.

Avoid working the soil to the same depth all the time, especially with machinery, as this could cause a hardpan layer to form at this level beneath the surface of the soil. Building raised beds will improve drainage and allow the soil to warm more easily.

On a large scale, investing in the installation of a tile drainage system may be the best answer to a waterlogged and poorly drained site. Clay tiles and perforated plastic pipes are among the most commonly used drainpipe materials. Although this solution may be expensive and entail a great deal of hard work, it can result in a permanent improvement, which might not be possible any other way.

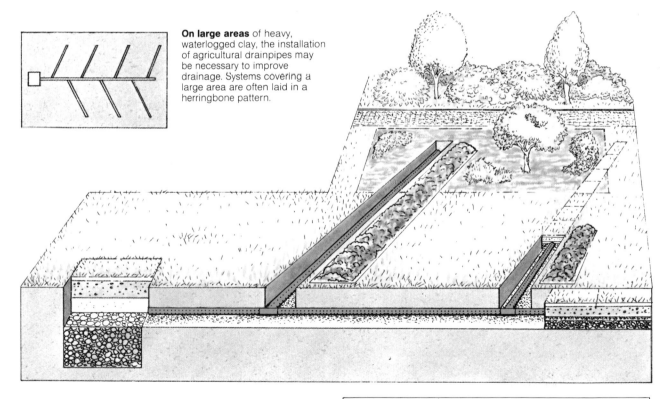

On large areas of heavy, waterlogged clay, the installation of agricultural drainpipes may be necessary to improve drainage. Systems covering a large area are often laid in a herringbone pattern.

If there is no natural outlet, such as a stream or pond, to which the water will be directed, an outlet can be created by breaking up an area of the impervious layer and filling it with loose, freely draining material.

Trenches for the drainpipes should be about 2ft deep and should slope gently down toward the outlet. It is important that you form proper, evenly sloped trenches before laying pipes. Generally, pipes should rest on and be surrounded by a layer of gravel or crushed stone.

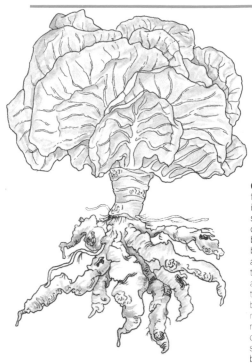

Clubroot is a fungal disease that is persistent in the soil and that causes the roots of brassicas to become distorted and swollen and the leaves to wilt and discolor. In time, the roots become a slimy mess from which millions of spores disperse into the soil to infect other brassicas.

 ## Once soil is contaminated with pests and diseases, is there any way of disinfecting it?

Most pest and disease organisms in the soil (with the exception of diseases like clubroot and onion white rot) can be controlled by using crop rotations and not growing susceptible crops in the same site for at least four to five years.

We don't recommend soil fumigants to the home gardener because they have only a localized and temporary effect, and because they can destroy beneficial plants and animals.

If you want to use contaminated garden soil for a potting mix, you should pasteurize the soil with heat to destroy most of the harmful organisms while leaving the humus and beneficial organisms intact. To do this, bake small quantities of the soil at 200 degrees F. for 30 minutes. Be prepared for the soil to release unpleasant odors as it heats.

 ## What is leaf mold and does it contain harmful pests and diseases?

Leaf mold is compost made solely from the leaves of deciduous trees and shrubs. It makes an excellent mulch. As a compost it is valuable for improving soil structure, as well as providing some nutrients.

Leaf mold does not contain harmful pests and diseases, although you will see all manner of fungi and microorganisms growing and insects crawling in it — just as in any type of compost.

Leaf mold composts more slowly in a compost pile than most other types of organic matter. Shredding the leaves will help it decompose more quickly, as will mixing it with grass clippings. Make sure that the leaves are kept wet, but not soggy, and add some soil to provide microorganisms. If you have large quantities of leaves, you may want to make separate compost piles just for them.

Don't use fresh leaf mold or composted leaf mold in a greenhouse or in a seedling container, where the combination of weak young plants and extra warmth could allow normally harmless soil organisms to cause damage to your seedlings.

Leaf mold can be made most quickly from small or shredded leaves. Any well-aerated bin can be used.

Fork leaf mold around roses, shrubs and fruit bushes as a mulch to protect the crowns in winter and to conserve moisture in the summer.

See also:
Starting seedlings pp 43, 142
Disinfecting containers p 43
Soil for hanging baskets p 50
Mulching p 57
Mulches p 122

What is best to use as a potting mix for seedlings and potting plants?

The ideal potting mix is light enough to be well drained and to allow for easy root growth but spongy enough to hold water and nutrients. If you tightly squeeze a handful of a moist well-made potting mix, it should crumble when you open your hand and tap the soil lightly.

Until the middle of this century, most potting mixes were soil-based, with materials such as sand, peat, and organic matter added in. More recently soil-less potting mixes have become popular, particularly with commercial growers. These soil-less mixes usually contain peat moss, vermiculite or perlite, and additional nutrients and conditioners.

Soil-based mixes contain a wider range of nutrients, on the whole, than soil-less mixes. Since these nutrients are in an organic slow-release form, a soil-based mix can provide a steady supply of nutrients, which means you need to give fewer supplemental feedings. You can make your own mixes fairly inexpensively or you can buy a premade soil mix.

A disadvantage to soil-based mixes is that they are heavy and much less convenient to handle. Also, they are not necessarily sterile, so the soil may contain diseases and weed seeds.

Soil-less mixes are more easily standardized in terms of texture and nutrients. They are lighter and are always free of pest and disease organisms.

Before you make your decision about a potting mix, consider what kind of soil your plants will do best in. When large plants in big pots are considered, for instance, the greater weight of the soil-based mixes is an important factor. Although a large pot filled with a soil mix may be heavy and inconvenient to move, there is less chance it will be knocked over accidentally.

Below are sample "recipes" for both a soil-less and soil-based potting mix.

Soil-less mix	Soil-based mix
2 parts peat moss	1–2 parts garden loam
1 part vermiculite	(larger amount for a heavier mix)
1 part perlite	1 part peat moss
1 tablespoon ground limestone/gallon	1 part coarse sand
2 tablespoons 20% superphosphate/gallon	4 tsp ground limestone/gallon
1 teaspoon 5–10–5 fertilizer/gallon	4 tsp 20% superphosphate or bonemeal/gallon

What is peat moss and when should it be used in the garden?

Peat moss is organic debris, primarily derived from sphagnum mosses, that has partially decomposed under waterlogged conditions. Horticultural peat moss tends to be fairly coarse and spongy, and light in comparison to its bulk. It has a low pH, 3.5 to 5.

Added to soil, peat moss will improve the ability of the soil to hold water. It will also lower the pH of the soil, or make it more acidic. Peat moss is often used in seedling and potting mixes. Its main drawback is that it has almost no nutritional value for plants.

Since peat moss is relatively expensive, we think that it is best used as a soil amendment only, in small areas that need improvement in soil structure or to be acidified for certain plants.

Peat moss can be very valuable in the garden as a mulch since it acts to slow down the evaporation of water. It is also an aesthetically pleasing material and is often used as a mulch for ornamentals.

The most convenient way to buy peat, if more than a small amount is needed, is in bales. In bales, the peat has been compressed and much of the water has been squeezed out, so the bales are lighter than bags and easier to transport.

15

How can I achieve the conditions that acid-loving plants, like blueberries and rhododendrons, need?

Plants that are acid-loving will generally thrive in a soil pH of 4.5 to 6.0. Increasing the acidity of the soil is not easy, but it is necessary if you want to be successful in raising blueberries and some of the most beautiful flowering shrubs, including rhododendrons, azaleas, and camellias.

Highbush blueberries
(Vaccinium corymbosum) are tall, vigorous growers (6–12ft) with abundant fruit production and bright autumn color.

In alkaline soils, these plants are unable to take up many of their required nutrients. In particular, they are unable to take up iron, which results in yellowed foliage and an inability to manufacture essential foodstuffs efficiently.

You can increase the acidity of soil by adding aluminum sulfate or agricultural sulfur. Although agricultural sulfur acts slowly and must be applied a year in advance of planting, we recommend its use because aluminum sulfate can cause a toxic build-up of aluminum in the soil. Sometimes adding additional iron in a usable form, such as ferrous sulfate, in the beginning of the growing season can be beneficial to these acid-loving types of plant.

If you have a relatively small area and it does not need a drastic pH change, you can incorporate peat moss, oak leaf mold, or sawdust to lower the pH. Remember, though, the decomposition of sawdust will tie up nitrogen in the soil, so add extra nitrogen at the same time.

If you are aiming for only a slight pH change, mulching with an acid mulch (pine needles, sawdust, peat moss) may be all that is needed.

Many gardeners prefer to provide a microenvironment for small acid-loving plants by building a small bed edged with rocks or logs and filling it with a peat and soil mix.

Some plants, such as *Erica carnea* (spring heath), a low-growing heather, have a fairly wide range of adaptability and can be grown in soils that are somewhat less acidic.

Some plants, such as spring heath, *Erica carnea*, are tolerant of somewhat higher pH levels. It grows about 12in tall and provides good ground cover. Foliage color ranges from yellow or bronze to light green, depending on the variety. Bushes are covered with small white, pink or red flowers from January to May, depending on the climate.

Compact, evergreen *Rhododendron yakushimanum* is ideal for growing in a tub or raised bed of acid soil in partial shade. It forms a rounded bush up to 3ft high, with a spread of 24–36in. Clusters of pink buds, paling to white as they open, appear in late spring.

See also:
Acid soils p8
Fertilizing lawns p102
Fertilizers and vegetables p121
Sidedressing vegetables p128

Heathers, camellias, dwarf conifers, rhododendrons and other plants that prefer acid soil can grow satisfactorily in a specially prepared raised bed containing a large proportion of peat moss or acidic soil.

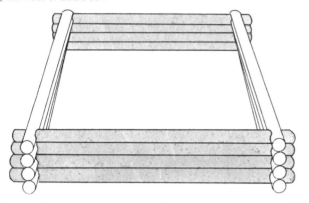

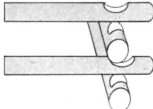

Railroad ties or treated wooden boards can be interlocked to form a sturdy bed. Put stones in the bottom for drainage before filling with soil.

 ## Do I need special fertilizers for each type of plant, or will a general mix do?

This is one of those areas where the distinction between what you should do and what you can get away with is fairly clearly defined. Although most gardening books suggest that your garden shed should bulge at the seams with specific fertilizer mixtures for each and every garden task, many gardeners find they can liberally and successfully use a general purpose fertilizer for a whole range of different purposes.

The numbers on a bag of commercial fertilizer refer to the relative percentage of nitrogen, phosphate, and potash. A fertilizer with an analysis of 5–10–5 (5 percent nitrogen, 10 percent phosphate, 5 percent potash) is a good balanced, all-purpose fertilizer that can be used on all crops, especially if you supplement it by incorporating organic matter into the soil. As a result of the constant supply of a balanced mix of nutrients from the organic matter, and the additional boost from the concentrated fertilizer at specific times, your plants will probably thrive.

If you apply a sufficient amount of a balanced fertilizer to meet the plants' need for nitrogen, it is likely there will be enough phosphorus and potash. In some instances, however, the particular need plants have for certain nutrients — for example, phosphorus to aid root development — means that a fertilizer containing proportionately more of that substance is required.

Here are some instances where a different fertilizer might be especially desirable.

☐ Young plants. Extra phosphorus is required by newly planted herbaceous perennials, trees, shrubs, and vegetable seedlings to assure good root development. You can apply a fertilizer such as 6–18–6 or sterilized bonemeal to satisfy this need. Provide extra phosphorus later for fruiting and flowering plants.

☐ Vegetables and fruits. As a general rule, we recommend applying the general, all-purpose 5–10–10 fertilizer or its equivalent in an organic mixture.

☐ Lawns. For spring and fall applications, we recommend a fertilizer that contains a high proportion of nitrogen.

☐ Trees and shrubs. Young trees and shrubs do best with a fertilizer high in phosphorus. Unless there is a soil deficiency, older plants will not need repeated fertilizing. We do recommend, however, that you maintain an organic mulch of leaf mold or compost.

 ## What is the meaning of the terms trace element or micronutrient?

The two terms mean the same thing: a chemical element required by plants in exceedingly small quantities and essential for healthy plant development. Normally, plants receive all the trace elements they need from the soil, particularly if organic matter is continually applied. Some inorganic fertilizers also supply micronutrients, although it is not always indicated on the label. Occasionally an element, such as boron or molybdenum, is deficient; if so it can be supplied in a fertilizer form.

How do liquid fertilizers differ from granular ones?

Liquid fertilizers are available either as a liquid concentrate or wettable crystals or powder, all of which are mixed with water before being applied. They can be organic (fish emulsion) or synthetically based.

Because nutrients are taken into plants in solution, in this way they are immediately available to the plant. However, they are quickly used or leached out of the soil and must be reapplied regularly. They should not be applied before planting or sowing since most of the nutrients will be washed from the soil before the plants have a chance to use them.

Additionally, because liquid fertilizers are so concentrated, there is more danger of overapplying and harming the plants, so use according to label directions.

Most of the granular fertilizers do not release their nutrients until they are wet. Some come in slow-release forms and, like most of the dry forms of organic fertilizers, are activated by such conditions as temperature, moisture and microbial activity. Although the rate of nutrient release is not always constant, and slow-release granulated fertilizers tend to be expensive, they can reduce the frequency of feeding.

Liquid fertilizers are diluted and watered at the base of plants or sprayed on the leaves. Granular fertilizers can be incorporated into the soil before planting or be used to sidedress the plants.

When a plant is listed as being hardy to a particular zone, what does it mean?

In the broadest sense, it means that the plant has the ability to survive the year-round climatic condition of a region. Although it more commonly refers to the plant's ability to survive the winter, a plant's hardiness also relates to other factors — including water needs, ability to withstand exposure to wind or sun, the length of the frost-free season, and so on. Another important factor has to do with the timing of the low temperatures. If the warm temperatures come in late winter and early spring and are followed by more very cold temperatures, the plant's growth may be prematurely stimulated.

Since it is impossible to take into account all of these factors, most hardiness maps are based solely on average annual minimum temperatures. You can use these zones as a general planning guide, but be aware that there are many minute climatic changes within each zone, especially where there are changes in altitude. It is probably worth experimenting with plants that are of borderline hardiness for your area since different strains and different cultural practices can all affect plants' hardiness.

In this book, when a zone is listed, it refers to the coldest zone in which a species is hardy.

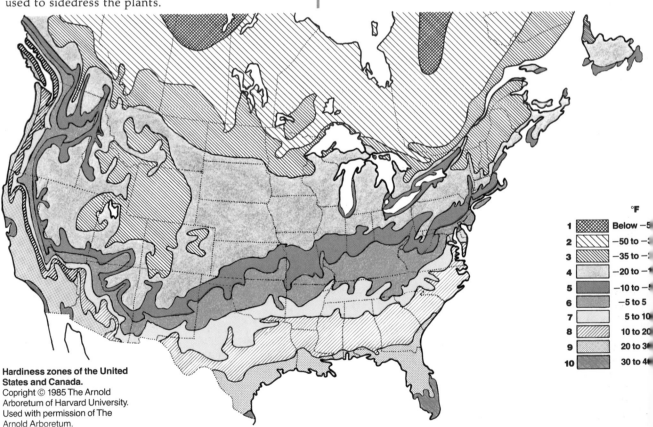

Hardiness zones of the United States and Canada.
Copright © 1985 The Arnold Arboretum of Harvard University. Used with permission of The Arnold Arboretum.

°F
1 Below −5
2 −50 to −3
3 −35 to −2
4 −20 to −1
5 −10 to −5
6 −5 to 5
7 5 to 10
8 10 to 20
9 20 to 30
10 30 to 40

See also:
Mulching p57
Lifting bulbs annually p69
Winter protection for shrubs p87
Winter protection for roses p97
Vegetables and frost p146

Is it necessary to protect certain plants by bringing them inside for the winter?

Plants are commonly classified as hardy, half-hardy, and tender. A hardy plant is one that will survive all year round in most areas, including the coldest of our climatic zones. A half-hardy plant will survive year-round in any of the moderate and warmest zones. A tender plant will survive outdoors year-round only in the very hottest zones. You may be able to grow half-hardy and tender plants in cooler zones, but you will probably have to bring them indoors for the winter.

Check with the nursery or seed company that sold you the plants, or consult any of the standard reference books regarding the hardiness of your plants.

Autumn frosts will blacken and kill the foliage of most half-hardy plants, such as dahlias and gladiolas. This is the time for you to lift tubers and corms and store them in a frost-free place for the winter.

If you want to experiment with overwintering a plant that is of borderline hardiness for your zone, cover the soil where it is growing with a protective mulch of peat or leaves or straw held down with a spadeful of soil. Even in quite northerly areas, sheltered gardens or sheltered corners in more exposed gardens may permit you to leave at least some nonhardy plants outdoors.

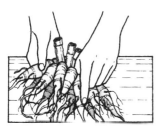

Tubers, such as those of dahlias, should be lifted carefully with a fork as soon as frost blackens and kills the foliage.

Trim the stems back to a few inches and dry the tubers upside down.

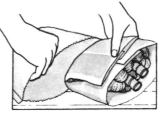

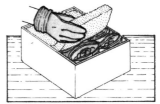

Tubers can be wrapped in paper, put into a box and stored in a cool (35–55°F.) dry, dark place for the winter.

What is the best way to protect outdoor overwintering plants?

If you live in an area with cold winters, many of your perennials will benefit from some type of protection from the excessively cold temperatures that come along with rapid temperature drops, from excessive winds, from alternate freezing and thawing, and from warm temperatures, which can encourage a plant to break out of dormancy too early.

In areas where a permanent blanket of snow falls before a rapid temperature drop, the snow will insulate the ground and help to keep temperatures even. This may be all the protection necessary.

In other areas, mulching plants in the fall with straw, corn stalks, evergreen branches, or dry leaves can provide effective insulation. Don't put the mulch on too early; let the ground freeze an inch or two first. This will allow plants to harden-off to lowering temperatures and give them adequate time to develop root reserves. Also, applying the mulch late discourages rodents from burrowing around the roots.

In some areas, you can hill soil around shrubs, such as roses, to protect the crowns from critically cold temperatures. Evergreens of borderline hardiness can be protected from winter sun and wind by making a shelter with pine branches or wrapping them with burlap.

Before you plant your garden, think about the site and how it will be affected by winter conditions. For example, hollows will collect cold air in winter and become frost pockets; these areas will need extra protection and tender plants should not be put in such areas. South-facing slopes are warmer, although this means plants could be stimulated to grow during a warm spell only to be damaged by subsequent freezing temperatures. This is why the best place for a tender plant may, contrary to expectation, in some cases be against the north side of a building.

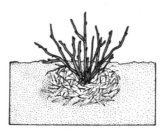

Insulating material like straw, packed around the crowns and between the stems of many herbaceous perennials and shrubs, can often be adequate winter protection.

LANDSCAPE PLANNING

The essentials
of design

Are there some sites or climates where a garden is impossible?

Definitely not! If you live on top of an exposed mountain, in the middle of a forest clearing, or out in the desert, gardening may *seem* pretty near impossible. But healthy gardens can and do exist in all these places.

If you have recently moved from a temperate area to one of climatic or geographic extremes, you are probably at a loss as to how to begin a garden — or even whether to attempt it. But, look around and you will see wild plants thriving. If nature can do it, so can you.

Where can I learn about garden and landscape design?

There are plenty of books and publications on garden and landscape design; the bibliography in the back of this book offers some suggestions.

Your local country Extension agent is an excellent source of information and publications. And if you are lucky enough to live near a botanical garden or an arboretum, you are sure to find useful publications and information there.

If you would like to study the subject a little more intensively, look into taking a course on landscaping or garden design at your local university or community college. Also, public botanical gardens and arboretums often offer classes for adults.

See also:
Saline soils/clay soils pp12–13
Landscape planning p22
Plants for boggy areas p41
Perennials for poor, shady sites p56
Shrubs for a shady site p79

Start by looking carefully at the types of wild plants that are obviously thriving. The cultivated forms of these plants or related but more desirable species can form the basis for your garden.

Now look closely at the particular features that make your situation so difficult. Is it the inadequacy of the soil, the length of the growing season, extremes of temperature, excess or lack of water, the wind? What can you do to lessen the influence of any of these factors or overcome the difficulties these factors represent?

As you plan your garden, be aware that site design and orientation are very important. You may want to construct or plant a windbreak. If you live on a slope, you will want to plant across the slope to avoid run-off and soil loss. Avoid planting in potential frost pockets. If your growing season is particularly short or particularly dry and hot, you may want to use plants that are naturally adapted to the climate or specifically bred for success in your area.

Consider drastic soil improvement as the first step in developing your garden. This could include extensive cover cropping, incorporating quantities of organic matter, or bringing in topsoil.

In an area of soil or climatic extremes it probably will not be practical, and may not even be possible, to grow a full range of garden plants. But working within the limitations of your site may make gardening even more rewarding for you.

A desert or mountaintop site might seem unsuitable for plant life, but carefully selected plants and thoughtful site preparation can result in thriving gardens in even these unlikely conditions.

Is it better to design your own landscape or to obtain professional help?

Most people who have some gardening experience are capable of planning a landscape of sorts. But few amateur gardeners have the combination of horticultural expertise, experience, plantsmanship, and artistic vision to make the most of a given site — and it is that ability to achieve more than the obvious that sets the professional garden designer apart from the experienced gardener.

Really, the question you should ask yourself is what are your expectations for your site and how far are you prepared to go to meet those expectations. Consulting a professional in no way discredits your own gardening ability. A good designer will always ask for your ideas and will be pleased to incorporate them into the final plan wherever this is possible.

Professional design and landscaping services do not come cheaply. However, you can obtain professional services at various levels. For example, you could ask a designer for a consultation visit, where the designer will simply walk through your site and discuss possible areas of improvement. Or you can hire a designer to come up with a set of drawings and plant lists. Alternatively you can employ a landscaping firm that will provide complete design, planting, and construction services. Naturally, this latter option will be the most expensive.

Before hiring a landscaper, ask for references. A good designer will always be happy to show you examples of his or her work. You should also obtain a complete estimate for the job, particularly when landscape construction is involved.

If in the end you decide you cannot afford professional help, or if you really want to do all the planning and planting yourself, remember that there are several excellent books and magazines on landscape garden design available for consultation.

How should I go about making a landscape plan for my new home?

Whether your new home is an old established homesite or a new building on an undeveloped lot, the initial planning stages will be very similar.

Start by making a reasonable "dream list" of all the features you would like to have on your site. Do you want an herb garden, a greenhouse, a garden shed? Do you want to plant roses, rhododendrons, or no shrubs at all? Are there particular types of tree that you have always wanted if only you had the space? Do you want to attract birds to your site? Include a swimming pool? Build a playground for the children? Once you have drawn up this basic list, give some thought to how much time you have to devote to maintaining your landscape and approximately how much money you will be able to spend on it — initially and over the next five years.

The next step is to look at your land from the highest vantage point you can find (usually this will be an upstairs window) and, with pad in hand, roughly sketch out the outline of the site. Then begin to fill in the details with the features you want to see in your plan.

No matter that you cannot draw; everyone can produce a sketch that they themselves can understand. As you fill in the details, you may come to the point where you realize that there is not enough room for everything you want. If that is the case, you can begin to rework your plan more realistically.

As you sketch out your plan, a number of questions will probably arise, and you will have to do some more detailed investigating (including referring to other parts of this book for guidance). What is the best position for a greenhouse? Which way does the prevailing wind blow, and which of the planned features is most likely to be affected by this?

Look carefully at the topography and drainage on the site. Can you plan around these existing conditions or will you have to invest in making drastic alterations? What type of soil do you have? Is it appropriate for growing the plantings you desire? Are there any existing trees and shrubs that you will want to incorporate into your plan?

Only when you have a fairly clear idea of what you want should you act. Begin your planting with the largest and most slow-growing items — the trees — followed by shrubs and hedging. Having established the framework of the garden, you can gradually move on to create a lawn and, eventually, flower and herb beds and a vegetable garden.

Transfer your design to graph paper when you are satisfied with your bird's-eye-view sketch, taking care to get the distance and dimensions of various features accurate. Bear in mind any slope of the land and don't crowd trees and shrubs, they may grow large quite quickly.

Try to imagine how your design will look when you are standing in the garden; remember any curve drawn on paper will be exaggerated in reality. Stick wooden pegs into the ground or lay a hose out to show the shape and position of beds, paths and so on.

See also:
Sizes of trees p24
Minimal attention landscape p26
Rock gardens p30
Water gardens pp32–3
Herbaceous perennial beds p54

Herb gardens p60
Shrubs, climbers, ground covers p78
Trees for small gardens pp112–13
Vegetables for a limited space p121
Espalier and cordon fruit trees pp132–3
Greenhouse considerations p140

? What is the best course of action when taking over an established site?

Do nothing immediately! That is the best advice we can give you. Drastic alterations made within weeks, or even days, of moving to a new site may be regretted in years to come. This applies especially to the removal of large trees and shrubs, for once gone, they cannot be replaced, and new stock will take many years to reach significant proportions.

Your first reaction on seeing a huge tree close to the house or shading a large area of the garden may be to decide it must go, either because it will damage the foundations of the house or because nothing else will grow on a sizable part of the yard. Neither of these things need be true. Many types of tree can grow quite happily and in close harmony with a building without posing any threat to the structure.

The effect of large plants on their neighbors depends greatly on the type of plant. Is it deep or surface rooting, evergreen or deciduous, and which side of the garden does it shade, for example? Above all else, therefore, wait for at least one season before removing anything large and woody.

It is a good idea to wait at least one growing season before making any major changes whatsoever. If you make your move in the winter, you may find it hard to identify all the leafless shrubs. And until you have lived through a spring, there is no telling what bulbous treasures the apparently barren earth may yield.

These cautions aside, the question remains of what areas of the original landscape plan to conserve and what areas to alter. So look at the existing design to see if it works as well as it should.

Is the herb garden close to the kitchen? Is the compost pile convenient for depositing household waste, yet screened from view? Are the perennial beds or small fruit plantings overgrown with tenacious weeds or in an unhealthy condition? In some cases, it is better to start fresh than to battle with an unhealthy patch.

Did the previous owner plan appropriately with regard to topography, drainage, and wind? Are the early spring-flowering shrubs at the far end of the yard where no one goes in muddy weather? Are the scented plants in positions where someone will appreciate the scent — close to a seat, a door, or a window? Have some of the shrubs, planted ten or twenty years ago, outgrown their original positions to the detriment of their neighbors?

Is there any way you can find out what the past cropping, fertilizing, and pest and disease control practices have been in the vegetable garden? If you can obtain this information, it can influence your decision to maintain the present vegetable patch or to start over at a new site.

If the overall design of the lot pleases you, but the plantings and gardens have not been well maintained,

A large tree close to the house can be an asset, even though, if they are shallow, the roots will deplete the soil for a distance and the branches will cast their shadow widely. The area beneath can provide a cool area for sitting or for growing plants such as ferns, some types of geraniums, or hostas which tolerate shade. Farther out, plants that prefer partial shade can be planted.

you may want to start on a restoration program.

Fruit trees can be pruned severely to restore their productivity. Spread out a drastic pruning program over the course of three years, pruning away only the dead branches during the first year and about a third of the extra branches each year after that. Balance the nutrition by removing all competitive weeds and by applying a moisture-retaining mulch and appropriate fertilizer (for example 15 pounds of 5–10–10 per large tree) spread under the drip line. Although applying pest and disease controls, fertilizing, and pruning can restore many fruit trees, some diseases, such as severe canker, cannot be cured; in some cases a neglected and diseased tree should be removed and burned.

Perennial beds of flowers, herbs, and vegetables should be weeded and heavily mulched. At the beginning of the growing season, apply a complete fertilizer. If the perennials are badly diseased or infested, check with an expert before you do too much renovation. Some diseases may not be curable. Spring is the best time to divide plants that have overexpanded in the perennial flower and herb beds.

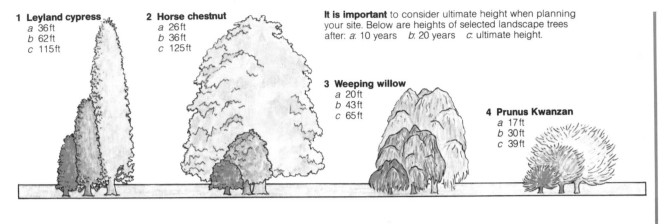

It is important to consider ultimate height when planning your site. Below are heights of selected landscape trees after: *a:* 10 years   *b:* 20 years   *c:* ultimate height.

1 **Leyland cypress**
a 36 ft
b 62 ft
c 115 ft

2 **Horse chestnut**
a 26 ft
b 36 ft
c 125 ft

3 **Weeping willow**
a 20 ft
b 43 ft
c 65 ft

4 **Prunus Kwanzan**
a 17 ft
b 30 ft
c 39 ft

5 **Bay**
a 13 ft
b 23 ft
c 59 ft

6 **Holly**
a 13 ft
b 20 ft
c 65 ft

7 **Paper bark maple**
a 10 ft
b 17 ft
c 39 ft

8 **Crab apple**
a 10 ft
b 13 ft
c 23 ft

9 **Royal azalea**
a 5 ft
b 10 ft
c 15 ft

Are there certain plants I might want to avoid in a new site?

When you select plants for a new site, your choices will be limited by your own likes and dislikes, the particular attributes of the site (whether it is rocky or shady, for example), and the climate. Beyond that there are a few other factors to keep in mind as you plan a landscape you will live with for many, many years.

Size It is pretty obvious that every plant you buy will grow larger when it is established. What is important to know is precisely how much larger, especially if the plant is a tree or shrub that will be an important and long-term feature of your garden.

Also, consider how fast the plant will grow. Will it reach its full height and spread in ten years or twenty years? How will this affect your plan? The illustration above shows how much some popular trees bought at a height of about 2 feet can grow. The Kwanzan cherry that seems so appealing in front of the house for a few years after planting will, quite possibly, be shading your bedroom windows within ten; and a weeping willow could be darkening the entire front garden after twenty. Better choices might be a crab apple or Japanese maple, *Acer palmatum.*

Don't forget to consider the ultimate size of herbaceous plants, especially when you are making a garden border. However, mistakes here are fairly easily corrected. It is a simple matter to dig up the offending plant and move it to a more suitable location.

Invasiveness Some plants, especially some herbaceous perennials, may not outgrow their welcome in terms of height or in the spread of individual plants. Nonetheless, they may reproduce too rapidly, either through the production of seeds or by rhizomes, runners, far-reaching roots or tiny bulbs, called bulbils. Such invasiveness is a feature of many of the most successful weeds, including quackgrass and nettles, but several choice garden plants are quite capable of turning on their owners in this way, too.

For this reason, carefully consider the invasive characteristics of such plants as bamboos and other ornamental grasses, horseradish, mints, comfrey, some of the St John's worts, some of the creeping campanulas, and bishop's weed, *Aegopodium podagraria,* when planting your site. Some of these plants are useful as ground covers, but become problematic when established among other plants.

Social undesirability Many plants have features that are downright undesirable. For example, silver birches, which are often hosts to aphids, are known to drip honeydew on people, cars, and garden furniture. Other undesirable traits include the messy yearly shedding of berries; mulberries are infamous for this.

Shrubs, like firethorn, *Pyracantha coccinea,* can have physically dangerous thorns or spines. Black walnuts exude substances that can have the effect of inhibiting the growth of some other species.

Other plants, such as yew, laburnum, privet, and some spurges, have poisonous parts, a problem in gardens where children will play. Many other plants, too, may be poisonous to animals or to humans if eaten in large quantities or will produce allergic reactions in some people when handled.

See also:
Containing invasive bamboo p24
Rose hedges p91
Screen for windy conditions p113
Edible hedges p114
Clipping hedges p116

Should I consider a windbreak for my landscape?

A windbreak consists of a screen of trees or shrubs or a wall or fence, usually set at right angles to the prevailing wind. It is constructed to lessen the wind's drying and cooling effect on vegetation, to lessen the physical impact of strong winds on plants, and to reduce erosion caused by wind. Appropriately placed, windbreaks can cut home heating costs and create areas of gentle breezes for comfortable sitting within the garden.

Generally, to be most effective, windbreaks should not be solid. Solid walls create an area of turbulence just behind the wall, whereas hedges and trees allow for a extensive area of gentle moving air. The sparser the planting, the more wind gets through, but the area of gentle breezes extends further. Windbreaks have an effect up to 10 to 15 times the height of the trees.

Which makes a better boundary a fence, wall, or hedge?

The best boundary for your garden depends on three broad areas of consideration: finances, aesthetics, and function. Look at the table below to see how the three types of boundaries compare.

At the same time, consider these questions. Is part of the function of the boundary to act as a barrier to animals? Hedges won't keep out woodchucks, and low fences won't discourage deer. Should your boundary also serve as a windbreak? Do you want to be able to grow climbing plants along the boundary?

If you are thinking of establishing a hedge but are worried about the length of time it will take to fill in, consider erecting a temporary fence that can be moved when the hedge is grown.

	Cost	Appearance	Practicality
Fences	Relatively inexpensive	Can be monotonous; good support for climbing plants; Chain-link are less aesthetic than wood	Quick to erect; take little space; can be somewhat unstable in high winds; wood fences tend to rot so may need periodic retreating and replacement
Hedges	Moderately expensive	Attractive, particularly flowering types; provide cover for wildlife; limited support for climbing plants; softens boundary	Slow to establish; take a lot of space; need clipping; can be good windbreaks; deciduous types less effective in winter
Walls:	Initially expensive	Attractive; excellent support for climbing plants; exclusive barrier	Fairly quick to establish; sturdy; need little maintenance; can create wind eddies

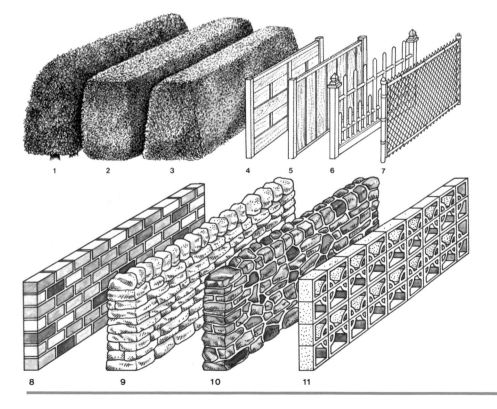

Although deciduous, beech, **1**, retains its dead leaves so long that it remains an effective screen in winter. Formal hedges of yew, **2**, and privet, **3**, are evergreen but need clipping to keep their shape and prevent them from becoming leggy. Wooden fences, **4**, **5**, **6**, of many different types take up far less room. Chain link fences, **7**, are easily installed, durable and relatively inexpensive, but much less aesthetic. Along with the wooden types, they allow air to circulate and sun to reach shrubs and climbers.

Brick walls, 8, have good clean lines and can be solid or with open geometric designs. Building drystone walls (closely packed stones with no mortar), **9**, calls for perserverance and skill, a job for the expert. Mortared walls, **10**, may be more easily mastered. Concrete comes into its own with the use of patterned blocks, **11**, that offer a good surface for plants to cling to and grow through.

Is it possible to landscape a site so that it requires only minimal attention?

Most people think that small is beautiful when it comes to saving time and energy on landscaping. While this is true to a certain extent, any garden can be planned for a minimum of maintenance, regardless of size.

The first step is to evaluate your land and its features (sun, shade, drainage, topography) so that you can work with, rather than against, those limitations. For example, plan to plant species that prefer wet areas in those poorly drained spots.

In many cases, putting in a big effort early on can pave the way for minimum attention down the road. Prepare your soil well in order to cut down on the need for fertilizing and caring for unhealthy plants later. Do a thorough job initially of clearing weeds, particularly when planting perennial beds. Mulch your plantings to cut down on the need for watering and weeding.

On a small site, a good-sized area can be made into a paved or graveled courtyard. With a large site, a lawn might dominate. Although lawns need mowing, they are certainly easier to care for than annual or perennial flower beds. The amount of mowing can be kept to a minimum by allowing the grass to grow long and just mowing pathways when possible. Consider also the value of plants such as ajuga, pachysandra, or vinca — hardy, maintenance-free ground covers — as alternatives to grass. A wildflower meadow is another option.

Within unmown grass, daffodils and other bulbs can be planted in drifts to naturalize and provide attractive early season color, while trees and shrubs not in need of careful annual pruning can be planted extensively. Those that grow fairly rapidly and supply good ground cover are especially valuable, and the enormous range of low-growing conifers merits serious consideration. Although many deciduous trees can thrive with a minimal amount of care, evergreen trees and shrubs tend to require less pruning than deciduous, are generally less susceptible to pests and diseases, can double as effective windbreaks, provide thick shade for weed suppression, provide year-round interest, and don't shed leaves that need to be raked.

Do not rule out roses for attractive color; but avoid the large or cluster-flowered modern varieties. Choose "old-fashioned" shrub roses, many of which will grow large. They need the bare minimum of pruning and can, by careful choice of varieties, be selected to bloom right through the season.

Clothe walls and fences with shrubs and climbers that do not need much attention to annual pruning — some of the vigorous clematis, such as *C. montana*, although ideally needing some pruning after flowering, can be allowed fairly free rein in unrestricted areas.

For the vegetable garden, plant in blocks or wide beds to allow for closer plantings, which will provide more weed-suppressing shade, allow higher yields, and

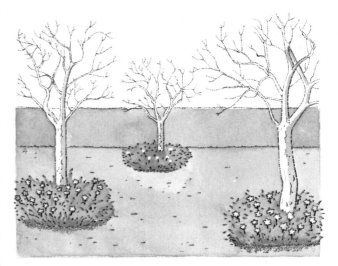

Planting bulbs for naturalizing in grass and around trees is an easy way of providing early color to your site.

Confine plantings to the edges of your site; lawns need less maintenance than beds. Plant good ground covers, such as low growing vinca, and use mulches to keep down weeds and hold moisture.

provide protection from the elements. Set out larger plants and do a minimum of direct seeding as that will increase your time investment. Mulching, again, will cut back on the need to weed and water.

In some areas, setting up a drip irrigation system could be an invaluable time-saver.

Before planning your labor-saving garden, ask yourself not only how much time you can spare throughout the season but also how that time is distributed between the days, weeks and months of the year.

See also:
Paved areas pp28–9
Water plants on the porch p32
Herbaceous perennial beds pp54–5
Bulbs to naturalize p68
Shrubs for weed suppression p87

Mulching p57
Mulches p122
Wide row and raised beds p120
Citrus in containers p132

Can a small site be designed so that it seems larger than it really is?

The art of creating an illusion is very much a part of landscape design and planning. When it comes to making a small site appear larger and less cramped than it is, there are a number of design principles you can use.

☐ Remember that you recognize a large area by your ability to see a long way. Avoid planting large trees and shrubs so that it is impossible to see farther than a few yards and impossible, therefore, to judge how much space lies beyond them.

☐ Fill as little as possible of the space with plants, while giving the impression that there are a great many of them. One way of doing this is to keep the center of the garden open and to confine most of the planting to the periphery.

☐ Create interest with the available plantings. Spectacular and pleasing features will draw attention away from size. Try to draw attention away from the boundaries of your garden by using plants of appropriate sizes.

☐ If there is an open space, such as fields and woods, beyond your garden, arrange your planting so that, although the boundary is obscured, the *vista* appears as if it is merely an extension of your property.

☐ Make use of curves in lawns, hedges, and shrubberies to suggest the presence of something beyond what can actually be seen. Try to convey by the slight hint of mystery that there is more to the garden, quite literally, than meets the eye.

☐ Consider raising at least some of your plants in containers. Suitable plants include many ornamentals, small fruits, trees, and vegetables. These can be placed on patios or hung in baskets to make effective use of limited space.

An illusion of size can be created by keeping planting to the periphery of the site, *above.* Curved lines, which partially conceal what lies beyond, stimulate interest and give a feeling of depth and extent.

A focal point, such as a bench, seen through a gap in shrubs or a hedge, can add visual interest. It also provides a spot from which to view the site from a fresh angle, making it seem bigger than it actually is.

 Can I use vegetables ornamentally in my landscape?

Yes, vegetables planted singly or in combinations can add a great deal of beauty to your garden. In some circles this is called edible landscaping (and usually includes fruits in the plan as well).

First you must overcome the tendency to consider vegetables *en masse* or in straight rows as they would be found in the vegetable garden. Instead, consider the plants individually or in imaginative combinations for their aesthetic appeal.

Some vegetables, such as carrots, chard, and red leaf lettuce, will be useful for the color, texture, or form of their foliage. The ornamental value of others may be in their flowers or fruit, as with eggplants, globe artichokes, and peppers. Some vegetable varieties, such as ornamental cabbages, have been specifically bred for their beauty, rather than palatability — they make particularly striking garden plants.

Where you plant these vegetables depends on your garden design. You can use vegetables to fill in tempo-

 What is the best material for the construction of paths, patios, and courtyards?

As with many aspects of construction, the best will depend largely on cost, and to some extent on the availability of resources. Here is a rundown on some of the more commonly used materials.

Concrete Inexpensive concrete is a rather plain material to use on patios, although it is slightly more acceptable for paths. The surface can be textured for greater interest by brushing or scoring it when wet, or by adding coarse gravel.

Gravel and stone chips Available in many different grades and colors, gravel and stone chips can be quite attractive. Angular particles tend to be more expensive and can be compacted when heavy-rolled, while rounded pea gravel types remain loose but give that appealing crunching sound when walked on. The loose types of gravel are among the cheapest materials, but they do need to be confined by raised edges to prevent them from spilling onto lawns. If the gravel is not laid deeply enough, weeds may find a way to grow through, and you will have the chore of removing them.

Sand and wood chips Less expensive than gravel and providing a soft and springy texture, sand and wood chips or shredded bark are often chosen for woodland paths. A major disadvantage is that such paths often suffer from weed growth and muddiness.

The appearance of concrete can be improved by brushing the surface with a stiff broom while it is still wet, which will also create a less slippery surface. It can also be scored to simulate the appearance of flagstone.

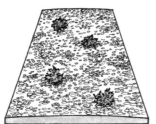

Gravel is cheap and easy to obtain, but it does shift, may need frequent raking to keep it level and may allow weeds to poke through.

Wooden slab paths look attractive but wood plays a more useful role as edging.

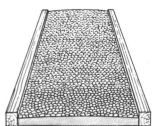

Railroad ties can provide an informal edging for confining loose gravel or woodchips on paths. They can also be used to make steps.

See also:
Wood preservatives p10
Landscape design p22
Rootstocks of fruit trees p130
Planting fruit trees in twos p131

rary gaps in a flower bed or between newly planted trees or shrubs. Pole beans or trellised cucumbers can provide a vertical dimension to a landscape, as well as a pleasing backdrop for a flower bed.

Combinations of vegetables and annual flowers can be highly effective. For example, planting onions with an annual, such as stocks, allows for the onions to provide the dominant foliage early in the season. When the onion tops die down, the stocks will be ready to flower and mask the dying foliage.

One cannot pretend that vegetables grown in this way will match in either quality or quantity those produced in a purpose-managed vegetable garden. But a group of globe artichokes or sweetcorn at the back of the herbaceous border and small groups of red lettuce, Chinese cabbage and carrots near the front, certainly bring a new dimension to vegetable growing. They will introduce novel foliage colors and patterns into your plantings, and they will serve as a talking point among your visitors.

What should I consider when planning for fruit or nut trees?

Fruit and nut trees do triple duty in a landscape plan — providing for ornamental interest, shade, and food production. The drawbacks are that they require more care and pruning (though nut trees less than fruit trees) than regular shade trees. The dropping fruits and nuts can also be messy.

If you are looking for quick results, fruit trees may be more to your liking than nut trees. While apples may start to bear in three years, nut trees from seedlings may take anywhere from seven to twenty-five years to begin to bear. However, many grafted nut trees are now available that will bear sooner (in three to five years for a black walnut), but they are more expensive.

On the other hand, nut trees are better shade trees and require less labor. You can find nut trees that are hardy in all of the United States, although pecans, for example, are primarily southern.

Fruit and nut trees require well-drained soils, although nut trees are somewhat more tolerant of wet. Both also need full sun and good air circulation.

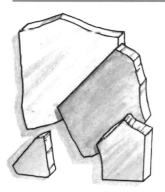

Slabs of different shapes, sizes and colors can be combined for variety. Plants such as low-growing species of thyme may be planted between the slabs.

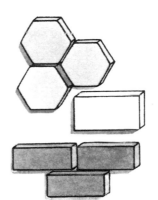

Bricks are difficult to lay well but can look magnificent in a variety of patterns.

Woods Short lengths of hardwood trunks, set vertically, can produce an extremely pleasing appearance, a fact known to Japanese gardeners for centuries. Unfortunately, such areas are better looked at than walked on, for they can be extremely slippery when wet. Another problem with wood is that it is not permanent. You can extend the life of your path by using rot-resistant wood such as redwood or cedar, but these tend to be very expensive. Other woods should be pressure-treated; paint-on preservatives are not as effective. Creosote is commonly used, but it can be harmful to plants.

Concrete and stone slabs Large, relatively flat slabs of flagstone and its cheaper substitute made of concrete are commonly used path and patio materials. The pieces can be rectangular or irregularly shaped so they can be set in a variety of designs. Concrete slabs are the least expensive and most readily available. Although they can look pretty dreary when first laid, they mellow surprisingly well.

Lay all slabs on a bed of compacted sand and do not cement between them. Instead fill gaps with compost and mat-forming plants tolerant of being stepped on, such as thyme, which will soften the look and add color and perfume. Slabs set in grass should be slightly below the lawn level so the mower will pass over the top.

Bricks Bricks are versatile in that they can be laid in interesting patterns and/or used to edge other types of pathways. Old bricks can be obtained fairly easily, but they often require cleaning and are usually unsuitable for paving, since they tend to crumble. Some of the modern durable bricks are less attractive and can be very expensive, but they are suitable for small areas.

Other materials Manufactured blocks are available in a vast range of sizes, colors, and textures. Some simulate natural materials and others are unashamedly artificial. Most are expensive, so before buying anything, try to see a sample area laid.

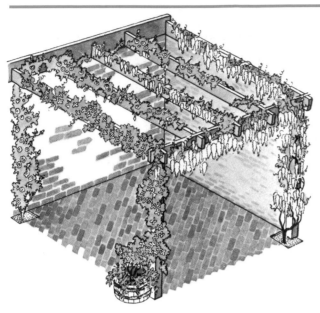

Arbors can be freestanding or can be effective as linking features where you already have two walls at right angles.

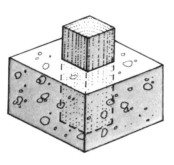

Treated wooden uprights can be set in concrete foundations about a foot square. Mesh can be attached to the uprights to provide support for climbers.

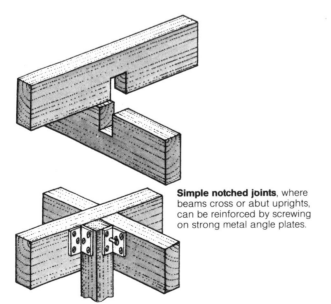

Simple notched joints, where beams cross or abut uprights, can be reinforced by screwing on strong metal angle plates.

What is an arbor
and how is one constructed?

An arbor is an open framework, without sides or roof, that is tall enough to walk under and that supports climbing plants.

Because arbors are permanent structures that are subject to the stresses of weather, and because they must be strong enough to support a great deal of plant weight, durability is important. If your plans are for vigorous, heavy vines, such as grapes or wisteria, you'll need more support than you would for light vines, such as morning glories.

Wood is one of the best construction choices for an arbor on the basis of aesthetics. It is best to use a rot-resistant wood, such as redwood or cedar. A sturdy structure can be built using 4 × 4s as the upright posts (sink them below the frost line), with 2 × 6s as cross pieces. If you want to add lattice work or other embellishments, try to incorporate them so they add to the stability of the structure, as well as provide additional support for your vines.

Any climbing plant is a suitable choice for an arbor. Remember that the structure will look pretty bare in the winter unless you include an evergreen climber, such as English ivy, *Hedera helix*.

You can realize high yields by growing grapes on arbors, although the growth habits of some varieties are better suited to arbors than others. Concord seems to benefit the most from such a setup.

Plants are generally set directly into the ground at the base of the uprights and then trained and pruned to climb onto the arbor. If you have the patience to wait for the results, you can plant something like wisteria and eventually train it over the entire structure — the results will be quite spectacular.

How should I go about
planning a rock garden?

Although rock gardens represent a considerable investment in initial work, once established, they become relatively low-maintenance gardens.

When planning a rock garden, first consider the site. Is there an existing rocky area — a slope or rock wall or stone pathway that you can make use of? Even if you don't have an existing area, you can create one. It is best, in that case, to start with a sloping site on which it is easy to build a natural-looking terraced garden. Although most of the true alpine plants (those that naturally grow in high altitude, rocky places) are sun and cool weather worshippers, there are a great many plants that will thrive in warm or shady rock garden

See also:
Plants to avoid p24
Herbaceous perennials p54
Climbing plants pp80–1
Child's vegetable garden p129

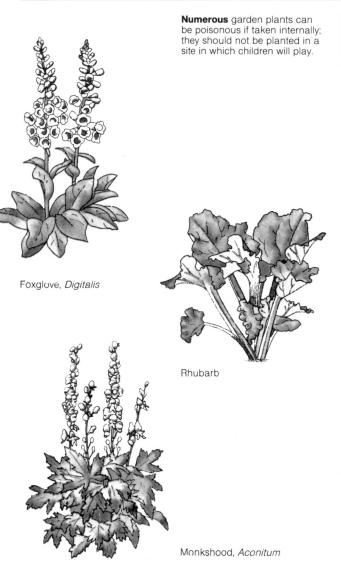

Numerous garden plants can be poisonous if taken internally; they should not be planted in a site in which children will play.

Foxglove, *Digitalis*

Rhubarb

Monkshood, *Aconitum*

What special considerations are there when planning a landscape in which children will play?

First, you will want to provide an area where children can play safely, without hurting themselves or your rare specimen plants. Second, you may want to consider setting aside a small area of the garden that the children can call their own.

Play areas are easily incorporated into a landscape plan. Generally all that is required is an open grassy spot, perhaps bordered with some shady trees for respite from the sun. Avoid planting thorny shrubs, such as firethorn, *Pyracantha coccinea*, nearby. You may also want to plan for some permanent play equipment, such as swings and climbing bars, as well as a sand box for younger children.

Since it is inevitable that children will play throughout the entire yard, you may want to plan your garden areas to have circular pathways, where children can run or ride without running into garden beds or boundaries.

Children should be discouraged from eating any plants in the garden. Many plants are toxic in varying degrees. Rhubarb leaves, monkshood and foxglove are three common examples. Of special concern should be yews, which have enticingly bright red berries.

We think it is an excellent idea to give children a small garden plot in which they can raise whatever plants they care to. Annual flowers and vegetables offer plenty of rewards for young gardeners. Not only can this serve to keep children from straying into delicate or dangerous parts of the main garden, a small children's garden can provide a special environment for the children to make exciting discoveries, take on new projects, and develop a sense of pride.

environments, so a variety of sites are possible.

Whatever the site, the first step is to clear the area of unwanted vegetation. If possible, dig out any old roots to avoid problems down the line.

The next step is to improve the soil texture and drainage by adding materials such as coarse sand and crushed rock or perlite. For a woodland rock garden, add leaf mold, compost, or peat moss.

Now you are ready to bring rocks to the area. When choosing rocks, it makes sense economically and aesthetically to use local rocks. Generally, the softer the rock, the more natural the weathered appearance and the more crevices for plant roots. The rocks should look as though they are naturally emerging from the soil. They should look permanent and stable. Packing soil between the rocks will help to stabilize them.

The rocks should be left to settle; if possible, it is best to leave them for an entire growing season so they can

stabilize. Spend some time getting rid of any perennial weeds that sprout up and repack the crevices with soil if the level sinks too far.

Your plantings should make use of the natural contours of the rocks. Use creeping, spreading, cascading, and smaller specimens to create a natural-looking scene. Some likely species for a sunny rock garden include wooly yarrow, *Achillea tomentosa*; columbine, *Aquilegia*; rock cress *Arabis*; wooly thyme, *Thymus lanicaulis*; hens and chickens, *Sempervivum tectorum*; prostrate juniper, *J. horizontalis*, and any of the sedums. For a shady rock garden, you may want to try bloodroot, *Sanguinaria canadensis*; woodland phlox, *P. stolonifera*; primroses, *Primula* spp.; wood anemone, *A. nemorosa*, and cyclamen. Learn about the individual cultural requirements of each species before planting. Some need special conditions, extra fertilizing, more dividing, less watering, and so on.

POOLS, PONDS AND STREAMS

Success with water gardens

What exactly is meant by a water garden?

Very simply, a water garden is one that is devoted to raising aquatic or waterside plants. These plants can be raised in or along the banks of a natural water source, such as a lake, pond, brook, stream, or bog. Or they can be grown in tubs, pools, or ponds specially created for growing water-loving plants.

The Japanese have known for centuries that water can add the interesting dimensions of sound and motion to a landscape, as well as provide an environment for some striking plants that one could not otherwise cultivate. Garden pools are also quite popular in Europe, particularly in England. In this country, constructing garden pools and cultivating aquatic plants in natural water sources is a relatively new development, but its popularity is growing rapidly. There are an increasing number of suppliers of water garden plants and paraphernalia.

What materials can be used to make garden pools?

Small garden pools are often incorporated into garden designs. They hold still or slightly moving water and provide a space for water plants, such as water lilies. If you don't have a natural water source and would like to create a space for aquatic plants, consider installing a small pool. Besides offering great rewards in terms of visual pleasure, pools often attract visits by wildlife, particularly birds.

Traditionally, garden pools have been dug out of clay. Where a garden lies on a firm clay subsoil, this method could still be used, though it means a lot of hard work and there is no guarantee that the clay will be absolutely watertight. First the clay must be "puddled," that is, pounded with a wooden mallet, then a spade, until it is solid and smooth. A minimum thickness of about 12 inches of clay is needed, and a firm edge to the pool must be built of rocks or flagstones.

Although it is sometimes suggested that the sole ingredient is clay, traditional puddled pools were usually lined with a mixture of clay, straw, and lime, which was stirred or kneaded together before the pure clay was hammered on top.

You will have to keep the clay wet throughout the operation — all in all a messy, rather difficult, though inexpensive operation, especially if you are prepared to provide the labor yourself.

See also:
Landscape design p22
Digging a pond p34
Plants for water gardens p36
Keeping pondwater clear p38
Water lilies for water gardens p39

What should I consider when deciding on a site for a pool or pond?

Most important is to avoid a site that is overhung by large deciduous trees, which will deposit vast quantities of leaves in the water every autumn. If the leaves are allowed to remain and decay, they will foul the water by using up oxygen at a time of year when oxygenating plants are unable to replace it. This will have serious harmful effects on plant life in general, and also on fish.

Although you could stretch nylon netting over the pool during the autumn, installing the netting is time-consuming and unsightly. Removing submerged leaves from the water is equally time-consuming, and messy as well. Also, tree roots can undermine a pool and cause cracks and leaks.

Sunlight is the most important single requirement for the correct functioning of a pool. There are almost no surface-living plants that are shade tolerant, while water lilies are particularly light-demanding, requiring six or more hours of direct sunshine a day. Many marginal pond plants (plants that grow at the water's edge), however, will do very well in the shade. Don't worry about the effect of direct sunshine on fish; they will find shelter beneath the leaves of plants and in the deeper parts of the pool.

If you are planning to dig a pond and leave it in its natural state, look for a site where the soil is heavy clay or the subsoil is fairly impervious. It is also best to dig where there is a high water table and/or an underground water source.

The slope of the land is another factor to take into account. Clearly, the pool or pond itself must be on level ground. But if you locate it at the base of a steep slope, water draining from the rest of the garden will create boggy conditions in the surrounding area, which is desirable only if you plan to have a bog garden.

You will also want a site that is protected from strong winds, particularly if the pool will provide the focus for a sitting area.

Remember that you will almost certainly want to drain a pool at some time (although not as a matter of routine), so you should plan some means of doing this. A pump will be essential if the pool is not sited so that a drain can be opened, allowing the water to run out naturally.

Of course, aesthetics are going to be a major deciding factor in site selection. A formal pool requires formal surroundings, a natural-looking pond requires a more rugged landscape.

Excavate a pool with sloping sides and rounded corners, leaving some shallow planting ledges. Remove stones and line the pool with about 2in of sand to prevent the rubber from wearing. Drape the sheeting over the pool, with twice as much extra around the edges as the pool is deep, and anchor it with heavy stones. Fill the pool with water to the level of the planting ledges.

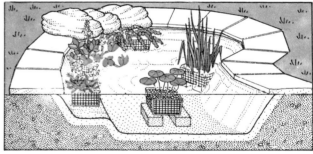

The weight of the water will stretch the rubber, and it will take on the shape of the pool. Cover 8–12in of sheeting at the edges with soil and rocks or slabs. Cut away any surplus material. Put plants in containers in position on the pool bottom and ledges and fill the pool. Always keep the water high since sunlight can rot the rubber.

Puddled clay was replaced by concrete, which isn't much easier to work with. The concrete mix must be just right and there is a significant difficulty in forming vertical walls. Properly done, however, a concrete pool is an excellent choice for a formal garden, which requires a pool with a defined outline.

Heavy plastic liners have replaced concrete for many pools. They are expensive, but much easier to use than concrete. A polyethylene sheet, the most obvious choice, is rarely satisfactory since even the heaviest gauge tears easily. At a somewhat higher cost, a pvc or vinyl sheet is much better. Best of all is butyl rubber, which is costly but extremely tough. Commercial reservoirs are sometimes lined with butyl rubber. All good aquatic suppliers stock pvc liners, and many stock butyl rubber; they will give details of how best to lay these materials. One important thing to remember is to leave a good overlap at the top so that earth and rocks can be used to anchor the liner around the pool's edge.

The simplest pool liners of all are the preformed shells, often made of fiberglass or polyester. They come in all shapes, but they tend to be shallow so they are not suitable for all aquatic plants. The other major drawback to preformed shells is that they rarely look natural and are very hard to disguise.

I'd like to dig a pond for game fish. Are there special requirements to consider?

Yes. Your climate, in combination with the depth of the pond, will affect the type of fish that you can successfully introduce, since different species prefer different conditions.

Trout, for instance, prefer ponds that are approximately 8 to 10 feet deep with relatively cool water (33 degrees F. in the winter, 75 degrees F. in the summer). In order to maintain these conditions, a trout pond should have a drainage system that allows the warmer water to be drained from the top.

A warmer climate and/or a shallower pond (4 to 8 feet) will provide good conditions for such fish as bass and bluegill. Catfish will thrive in even shallower ponds — as little as 2½ feet of water. Such a pond would require a drainage system that could draw off the cooler water from the bottom.

For any fish pond, dig the pond with vertical, as opposed to sloping, sides to cut down on the growth of water weeds, which do not provide food for the fish and use up oxygen upon decaying.

What is the standard procedure for digging a pond?

Your local soil conservation service can help you through all the stages of pond construction — including site selection, design, and working with the contractor — so check with them first. Some states also have water authorities that regulate water use, so they must be contacted as well.

The first step in the actual construction of a pond is to select a site. A low, wet, sunny basin is ideal. The soil conservation officer will bore a hole into the soil to determine if you have the necessary layer of impervious clay to hold the water. They will also determine if you have a high enough water table or sufficient underground water source to supply the pond.

If you don't have underground water, you can utilize natural run-off. However, it is undesirable to have any surface run-off water that is contaminated by farmyard manure or pesticide use. If you have neither underground water nor surface run-off, you can have water piped in from man-made wells. However, this will greatly increase the cost of the pond.

The next step is to clear the area and remove stumps and trees from the perimeter of the pond. Leaves that fall into the pond decay and deplete the oxygen, so it is best to remove any overhanging trees.

You can construct an excavated pond, where material is removed from the pond site and may be used to build up the embankment; or you can make an embankment pond, made by building a wall or dam across a stream or at the foot of a slope. Embankment ponds are generally more expensive to build.

Plan to install a drainage system to take care of overflow problems. A spillway is also important for large overflows, particularly in the spring.

Is moving water beneficial for water-based gardens?

The sight and sound of moving water adds a nice dimension to a water garden. Moving water is also valuable for oxygenating and cooling the water.

However, many aquatic plants, especially water lilies, do not enjoy turbulent water. If you are growing these types of plants, situate the recirculation pumps or cascades carefully so as not to disturb the plants.

Many of the marginal plants (see illustration) are adapted to stream-side conditions, and some plants, such as bulrushes and nuphar type lilies, are likely to succeed in gently moving water.

An artificial waterfall can be made on a natural slope or on one formed from the soil excavated when you dig your pool. Concrete is often used to determine the course of the flow and butyl rubber to line pools on various levels. These materials can be hidden with soil and rocks and can eventually be masked by moss and careful planting of water-loving plants.

Water flowing down a waterfall can be returned to the top by a submersible electric pump in the lowest section. The modern types are very safe and easy to install.

See also:
Pond site p33
Keeping pondwater clear p38
Stream-side planting p40

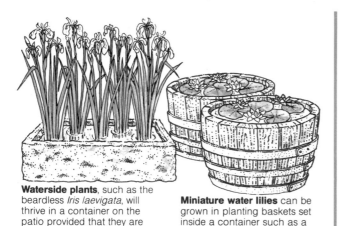

Waterside plants, such as the beardless *Iris laevigata*, will thrive in a container on the patio provided that they are rooted in rich soil and always have 2–3in of water covering their roots.

Miniature water lilies can be grown in planting baskets set inside a container such as a half-barrel. Add oxygenating plants, a pair of small fish and a few water snails.

If your heart is set on installing some form of water movement, remember that providing an electricity supply to a pool and connecting cables that will be in contact with water is definitely a job for an electrician. A large range of suitable pumps is available; select one of appropriate power — if possible, one of the modern, low-voltage models that operates through a transformer.

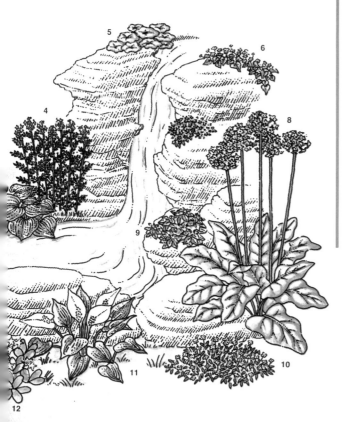

Can I grow water plants in containers on my porch?

Yes, and most water gardening supply companies sell some form of small barrel or container, although containers of ceramic, wash tubs, or wine barrels can also be used. The container should hold at least four gallons. Thoroughly scrub any container before using. If you think there is a danger of leaking, line the container with a pvc lining.

Some of the small aquatic plants, such as dwarf lotus and water lilies, are good choices for a small container. Balance your plantings with oxygenating plants, such as anacharis, which absorb water impurities and liberate oxygen. A few small fish and some water snails can also be included in your container water garden.

How do I prevent frost damage to my pool during the winter?

If you live where the winters are harsh, your best bet is to drain the pool and keep any fish and oxygenating plants in indoor tanks. Lilies and other aquatics can be kept in a cool, damp basement until spring. In many cases, they will also survive if left in a drained pool and mulched.

In more moderate climates, you can keep the pool filled. Keep some object floating in the water. If a freeze occurs, pouring boiling water over the object to free it from the ice. This will open up a hole to allow oxygen to reach plants and fish. Never hammer a hole in the ice as this could send out shock waves that could damage the fish and the pool itself.

The best method for keeping a pool frost free, and an easy one to arrange if you already have electricity for the pump, is to fit a small, thermostatically controlled heater in one corner of the pool. Some pool owners routinely disconnect and remove the pump during the winter and connect the heater to the same supply. Set the heater to maintain the temperature over a small area of the surface at just above freezing.

Plants pictured left are **1** Yellow flag, *Iris pseudacorus*; **2** Tibetan primrose, *Primula denticulata*; **3** Plantain lily, *Hosta sieboldiana*; **4** Jacob's ladder, *Polemonium caeruleum*; **5** Umbrella plant, *Peltiphyllum peltatum*; **6** Marsh marigold, *Caltha palustris*; **7** Dalmatian bellflower, *Campanula muralis*; **8** *Primula florindae*; **9** Water mint, *Mentha aquatica*; **10** Wall rock-cress, *Arabis caucasica*; **11** Water arum, *Calla palustris*; **12** Bog bean, *Menyanthes trifoliata*.

What plants should I buy to stock a new pool or pond?

A variety of plants are critical to the health of the pool or pond. Certain essential plants must provide oxygen and dispose of waste substances. Without this accomplished, the ornamental plants and the fish will not survive. Not only do you need a variety of plants, but you need them in proportion to the size of the pool and to the volume of water it contains.

The essential water plants are the submerged oxygenating plants. Not many will be visible, but they help to keep everything else alive. It is also important to choose a balance between the so-called marginal plants that have their roots in the mud at the edges of the pool but their heads up in the air (some of the aquatic irises, for example); true pond plants, such as water lilies, which root in the bottom of the pool but whose leaves float on the surface of the water; and floating plants, such as water soldier, *Stratiotes aloides.*

The table below gives the types and quantities of plants suitable for pools of different sizes. A small pool measures 5¾ feet by 4 feet with a depth of 12 inches; a medium-size pool, 10 feet by 5¾ feet with a depth of 18 inches; and a large pool, 14 feet by 10 feet with a depth of 22 inches. Depths are those in the center of the pool; much shallower water is needed at the edges for marginal plants to establish themselves successfully. If your pond is larger than the size given for a large pool, just increase the number of plants proportionately.

Type of plant	Suitable plants	Small pool	Medium pool	Large pool
Oxygenating plants	*Elodea (= Anacharis) canadensis* — Canadian pondweed *Myriophyllum spicatum* — Milfoil *Cabomba caroliniana* — Carolina fanwort *Hottonia palustris* — Water violet	10 bunches	25 bunches	80 bunches
Marginal plants	*Alisma plantago aquatica* — Water plantain *Butomus umbellatus* — Umbrella rush *Caltha palustris* — Marsh marigold *Iris laevigata* — Bog iris *Menyanthes trifoliata* — Bog bean *Myosotis palustris* — Water forget-me-not *Pontederia cordata* — Pickerel weed *Sagittaria sagittifolia* — Arrowhead *Veronica beccabunga* — Brooklime	6	8	20
Other pond plants	*Aponogeton distachyum* — Water hawthorn *Sagittaria natans* — Arrowhead *Orontium aquaticum* — Golden club *Nymphoides peltata* — Water fringe	1	2	6
Floating plants	*Azolla caroliniana* — Fairy fern *Hydrocharis morsus-ranae* — Frogbit *Stratiotes aloides* — Water soldier	4	7	20
Water lilies	Requirements vary too much and are detailed separately on p39			

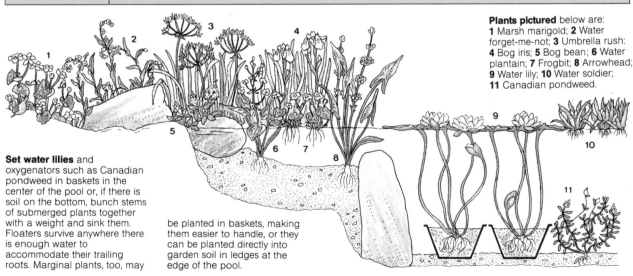

Plants pictured below are: **1** Marsh marigold; **2** Water forget-me-not; **3** Umbrella rush; **4** Bog iris; **5** Bog bean; **6** Water plantain; **7** Frogbit; **8** Arrowhead; **9** Water lily; **10** Water soldier; **11** Canadian pondweed.

Set water lilies and oxygenators such as Canadian pondweed in baskets in the center of the pool or, if there is soil on the bottom, bunch stems of submerged plants together with a weight and sink them. Floaters survive anywhere there is enough water to accommodate their trailing roots. Marginal plants, too, may be planted in baskets, making them easier to handle, or they can be planted directly into garden soil in ledges at the edge of the pool.

See also:
Ponds for game fish p34
Water gardening in containers p35
Water lilies p39
Stream-side plants pp40–1

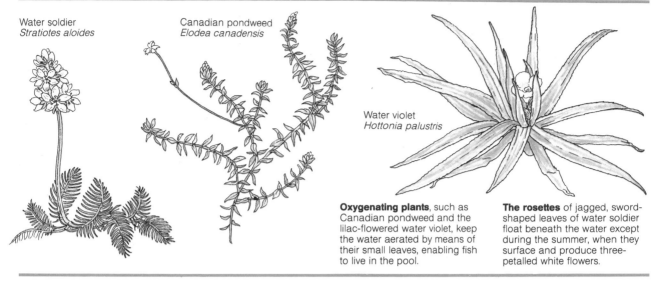

Water soldier
Stratiotes aloides

Canadian pondweed
Elodea canadensis

Water violet
Hottonia palustris

Oxygenating plants, such as Canadian pondweed and the lilac-flowered water violet, keep the water aerated by means of their small leaves, enabling fish to live in the pool.

The rosettes of jagged, sword-shaped leaves of water soldier float beneath the water except during the summer, when they surface and produce three-petalled white flowers.

 ## Can I put fish into my pool the same time as the plants?

No. It is important to give the plants and the water ample time to settle down before the fish are introduced — three or four weeks at least. This also gives the plants time to root properly.

Choose lively fish with firm, well-expanded fins. However healthy the fish may seem, movement to a new environment can be a stress on their systems, and they may become more susceptible to diseases. Therefore, it is generally recommended that you mix a commercial parasite control with the water when you introduce the fish.

As with plants, it is important to choose the right quantities of fish for the size pool, as well as the right types. Choose pond fish that are suited to outdoor life; most aquarium fish won't survive in a pool or pond. You will need some bottom-living scavengers among the fish, such as tadpoles, freshwater mussels, and snails (preferably ramshorn snails). The following numbers of fish, such as goldfish, golden orfe, and shubunkins, should be adequate for pools of roughly the sizes indicated.

Small pools
10 fish 3in long
1 scavenger fish
Medium pools
20 fish 3–4in long
3 scavenger fish
Large pools
25 fish 5–6in long
5 scavenger fish

 ## What is the actual method of planting?

Water plants need something to root in just as much as any other plants do (floaters are the exception), but there are certain rules that apply specifically to water plants. Always plant them in damp soil, not in organic compost, manure, or leaf mold, which will rot in the water and deplete the oxygen. Put a layer of gravel over the soil; otherwise the fish will stir up the soil and make the whole pool cloudy.

Depending on your climatic zone and the hardiness of the plant, planting is best done between April and mid-August into loam-filled ledges built into the sides of the pool or, more conveniently, into plastic planting baskets lined with fine nylon mesh to prevent the soil from washing out. Spread the roots out well — don't cover the crowns completely. Position the baskets at the recommended planting depth for the particular species.

If, after receiving your plants, you are unable to deal with them promptly, make sure that they are kept in buckets of water and never allowed to dry out.

Baskets of water lilies should be placed on bricks and only gradually lowered to the bottom of the pool, otherwise the plants may not flower in their first season.

How can I keep the water in my pool and pond clear and weedfree?

If you have a new pool or pond, and you are combining numerous plants, fish, soil, and water, it will take some time for a natural balance to establish itself. Even once it's established, cloudiness will occasionally occur, generally increasing during the summer, and will continue that way periodically.

Often this cloudiness is caused by a natural build-up of microorganisms. With a careful balance of plants, including oxygenators, and careful attention paid to preventing organic matter (dead leaves, manure run-off) from contaminating the water, there is no cause for concern. In time, clarity will return.

But whenever light and water combine, you will have algal growth, although that doesn't necessarily mean that you have an unhealthy system. Algae are simple types of plant life that absorb nutrients from the water and give off oxygen as a by-product. They range in size from microscopic to huge seaweeds. Excessive algal growth will interfere with the clarity of the water. While the free-swimming types of algae will make the water appear uniformly green, filamentous algae look like strands of moss.

The best way to prevent the excessive build-up of algae is to keep a good balance in your system, which might include oxygenating grasses (they absorb carbon dioxide that algae need so there is less for the algae to thrive on), aquatic plants, snails (which are scavengers), and fish so that levels of light, nutrients, oxygen, and carbon dioxide will be moderated. Keep the water clear of old leaves and foliage, which supply nutrients for algae to grow on.

If there is excessive growth, particularly before the various elements have been able to balance, you can use chemical algicides. However, many may be toxic to certain plants or fish, so check carefully before using them. Filamentous algae strands are best controlled by being mechanically removed — scooped out of the water. Even if the algicides worked on these algae, they would leave behind too much material, which would decay and foul the water further.

The pH factor can also affect the balance in pools and ponds — 7.5 to 9.5 is a desirable range, with 8.0 giving good plant growth with the least algal growth. Water garden catalogs carry clarifiers that affect the pH. Or add small quantities of baking soda (1 teaspoon per 100 gallons of water) to raise the pH.

Aside from algae, aquatic plants, such as duckweed, can fill a pool or pond with green growth. Duckweed reproduces at a prodigious rate, simply budding off new plants without producing seed.

Although chemical controls are available, and some are relatively harmless to fish and other plants, they have many drawbacks and must be judiciously applied. Chemical controls may well prove to be only a short-term solution that negatively affects the pond balance. On a small scale, mechanical control may be most effective. But it will be impossible to remove all of the weed. And even one plant left behind will soon start up the colony afresh, so removing the duckweed will become a regular chore.

To remove duckweed or filamentous algae mechanically, scoop the growth out with a wooden rake. Be sure not to use a sharp metal tool, however, especially in a pool with a plastic lining. One injudicious swipe could be disastrous.

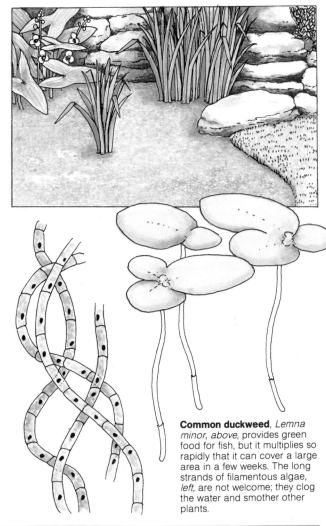

Common duckweed, *Lemna minor, above*, provides green food for fish, but it multiplies so rapidly that it can cover a large area in a few weeks. The long strands of filamentous algae, *left*, are not welcome; they clog the water and smother other plants.

See also:
Water lilies in tubs p35
Planting water plants pp36–7
Sites for pools and ponds p38

Which types of water lily will give the best color?

There are many different varieties of water lily, varying not only in color, but also in vigor of growth, preferred depth of water, flowering time, and length of flowering season. How many plants and which varieties you choose depend primarily on the size and depth of your pool. In a small pool, there will probably be room for only one or two plants of the less vigorous varieties. Some plants suitable for the size and depth of water of different pools are given below. But remember, to obtain a particular water lily hybrid, you may have to order from a specialist nursery.

A SAMPLING OF WATER LILY VARIETIES (NYMPHAEA)

White varieties

M	*alba*	medium-sized flowers; needs really deep water
M	*marliacea* Albida	huge waxy flowers with yellow stamens
M-L	*odorata* Gigantea	pure white flowers; strong scent
S-M	*tuberosa*	white; good for small ponds

Pink varieties

L	Hollandia	very large, profuse flowers
S-M	*marliacea* Carnea	pink tinged; for shallow or deep pools
M	Pink Opal	dark pink star-shaped flowers with bronze leaves
M-L	Rose Arey hybrid	pink flowers open in the morning; one of the earliest bloomers

Red varieties

M-L	Sultan	cherry red flowers; a prolific bloomer
M-L	Escarboucle	crimson red with orange stamens; a magnificent lily
M	James Brydon	rich red with orange stamens; tolerates some shade
S-M	*ellisiana*	vivid, dark red flowers; excellent for small pools and tubs

Yellow varieties

S-M	*odorata* Sulphurea Grandiflora	fragrant; good for small pools
S-M	*marliacea* Chromatella	free flowering; soft yellow
M-L	Sunrise	dark green leaves; large (12-in) flowers
S	*pygmea* Helvola	marbled leaves and soft yellow flowers

Spread

S	1–6 sq ft
M	6–12 sq ft
L	12 + sq ft

Nymphaea alba
White with yellow stamens

Nymphaea marliacea
Chromatella
Soft primrose yellow

Nymphaea
James Brydon
Rich red with orange stamens

Nymphaea Escarboucle
Crimson with orange stamens

There is a small stream flowing through my land; how can I make the most of it?

Lucky gardener! A small stream permits you to grow plants that you would otherwise find it difficult to accommodate, while the sound of gently running water adds to the enjoyment of any garden — especially when it is from a natural source, rather than originating from an artificial fountain.

While planting along stream margins is a fine practice, damming a stream in order to grow water-loving plants can have serious implications. Not only could this drastically alter the ecosystem and impede water flow, it could affect owners of adjacent land, and there may be legalities involved. So check with local water authorities before doing anything that affects the natural course of the stream.

There are other considerations as well. The pretty little brook that trickles so peacefully through your garden in summer may be a torrential drainage channel during the spring run-off. Before doing any planting, be sure you know how much the water course widens over the seasons, and bear in mind the ability of the stream to tear out delicate waterside plants before they have had time to become established.

Unlike a formal garden pool, a stream-side habitat will have natural vegetation of its own. This has two implications. There may already be many beautiful plants adorning the water's edge — flowers that would be folly to remove — purple loosestrife, marsh marigold, and meadowsweet, for example. These may not be apparent in winter, so before you start planning in detail, wait for a summer to pass and reveal what is there already. The summer will also reveal what waterside weeds are present. These will have to be removed by hand as chemical weedkillers should never be used near a stream.

Despite the ease with which some plants establish naturally in running water, it is usually difficult to persuade them to do so. You may be successful with water crowfoot, *Ranunculus aquatilis*, if you anchor them firmly, but it will usually be more rewarding to confine your planting to the water's edge and the banks.

Suitable plants can be bought from special nurseries — don't uproot plants from natural river banks. Choose a range of plants to include those that prefer to be in shallow water at the stream's edge to those that like wet soil but do not like to be immersed. Include some that need somewhat drier conditions, farther away from the water, but can tolerate an occasional drenching. The marginal plants suggested for planting in the water at the edge of a pond can be used at the side of a stream too, but there are many others.

See also:
Water plants pp34, 36
Irises pp36, 73

Flag
Iris pseudacorus

Primula rosea

Plantain lily
Hosta sieboldiana

Common calla
*Zantedeschia
aethiopica*

Plants pictured are: **1** Black bamboo, *Phyllostachys nigra;* **2** Flowering rush, *Butomus umbellatus;* **3** Astilbe arendsii; **4** Sweet gale, *Myrica gale;* **5** Plantain lily, *Hosta sieboldiana;* **6** Sweet flag, *Acorus calamus;* **7** Flag, *Iris pseudacorus;* **8** Globe flower, *Trollius europaeus;* **9** Royal fern, *Osmunda regalis;* **10** Tibetan primrose, *Primula florindae;* **11** Common calla, *Zantedeschia aethiopica;* **12** Gunnera manicata

What should I plant in a boggy part of my site?

The small area a few feet away from the edge of a stream, where the soil is spongy, porous, and wet is the ideal habitat for a wonderful range of bog plants, but a bog garden can be constructed anywhere that water is continually available. This might be close to a garden pool or pond in a low-lying hollow, or at the foot of a slope.

When choosing bog plants, use the same criteria as you would when planting any mixed group. Be aware just how big some of these species can grow — *Gunnera manicata* is the extreme, having leaves more than 10 feet in diameter — and ensure they will not shade out more modest plants. Try to select for continuity of flowering and to avoid color clashes here just as you would in a herbaceous border.

There are dozens of plants to choose from. Here is a list of a few popular ones.

Astilbe These invaluable plants with feathery flowers are available in a wide range of varieties. They come in such vibrant colors as the crimson Fanal, the salmon-pink Peach Blossom, as well as in white. The height of astilbe ranges from 6 inches to 4 feet.

Gunnera For the biggest gardens only, these magnificent plants have huge kidney-shaped leaves and tall, bottle-brush flower spikes. Gunneras are not very cold hardy; if grown north of zone 7, a heavy winter mulch must be applied.

Hosta, Plantain lily Hardy to zone 3, these versatile foliage plants are available in many shades of green and with variegated leaves. The plants grow from 1 to 2 feet tall. They are readily propagated by division.

Iris Many species are suited to bog conditions, as well as to stream-side areas. They all have the typical iris flowers of blue, purple, or yellow, with heights ranging from 6 inches for the crested iris to 42 inches for the Eolian iris.

Pontederia cordata, Pickerel rush Well-suited to zones 3 through 9, this plant has dark green heart-shaped leaves with blue or white flowers on spikes.

Primula There is an enormous choice among the bog primulus in terms of color, size, and form. For a start, among the dozens of different forms and species, try *P. rosea*, which grows 6 inches tall with deep carmine-red flowers. Then consider *P. florindae*, which resembles a cowslip 2 foot tall. *P. bulleyana* has tiers of orange-yellow flowers and grows up to 2 feet tall.

Thalia dealbata, Water canna A typical bog plant, native to swamplands and marshes, it grows readily in zones 7 to 9. A large variety is available.

Trollius europaeus, Globe flower A hardy buttercup-like plant with golden, yellow, and orange flowers. These will grow up to 42 inches tall.

ANNUALS AND BIENNIALS

Creating a profusion of color

What is meant by annual, biennial, hardy, half-hardy, and tender?

You will find all of these terms in seed catalogs; and, unfortunately, they aren't applied in any standard fashion.

An annual is a plant that completes its life cycle from seed to seed within the space of one season. This usually means that if you plant annuals you will need to start fresh each year with new seeds or plants, although some annuals will self-sow, sparing you the necessity of replanting. And some plants, potentially grown as perennials in some parts of the country, will be grown as annuals since they perform better if sown fresh each season. This category of plants includes snapdragons and verbena.

A biennial is a plant that requires two seasons in which to complete its life cycle. The plant establishes itself in the first year, then flowers and sets seed in the second. Some well-known biennial garden flowers are sweet william and foxglove. But to add to the confusion, many of the plants grown as biennials are actually perennials.

When you plant biennials, it is important to follow the recommended sowing dates; generally, the plants need time to establish a good size before winter, but they shouldn't be planted so early that they flower or become too leafy before winter.

Superimposed upon the annual/biennial distinction is the division of plants into the categories of hardy, half-hardy, and tender. These terms are given to help guide planting times, although in mild climates, the terms don't matter much — and many sources don't use the half-hardy distinction.

A hardy plant is one capable of surviving outdoors in a particular climate with no protection. It can survive some frosts without being killed or badly damaged. Hardy annuals include calendulas, cornflowers, sweet peas, larkspurs, nasturtiums, and godetias — they can be safely sown outdoors early in the season or even, in some instances, at the end of the preceding season to obtain an even earlier start.

A half-hardy annual is one that will grow outdoors during the summer but cannot be transplanted or directly seeded outside until the coldest part of the early spring and the danger of frost has passed. Most can, however, withstand long periods of damp, cold weather. Many of the most popular bedding plants fall into this category, including marigolds, snapdragons, impatiens, nemesias, petunias, and salvias. But some plants grown as half-hardy annuals, such as geraniums, are actually half-hardy perennials.

Tender annuals cannot be transplanted or directly seeded into the garden before the soil has warmed. They require a long, warm summer for good flower production. In areas with short growing seasons, tender annuals must be started early indoors. Heliotrope is commonly regarded as a tender annual.

See also:
Disinfecting soil p14
Potting mixes p15
Hardiness p18
Hardening-off p44

Germination of seeds p44
Saving seeds p45
Starting seedlings p142
Cold frames p144

Should annuals and biennials be started as transplants indoors or sown directly in the garden?

Each method has its advantages; the answer really depends on the resources at your disposal, how early you want blooms, the time you have to spare, and your climatic zone.

Half-hardy and tender annuals must not be placed in the open garden until the danger of cold and frost has passed; so to obtain the earliest flowering, you must put them out as plants rather than as seeds. With fast-growing, half-hardy annuals, such as strawflowers and asters, transplants may come into bloom several weeks earlier than direct-sown plants. And some plants, if directly sown, such as ageratums and petunias, may not reach the flowering stage before the first fall frosts.

The general rule for half-hardy and tender annuals is to start seeds indoors — in a greenhouse, under grow lights, or even on a sunny, warm window ledge — or in a cold frame outdoors. The information provided on the back of seed packets will tell you how many weeks before your last spring frost date to start the seeds. You can sow hardy annuals outdoors as soon as the soil begins to warm up; there is no need to wait until the danger of frost has passed. Even so, it is possible to achieve an earlier start and the earliest flowering by starting some seeds indoors in the same way as half-hardy varieties.

If you live in a warm climate, you can sow many hardy annuals in the fall for early growth and blooming during the cooler parts of spring and summer. Even if you live in the North, you can try this method with some flowers, such as sweet peas.

Many people who don't have the time or the space to start plants indoors are happy to buy started plants at nurseries, although their selection tends to be limited to the most common bedding plants. If you compare buying transplants or starting your own transplants to direct seedings, you will find that, in general, direct seeding involves less expense for materials, less handling of plants (some plants will be set back by transplanting), but more time spent initially in weeding the flower bed. Also, with tiny seeds, the yield for directly sown seeds may be reduced because of damage caused by animals and the elements.

Loosely fill a container with moist soil mix, level it and firm it down to about ½ in from the top. Broadcast the seeds randomly or in straight rows. Cover lightly with soil mix, but check with the packet since some may not need covering. Water with a gentle sprinkling head or set the flat in shallow water for 10 minutes.

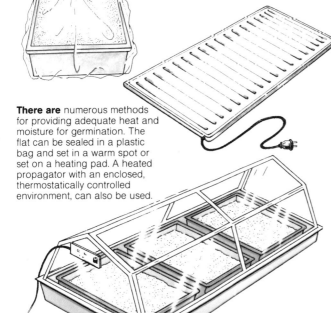

There are numerous methods for providing adequate heat and moisture for germination. The flat can be sealed in a plastic bag and set in a warm spot or set on a heating pad. A heated propagator with an enclosed, thermostatically controlled environment, can also be used.

What is the best way to disinfect a container for starting seedlings?

Clean, fresh potting mix and a more or less sterile container are essential if you are to avoid incubating pests and diseases along with your tender young seedlings. The best way to clean a container is to scrub it thoroughly with a stiff brush and hot, soapy water. Remove all traces of old soil and roots. Then soak the container in a mild bleach solution (1 part bleach to 10 parts water). Allow wooden containers to soak for about 30 minutes, while containers made of nonporous materials, such as plastic, need only soak for 10 minutes. Rinse the containers in clear water before using.

What does hardening-off mean and how do I do it?

Hardening-off is the process of taking plants that have been grown under protection indoors and gradually accustoming them to the outdoors.

This process is necessary because, when plants are grown with artificially high warmth and moisture (as in a greenhouse), their cells tend to be relatively large, their tissues contain an abnormally high amount of water, and the outer surfaces of the plant are thin. When such plants are then placed outside, they are prone to desiccation (drying out), to cold damage, and, because of their cell structure, to be physically unstable.

But, if you only very gradually expose these tender plants to outdoor conditions, as they continue to grow, the new cells that they form will be smaller, thicker

walled, and generally more able to tolerate harsher conditions.

The best way to harden-off plants is to place them in a cold frame — an unheated, usually wooden enclosure with a removable glass cover. A temporary cold frame can be made by placing a storm window or door over hay bales, which form the walls. The glazing ensures some increase of the outside temperatures and helps to trap some warmth for night-time protection. During the day you can raise or remove the cover completely (depending on the weather), until after about two weeks, the plants can safely be exposed fully to the outside environment.

If you have neither the space nor the materials for a cold frame, you can harden-off your seedlings by placing them outside in a sheltered spot for progressively longer periods each day.

Why do some seeds germinate more successfully than others?

Seeds are marvelously adapted to be successful in their native habitats. Unfortunately — or fortunately, depending on your point of view — this sometimes means that the seeds don't readily respond to conditions in a typical garden. For example, most seeds have some intrinsic mechanism to prevent or inhibit germination until growing conditions are just right for the tender young seedling. Thus, the seeds of most plants won't germinate when they fall from the parent in the autumn because the subsequent winter temperatures would kill the young plants.

Similarly, the seeds of many plants that originate from extreme climates have hard, thick coats, which enable them to survive especially high or low temperatures. Plants that live in climates with marked seasonal rainfall often produce seeds with a thick coat. In that way, a single shower of rain, which would not provide sufficient moisture for the seedling to live for long, will not stimulate germination. The thick seed coat can be softened and penetrated only by a prolonged downpour, ensuring that the seed will not germinate until the environment contains enough moisture for the survival of the resulting plant.

Thus, some seeds germinate easily with moderate moisture and warmth, others require prolonged exposure to the same treatment, while yet others require special treatment. Some seeds require light and should not be buried, while others germinate best in the dark.

Among the more common tricks to promote germination that you will find suggested on seed packets or in gardening books are to place seeds in the refrigerator or freezer, in order to mimic a natural cold spell. Some seeds, such as parsley, which have hard seed coats, benefit from being soaked in warm water overnight before sowing. Some hard-coated seeds, such as sweet pea and morning glories, will germinate faster if scarified (chipped with a file or razor) so there is an opening in the seed coat.

It is worth mentioning, too, that some tiny seeds, such as those of lobelia and fibrous-rooted begonia, bear special treatment of a different nature. These seeds contain insufficient food reserves to enable the seedlings to reach the light if they are even slightly buried. They should be scattered thinly on the soil surface, and kept moist. Seed catalogs and packets are generally the best sources of information on encouraging germination for specific seeds.

Extremely small seeds can be mixed with sand before being sprinkled on the surface of your soil mix, **1**, or shaken off a sheet of paper. Don't cover them with soil mix. Soak large or hard seeds for twelve hours before sowing, **2**, Hard seeds, such as sweet pea, will germinate more easily if the seed coat is nicked with a sharp knife, **3**.

 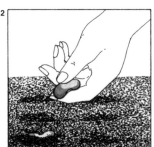 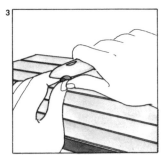

See also:
F1 hybrids pp118–19
Seedling wilt and damping-off p147

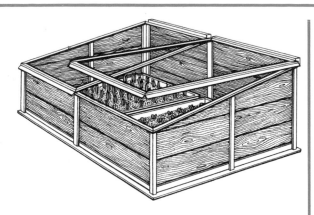

Gather seed heads and pods when they are almost dry and spread them out on trays in the sun or bunch the stems and

hang them up with their heads in a paper bag. Shake the bag occasionally so the seeds drop into it as they dry.

Seedlings raised indoors or in a greenhouse should be hardened-off before being planted in the garden. This can be done in a cold frame

by raising the lid for a longer period of time each day to expose the plants to wind, sunlight and temperature variations.

Store properly dried seeds in a cool, dry place or a refrigerator in clearly marked envelopes, paper bags or sealed containers.

 ## Can I save the seeds from my annuals to plant next year?

There are few more satisfying aspects of gardening than collecting seed from a plant in your garden, and sowing it the following year to produce a fresh crop. Saving seeds has the additional advantages of saving money and enabling you to grow and preserve varieties of plants that may not be offered for sale commercially.

Anyone interested in crossing plant varieties in the hope of producing improved hybrids will have to save seeds as part of the process. Such deliberate crossing of varieties provides an addictive challenge, but the many natural hybridizations that occur in the garden during the course of the summer mean that anyone sowing seed from their own plants always stands a chance of finding something new. Here are some guidelines.

☐ Never save seed from a variety that is described as an F_1 hybrid, for the resulting plants will contain a different genetic make-up and bear little resemblance to the parent. F_1 hybrid seed must be raised from new crossings each year, which is why it tends to be more expensive than other seed.

☐ Never save seed from plants that are in any way sickly or abnormal; they may well be diseased and the affliction could be passed on.

☐ Always store well-dried seeds in a sealed container in a cool, dry spot.

☐ Don't offer for sale seed that you have saved since it might be a protected variety, and there are legalities concerning who may sell such seeds. However, exchanging seeds with friends or through seed exchange organizations can allow you to help in maintaining diverse varieties.

 ## Is it possible to introduce diseases into my garden with poor-quality seed?

Yes, it is; but with modern methods of commercial seed production, it is unlikely that you will introduce any serious problems with store-bought seed. Vegetable seed especially is tested to ensure that certain defined standards of purity are attained. The risks will be higher for you if you save seed from your own plants, and it is sensible to take precautions.

Don't collect seed from poor or sickly plants. First, the seed may, like the parent, lack general vigor. Second, it is possible that virus contamination is responsible for the poor growth, and many plant viruses can be transmitted from one generation to the next within the seed.

The most common problem with home-produced seed is probably damping-off of the seedlings, for many species of microscopic fungi can adhere to the seed coat and show themselves when the seeds are sown and incubated. To prevent this, before you sow them, you can dust your home-grown seed with an approved fungicide for treating seeds.

Which annuals or biennials will produce a long season of blooms?

Many flowers will produce blooms for long periods in most of our climatic zones, if the timing of starting seeds or setting out transplants is done properly.

In the northern areas that experience relatively early fall frosts and long winters, hardy annuals should be planted in early spring, and more tender annuals should be set out after all danger of frost has passed.

In the South and Southwest, many annuals will produce a long season of blooms if planted in the fall for winter and spring flowers. It is important to time your plantings so that cool-season plants mature before the heat of the summer. To maintain long bloom periods, it is sometimes necessary to do a second planting to mature in the fall after the summer heat has spent the first flush of flowers.

Regardless of where you live, the process of deadheading, or removing old flowers once they are past their prime, is a method of prolonging blooming.

Here is a list of plants that have proved to produce a long season of blooms in most parts of the country.

Ageratum, *Ageratum houstonianum* This dwarf, compact plant (4 to 8 inches) should be treated as a tender annual. Plants must be started indoors about eight weeks before they can be set out. They do well in sun or half-shade and produce tight clusters of blooms, usually blue, although Summer Snow is a widely available white variety. Ageratum is not very heat resistant; in hot climates, it should be planted for spring and fall blooms.
Calendula, *Calendula officinalis* Also called pot marigold, this hardy annual grows 1 to 2 feet high and blooms from spring until fall during cool weather. In warm areas, sow seed in August or September for Christmas blooms. In areas with a snow cover, sow in September. The plants will grow a little, then go dormant, and resume growth in the spring. Pacific

Beauty (2 feet) is a popular variety of mixed colors; Gypsy Festival is a dwarf variety (12 inches) that also grows in mixed colors.
Celosia A tender annual, celosia comes in two types: *C. cristata* blooms with a flat, velvety flower head that resembles a crest or a lump of coral, while *C. plumosa* has feathery plumes. The colors include yellow, orange, pink, and fiery red, while the height runs from 6 to 30 inches. Jewel Box is a dwarf variety with large, thick, colorful crests. Among the plumed types, Fairy Fountains is a popular dwarf (12 inches).
Cosmos You can have your choice of colors with this half-hardy annual. *C. bipinnatus* varieties, such as Sensation Mixed Colors (4 feet) produce white, pink, and red flowers. *C. sulphureus* varieties bloom with yellow and orange flowers. Diablo (4 feet) offers deep orange flowers, while Sunny Bold (1 foot) offers yellow flowers. The *C. sulphureus* varieties are somewhat more heat-tolerant.
Globe amaranth, *Gomphrena globosa* A tender annual even in hot climates, this bushy, spreading plant does well in a hot, dry, sunny location. It produces 1-inch clover-type, usually purple flowers. The size ranges from the dwarf Buddy variety (6 to 8 inches) with purple

Cosmos
Cosmos bipinnatus

Sweet alyssum
Lobularia maritima

Pot marigold
Calendula officinalis

See also:
Hardy, half-hardy, tender plants p42
Less common annuals p48
Annuals in hanging baskets p50
Annuals as dried flowers p52
Starting seedlings p152

flowers to Haageana Aurea (2 feet), with deep reddish-orange blossoms.

Nasturtium, *Tropaeolum majus* A very easy to grow half-hardy annual, nasturtium flowers and foliage look good in borders and in hanging baskets. Climbing varieties (up to 8 feet tall) can be trained up a trellis. Under cool conditions, the flowers will bloom continuously. Nasturtiums tolerate drought and poor soils.

Petunia, *Petunia × hybrida* Grown as half-hardy annuals, petunias come in many varieties, offering a choice in flower size, color, and shape. The varieties fall into two categories, both having single and double flowers. The grandifloras have large, spectacular flowers, yet are less vigorous than the multifloras, which produce small flowers but bloom profusely.

Phlox, *Phlox drummondii* A hardy, heat-resistant annual, phlox will produce early blooms of white, blue, pink, red, and lavender. Although the flowers may diminish somewhat in the heat, they will pick up later in cooler temperatures. The height range is generally 6 to 20 inches. Most have clusters of rounded flowers.

Snapdragon, *Antirrhinum majus* Technically a tender perennial, snapdragons are primarily grown as annuals.

They have colorful flowers that grow on spikes and open from the bottom to the top and are available in a range of sizes from 8 inches to 4 feet. Snapdragons have a long blooming period and, if cut back after the flowers fade, may produce a second crop. Rockets is a popular tall variety, while Floral Carpet (8 inches) is good for low borders.

Sweet Alyssum, *Lobularia maritima* A low-growing hardy annual that spreads readily, sweet alyssum is nice for a low border or a ground cover. An attractive combination is the white Carpet of Snow with Wonderland Rose, a bright, cherry red variety.

Verbena, *Verbena × hybrida* Grown as a tender annual, verbena is a heat-tolerant plant that produces bright flower clusters good for beds and hanging baskets. Trinidad is a rich rose pink variety (10 inches) that is extremely long-lasting and able to survive light frosts.

Celosia
Celosia plumosa

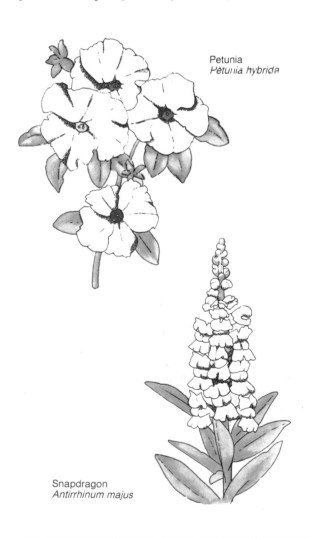

Petunia
Petunia hybrida

Snapdragon
Antirrhinum majus

Nasturtium
Tropaeolum majus

47

What should I look for when buying flower transplants?

Although instant color is tempting, avoid plants that are already in bloom. They will not do as well as younger plants. Older plants (check with the nursery to find out how old the plants might be) tend to suffer more from transplant shock than younger plants.

Look for stocky, compact plants with a healthy green color. Plants that are tall and leggy may have been grown under inadequate, stressful conditions and be less sturdy and more prone to pests and diseases.

Check the undersides of leaves for evidence of pests, such as aphids and whiteflies. Even if the leaves don't appear damaged, it is best to avoid infested plants since the pests may have transmitted diseases.

Check with the salespeople to see if the plants have been hardened-off. If not, plan to do this yourself to increase the likelihood of successful transplanting.

Can you offer some tips for successfully transplanting seedlings?

First, timing is important. Don't set out tender annuals before the danger of frost is past. And don't neglect the hardening-off process.

If your transplants are in a crowded container and the roots are bound up and intertwined, cut through the soil between the plants with a knife a few days before transplanting. This will allow time for the roots to recover from the disruption before you set them out.

The best time to set out plants is on a drizzly, cloudy, and windless day. If those optimal conditions don't exist, transplant in the late afternoon or evening.

If you are adding fertilizer to the soil, mix it in well so that it doesn't directly contact the roots.

Moisten the soil in the container before transplanting so the soil will cling to the roots. Dig a plant hole so that the seedling is set at the same depth as in the original container. Firm the soil around the plant and leave a slight depression to catch water.

Water your transplants immediately and shade them if it is a sunny day. Newly transplanted seedlings will benefit from a dilute application of a high-phosphorus fertilizer (or a dusting of bonemeal in the hole to aid in good root development).

Can you recommend some out-of-ordinary annuals for a flower garden?

It's unfortunate that most commercial nurseries stock the same limited varieties of annuals year after year. There are many more worthy annuals that could hold a spot in your garden. To add some diversity of color and shapes to flower beds, consider some of the annuals listed below. Some can be found as seedlings if you seek them out; all are available as seeds through catalogs.

Annual larkspur, *Consolida ambigua* This hardy annual is related to delphiniums. It produces 1-foot to 2-foot spikes of violet, rose, purple, pink, or blue flowers. The plants prefer cool weather for flowering. Giant Imperial grows 4-foot plants with mixed colors.

Annual tree mallow, *Lavatera trimestris* Tender annuals closely related to hollyhocks, tree mallows grow to 5 feet, with long-blooming, pink and white flowers. It can act as a quick-growing screen.

Bells of Ireland, *Moluccella laevis* What is most interesting about these plants are the calyxes, which look like bell-shaped flowers. The flower spikes grow 2 to 3 feet high. These tender annuals are excellent for cutting.

Flowering tobacco, *Nicotiana alata* Grown as a tender annual, nicotiana produces brilliant flowers; several varieties produce green blooms. New semi-dwarf varieties, such as Nicki, grow to 18 inches.

Heliotrope, *Heliotropium arborescens* Grown as a tender annual, heliotropes make excellent flowers for containers. The 1-foot to 2-foot plants produce clusters of small, fragrant flowers.

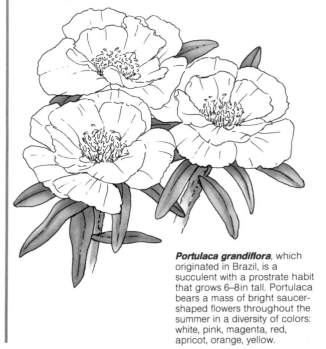

Portulaca grandiflora, which originated in Brazil, is a succulent with a prostrate habit that grows 6–8in tall. Portulaca bears a mass of bright saucer-shaped flowers throughout the summer in a diversity of colors: white, pink, magenta, red, apricot, orange, yellow.

See also:
Hardening-off p44
Annuals for hanging baskets p50
Annuals as dried flowers p52
Starting seedlings p142

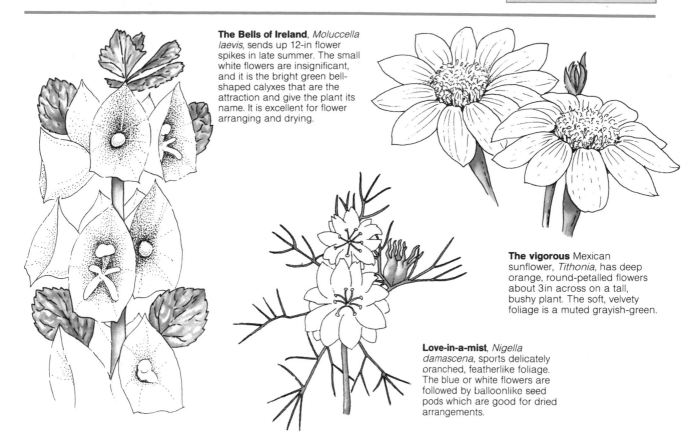

The Bells of Ireland, *Moluccella laevis*, sends up 12-in flower spikes in late summer. The small white flowers are insignificant, and it is the bright green bell-shaped calyxes that are the attraction and give the plant its name. It is excellent for flower arranging and drying.

The vigorous Mexican sunflower, *Tithonia*, has deep orange, round-petalled flowers about 3in across on a tall, bushy plant. The soft, velvety foliage is a muted grayish-green.

Love-in-a-mist, *Nigella damascena*, sports delicately branched, featherlike foliage. The blue or white flowers are followed by balloonlike seed pods which are good for dried arrangements.

Love-in-a-mist, *Nigella damascena* An old-fashioned garden annual, nigella has jewel-like flowers of mixed colors, very finely divided leaves, and grows to a height of about 18 inches. It is prized for its unusual seed pods.

Mexican sunflower, *Tithonia rotundifolia* A very tall, tender annual, growing 30 inches to 6 feet high, tithonia produces masses of rich orange daisylike flowers over a long season. Torch (4 to 6 feet) has the richest color flowers, while Goldfinger is very compact (30 to 42 inches).

Monkey flower, *Mimulus cupreus* Prized for its brilliant, velvety, speckled, red and yellow tubular flowers, mimulus flowers best in cool weather and does well in partially shaded areas. This tender annual grows to a height of 12 inches.

Moss rose, *Portulaca grandiflora* Succulent, needlelike leaves, with brilliant flowers that resemble miniature roses, characterize this low-growing (6 inch), spreading, tender annual. Sundance is bred to stay open for most of the day, while many other varieties tend to close early.

Nemesia, *Nemesia strumosa* This tender annual doesn't do well in the heat or humidity of summer and prefers cool, dry weather. The bushy plants grow 1 to 2 feet tall, and the flowers resemble small, tubular pansies, in colors of red, yellow, pink, rose, and light blue.

Ornamental cabbage, *Brassica oleracea* var. Although they don't produce flowers, ornamental brassicas make a wonderful addition to a flower bed, providing a variety of attractive leaf colors and textures on plants ranging from low-growing rosettes to the much taller kale plants.

Ornamental pepper, *Capsicum annuum* These tender annuals aren't much for flowers, but the vivid red and yellow fruits provide plenty of visual interest. The small pepper plants (9 to 12 inches) can also be grown indoors in containers.

Pincushion flowers, *Scabiosa atropurpurea* A hardy annual, the flowers, which are good for cutting, are brightly colored (purple, rose, white) and resemble pincushions. The size ranges from Dwarf Double (18 inches) to Giant Imperial (3 feet).

Spider flower, *Cleome* spp. Consider the shrubby cleome for a dramatic backdrop. The tall (3-foot to 4-foot) plants have spiderlike pink and white blooms. A warm-season annual, cleome tolerates heat and dry weather.

Toadflax, *Linaria marocanna* A hardy annual, toadflax produces bright flowers in mixed colors and resembles the snapdragon. The plants grow 8 to 12 inches high and prefer cool weather for flowering. Toadflax has few pest or disease problems.

Velvet flower or **painted tongue**, *Salpiglossis sinuata* A cool-season tender annual, this has velvety, funnel-shaped flowers variegated with rich colors.

A hanging basket can be made at home by lining a wire basket with sphagnum moss, *above*, or with plastic, *below*, punctured for drainage.

Be sure to overlap the moss adequately so that it will hold soil. Then, fill the basket with your soil mix.

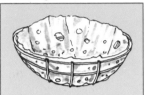

Insert plants into the sides, firm and add more soil for the next level of plants. Fill soil to within ½ in of the top.

If you go away for a few days, set the basket in the shade on top of a bucket of water with the bottom just touching the water, which will be drawn up by the soil as it dries out.

Which annuals will produce color throughout the season in hanging planters?

What you are looking for is a mix of plants that will give color throughout the season, without any replanting and with a minimum of deadheading or other routine attention. The plants should be compact and represent a range of growth habits, including upright, climbing, and trailing. The old faithfuls most frequently found are lobelia, alyssum, and dwarf petunias.

Many people forget to include twining plants to take advantage of the potential offered by the support chains. Sometimes called black-eyed susan, *Thunbergia alata*, is a very appealing half-hardy annual that blooms continuously with rather uncommon, rich orange-cream flowers with a dark center. It is easily grown from seed, but needs full sun and may not be successful in colder areas of the country.

Thunbergia can be allowed to trail downward, but that role is usually filled by trailing lobelia, perhaps one of the Cascade varieties (among which is a real red, Ruby Cascade) and by ivy-leaf geraniums, which come in red and white bicolored forms.

Nasturtiums can be used to trail, but they sometimes fail to produce their best because the potting mix is too rich. The liquid feeding and constant attention to watering that are so important for successful hanging pots are not really to their liking, so they may be grown best by themselves. Other useful trailing plants are pendulous begonias and some of the trailing campanulas.

Foliage plants add a lot of interest to a planter. There are many attractive variegated ivies that will trail over the edge and can be replanted year after year. The gray-leaf trailing ground ivy, *Nepeta hederacea*, grows faster and longer than many of the other trailing forms and will almost reach the ground in favorable situations.

A planter might feature such plants as coleus, heliotrope, or bright, cascading varieties of petunias that will flower all season. Dwarf cascading fuchsias or a small-leaf variety of impatiens (such as Elfin) are also

See also:
Germination of seeds p 44
Annuals for a long season of
  bloom pp 46–7
Native perennial wildflowers p 63
Foliage plants pp 64–5

nice for a centerpiece. Around the central plants may be planted almost anything that takes your fancy. Don't forget to make sure the planter is attractive to look at from all angles.

Many of the plants used in hanging pots also can be used for window boxes, but some more substantial types, such as salvias, the more robust fuchsias, and additional geraniums can be included. Experiment also with compact annuals.

Containers for hanging plants can include slatted wooden tubs (redwood is the least susceptible to decay), clay pots, plastic pots, brass containers, or wire baskets. Your choice will probably depend on which fits best in your setting, expense, time investment (for example, clay pots will have to be watered more frequently than plastic) and, to some extent, what is being planted (for example, Christmas cactus thrive in open-sided containers since they don't like to be too moist).

Your container should have drainage holes in the bottom. You will probably want to have a dish or saucer (or pot within a pot) to catch draining water. If you can't have drainage holes, place several inches of stones on the bottom to allow water to collect below the plants and evaporate. If you are using a wire basket, line it with sphagnum moss or a plastic liner that has drainage slots cut into it.

Use a good, well-drained potting mix (either soil-less or soil-based). And don't forget that the constant watering needed by hanging baskets during the summer results in nutrients being leached out from the soil. A regular application of a liquid fertilizer is essential. Protect the planter from sun and wind.

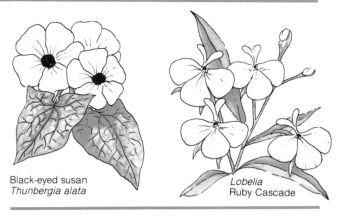

Black-eyed susan
Thunbergia alata

Lobelia
Ruby Cascade

? Which annuals and biennials will reseed themselves? Can they be established in a natural setting?

There are a number of annuals and biennials that will readily produce seed and self-sow in the course of a growing season. These include alyssum, ageratum, California poppies, petunias, nasturtiums, calendula, cleome, forget-me-not, foxglove, sweet william, and hollyhocks.

The degree to which a plant will successfully self-sow is determined by many factors, including variety, climate, and tolerance to germinating conditions. Climate, of course, is critical, since only the hardiest will reseed in certain areas. Success is more likely where the soil is not disturbed or heavily mulched.

Some of these annuals can be seeded in a "natural" setting, such as a meadow or open slope, although the chances of the annuals reseeding and competing with other plants is limited. Over time, they will have to be replanted.

Wildflower mixes that are advertised by seed companies generally contain a certain proportion of both annual and perennial seeds that are appropriate for particular climates. The annuals will offer color mainly for the first season. Although the annuals may reseed naturally to a degree, it is the perennials that will take over after that.

It isn't always desirable that annuals self-sow. Volunteers from hybrid varieties won't necessarily breed true and may produce poor-quality flowers.

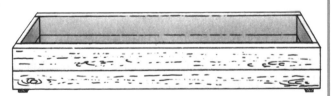

If you treat your wooden window boxes to prevent rot, make sure to use a substance that is not harmful to plants. Window boxes should have drainage holes in the bottom and be raised up to prevent the wood underneath from rotting. Plastic boxes can be used alone or can be placed inside more aesthetic wooden boxes.

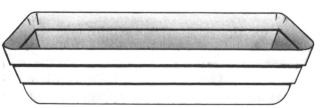

I want to grow annuals to use as dried flowers. What do I need to know?

There's nothing special about *growing* an annual that is slated to be dried — each plant variety will have its own cultural requirements — the difference lies in harvesting and post-harvest care. How successful you will be in drying flowers will be affected by the humidity at the time of harvest and drying, time delays before drying, the timing of the harvest, and light.

Harvest your flowers on a dry, sunny day just before the peak bloom. They will continue to open somewhat after you cut. If you cut too late, the flowers won't last as long or look as nice.

Hanging is the traditional, tried-and-true method of drying flowers. It is a particularly good method for those that are everlastings, meaning plants that have flowers with papery parts that retain their forms and colours after being dried, such as statice and straw-flowers. Others, like celosia, will dry well this way also. You must hang your flowers immediately after harvest. Group the flowers in bunches — don't make the bunches too big or the air circulation will be limited. Remove the lower leaves so the biological processes slow down. With flowers like strawflowers, it is best to attach wired stems because their own stems won't hold up. Use florists' wire and attach it just after picking, before the flowers are dried. Then hang the flowers in a dark, dry, well-ventilated area. An attic is often ideal.

For certain flowers, such as larkspur, marigolds and hollyhocks, the best drying method is to cover the

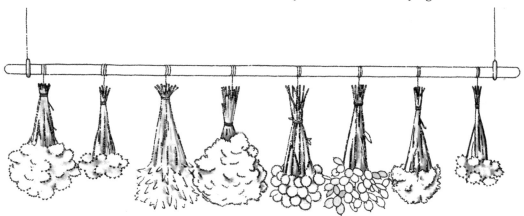

Hang drying flowers upside down in bunches in a dark, dry well-ventilated area. The smaller the bunches, the better the flowers in the center will dry.

I've often found green bugs on the leaves and stems of my annuals. What are they?

It sounds as though your plants are hosting aphids — a fairly common insect pest. They are soft-bodied green, yellow, or dark insects that suck the juices from the leaves and buds.

In small numbers, aphids do little damage, but they are extremely prolific. When their numbers increase, they can do enough damage to cause yellowing of the leaves, leaf drop, and stunting. Perhaps more serious is the ability of aphids to transmit viral diseases, such as mosaic and yellows. Aphids also secrete a sticky honeydew substance that may develop a sooty mold fungus.

The best defenses against ravaging insect attacks are to keep your plants in a healthy state and to remove all infected plant debris, since the eggs can overwinter, even in cold climates. Aphids are also attracted to high nitrogen levels and tender growth, so overfertilizing with nitrogen could render your plants more susceptible to aphid attacks.

If your plants become severely infected, you can treat them with an insecticidal soapy spray, a botanical insectide, or an approved chemical insecticide. Many gardeners have had success against aphids with home remedies, such as garlic spray.

See also:
Less common annuals p52
Perennials as dried flowers p60
Aphid control p95

flower completely with a drying agent, such as a mixture of dry sand and silica gel. Layer the mixture in a container and carefully place the flowers on top, then cover with more of the mixture. Cover the container and place in a dry, warm place. After five days, feel the petals — if they are dry, carefully remove and mount on stems. Other materials that can be used as drying agents include cornmeal and borax, although they tend to get lumpy. You will need to experiment with this method before you can rely on it.

Acroclinium, *Helipterum roseum* A daisylike, papery, white or pink flower with a yellow center. The flower appears early and is rather short-lasting. It can be picked in bud and will look especially nice in a bunch with other flowers.

Annual statice, *Limonium sinuatum* Commonly grown, annual statice makes a lovely dried flower. The colors range from blues, purples, and rose to yellow. Although easily grown, it does not do well when the summer is very rainy.

Bells of Ireland, *Moluccella laevis* This plant is treasured, not for its insignificant flowers, which grow on a 2-foot or 3-foot flower spike, but for its green bell-shaped calyx that surrounds the flower. It blooms in late summer. Pick when open and stiff.

Globe amaranth, *Gomphrena globosa* The timing of the harvest of these vibrant purple, pink, and white clover-type flowers isn't very important. The flowers change very little when dried.

Honesty or **money plant**, *Lunaria annua* The biennial money plant produces flat, papery pods that resemble silver dollars.

Immortelle, *Xeranthemum annuum* Growing 3 feet tall, this plant produces pink, white, and purple star-shaped papery flowers. Keep picking until the frost.

Larkspur, *Consolida* spp. Although not everlastings, larkspurs dry well. The colors include many blues, and purples, as well as white and pink. If picked too late, the flowers will fall off easily.

Love-in-a-mist, *Nigella damascena* Wait to harvest this plant until the seed pods appear; they are especially good in dried arrangements. The flowers are best dried in sand or some similar substance.

Ornamental grass There are several species of annual grasses, such as hare's-tail grass, *Lagurus ovatus*, that make attractive dried specimens. Many will reseed themselves and come up again the next season.

Rodanthe, *Helipterum manglesii* This plant grows 18 inches tall and produces small pink or white flowers with silvery buds. It has an early, short flowering season.

Strawflowers, *Helichrysum bracteatum* Strawflowers come in a large variety of colors. The plants are long-blooming if you keep them picked. Harvest in bud or before the center is visible. Attach wire stems to the flower heads. The size ranges from the bright, compact Bikinis (12 inches) to *Helichrysum monstrosum* (30 inches).

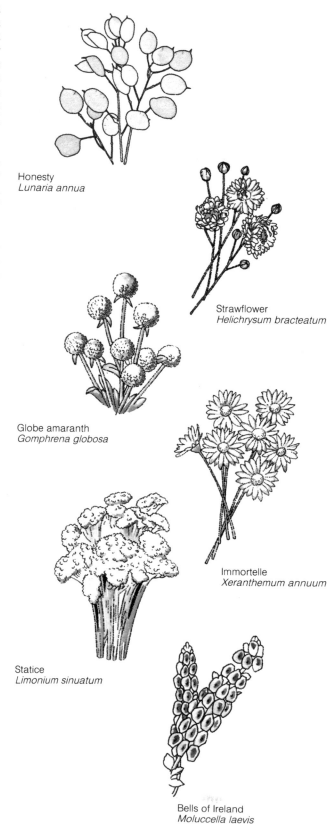

Honesty
Lunaria annua

Strawflower
Helichrysum bracteatum

Globe amaranth
Gomphrena globosa

Immortelle
Xeranthemum annuum

Statice
Limonium sinuatum

Bells of Ireland
Moluccella laevis

53

HERBACEOUS PERENNIALS

Plants for beds and borders

 What should I consider when planting a bed or border of herbaceous perennials?

Herbaceous perennials are nonwoody plants that will appear year after year, and, in most cases, die back to dormant roots during the winter. Most will live for a long time, provided they are cared for and divided at intervals.

If you are planning a perennial bed, you will probably want to plant a variety of specimens of varying heights, spreads, flowering seasons, and colors. And you may want to include in your planting some annuals, summer bulbs, and low-growing shrubs to provide a full season of interest. A bed at least 6 feet wide is nice, particularly if you include large plants and low shrubs, but the bed can be much narrower and still be very pleasing.

Since the plants will be in the same spot for a long time, good site selection is the key. The site should be well drained, with rich loose soil. Take the time to spade it deeply, clear it of perennial weeds, and incorporate plenty of organic matter into the soil. Trees or shrubs can be used as a background, but put the bed several feet away so there won't be root interference. The site should have at least a half day of sun, although more would be advantageous.

As you develop your plan, start small; you can continue to add more specimens as you see how well your plan is working. Here are some tips for selecting an aesthetically pleasing mix of plants.

- ☐ Select for colors that compliment each other (for example, blues, purples, and pinks) rather than shocking contrasts.
- ☐ Sizable clusters of different plants generally look better than individual plants scattered here and there. The sizes of clusters should vary. Allow one clump of plants to drift naturally into another.
- ☐ Plan for a continuous season of flowers with plants that bloom at different times.
- ☐ Vary the height of the plants. Don't limit yourself to tall plants in the back and short ones in the front; experiment. If the bed can be viewed from both sides, the tallest plants should be planted toward the middle.
- ☐ Some perennials, such as bee-balm, Silver King artemesia, and mint, can be invasive. One technique to prevent them from spreading is to grow these plants in containers that are sunk in the ground. When the plants become overcrowded, dig up the container and separate the plants.

In the North, plant your perennials in the spring for the greatest chance of success. Fall plantings are fine in most places, but allow at least two months before the cold sets in for the plants to develop root reserves.

See also:
Dividing chrysanthemums p59
Perennials for all-season color p59
Foliage plants p64
F1 hybrids pp118–19
Starting seedlings p142

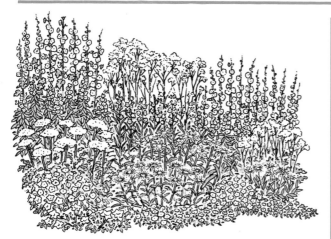

This herbaceous perennial bed contains hollyhocks and meadow rue for height, with purple phlox, blue canterbury bells, spiraea, golden yarrow and shasta daisies at the next level. The lower-growing plants in front include carpathian bellflower, gentian and colorful rock roses.

This less formal bed has a framework of shrubs: hydrangea, buddleia and potentilla, interplanted with red poker plants, coneflowers, phlox and heliopsis. Also included are crane's bill, oriental poppy and sedum. In front are masses of purple bellflowers, yellow sundrops and pink thrift.

 ## Is it better to grow herbaceous perennials from seed or to buy plants?

A glance through the catalog of any commercial nursery that sells perennial plants will tell you that stocking a garden this way can be very expensive. The high price per plant means that most gardeners can afford only a few each season. Obviously seeds are less expensive.

Unfortunately, you cannot always achieve the same results with seeds. First, only a limited range of varieties of each type of plant is available in seed. Often these are not the best varieties because many plants do not come true from seed and must be propagated by cuttings. Also, most of the perennials offered as seed are hybrid mixtures, which will give rise to plants in a range of colors and of varying quality. But if you don't mind taking a risk, you stand a good chance of producing at least some good individuals from seed.

Start perennials from seed during the summer and plant them out in early fall in time to become established before winter. Or start them sometime between late winter and early spring for spring planting — although few plants raised from seeds can be guaranteed to flower in the first season. This is another area where plants can offer a big advantage.

Remember, too, that having paid for a single initial plant, you will be able to increase your stock by cuttings or division. And there are few more satisfying and enjoyable ways of increasing your range of perennials than by exchanging cuttings and divisions with gardening friends and neighbors.

 ## When should I divide my herbaceous perennials?

Once you have established a perennial bed, it is a good idea to divide the plants regularly to rejuvenate them, control spreading, and increase the blooms.

Perennials should always be divided when dormant, either before or after flowering. If a plant is lifted during the period of active growth, it will wilt and die fairly soon as the plant will have experienced extensive root disturbance.

Generally, plants that bloom in the spring or summer will do well if divided in late summer or early fall. It is important, however, that the plants have a couple of months to settle in and recover before winter. If the plants bloom late, or if you have an early winter, don't divide them until spring.

Those few perennials, such as peony and hellebores, that resent disturbance (usually because they have thick, fleshy roots) should be moved in spring shortly before growth recommences. They should be divided only infrequently and cautiously.

How often you divide depends on many factors, including soil, growing conditions, species, and variety. In general, plan to divide your perennials every two to four years.

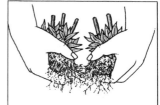

Divide an overgrown clump of perennials by pushing two spading forks into the crown and forcing the handles apart to separate the roots. Pull the clump apart and clear out any dead sections before replanting young rootstocks.

Is it possible to grow herbaceous perennials satisfactorily in a poor, shady site?

Shady? Certainly. Poor? With severe limitations. Many perennials will tolerate shade, although your choices of plants will be limited. The list below gives some suggestions for shade-tolerant perennials. There are shade-tolerant shrubs that you might also want to include.

Aconitum, Monkshood Zones 3 to 9. Monkshood prefers rich soil and does well in partial shade. The foliage is similar to that of delphiniums, with lovely blue, purple, yellow, or white flowers on 3-foot to 5-foot spikes. Try Bressingham Spire for deep violet flowers on 3-foot spikes or *A. naphellus* Album for white flowers on 3-foot to 4-foot spikes.

Ajuga, Buglewood Zones 3 to 9. Preferring good soil, this plant does well in shade or sun, spreads quickly, and makes an excellent ground cover and good rock garden plant. It is evergreen in mild climates. For a nonspreading species with blue flowers, try *A. pyramidalis*.

Alchemilla vulgaris, Lady's mantle Zones 3 to 9. Invaluable for its fresh green, ground-covering foliage and greenish flower sprays in the summer, lady's mantle tolerates partial shade. It grows to 18 inches.

Astilbe, False spirea Hardy to zone 5. Astilbes do well in good moist soil and partial shade. *A. × arendisii* grows 2 to 3 feet tall and has feathery, plumelike flowers in white, pinks, and reds. Fanal is a popular variety with brilliant red flowers, Rheinland has pink flowers, and Deutschland has white ones.

Asarum, Wild ginger Zones 4 to 8. This woodland perennial is shade-loving and prefers a good, rich soil. It grows low to the ground with rapidly spreading rhizomes, kidney-shaped leaves, and hard-to-see, brown, bell-shaped, drooping flowers.

Campanula, Bellflower Zones 3 to 9. These plants do well on moderately rich, well-drained soil, and many species do well in half or light shade. They produce blue or white flowers. *C. carpatica* grows to 12 inches tall and has lovely blue blooms all summer. This is an excellent choice for edging.

Cimicifuga simplex, Bugbane Zones 3 to 9. In partial shade this plant produces narrow, graceful, 5-foot spikes of tiny white flowers in late summer or autumn.

Geranium Some geraniums will thrive in partial shade. *G. macrorrhizum* will thrive in half shade and is drought-tolerant. It grows about 10 inches tall and produces magenta, pink, or bluish white flowers.

Digitalis, Foxglove Zones 3 to 8. Some foxgloves are perennials while others are actually self-sowing biennials. They all do best in damp, rich soil and partial shade. The flowers come in purple, white, rose, and, more rarely, yellow.

Helleborus Hardy to zone 3. You can grow helleborus

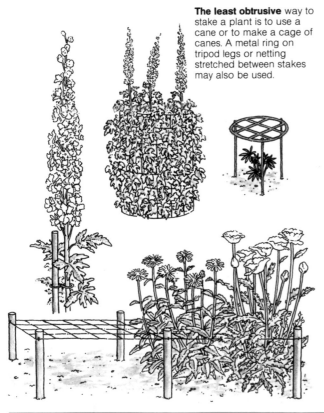

The least obtrusive way to stake a plant is to use a cane or to make a cage of canes. A metal ring on tripod legs or netting stretched between stakes may also be used.

Is there an easy way to tie in and stake herbaceous perennials?

Almost every gardener faced with this problem has asked how such plants survive in the wild where there is no green-fingered human with a ball of green twine to keep them upright. The answer to this is three-fold. First, many of the cultivated varieties of plants grown in gardens have been bred deliberately to produce larger-than-normal flower heads and so are less stable than their wild counterparts.

Second, most natural plant communities do not have bare spaces between the plants, which are held upright and protected from wind by their neighbors. And, third, toward the end of the season, many wild plants actually do fall over, spilling their seed as they do so. With no fastidious gardener's eye to offend, they thus perform their natural function perfectly well.

What does this tell you about the management of herbaceous perennials? It should tell you to look carefully before selecting varieties that appeal to you, for modern hybridists are well aware of the instability of many of the older forms and are constantly trying to improve their robustness. It explains why beds should be designed so as to achieve the optimum density of planting consistent with good growth, and why isolated

See also:
Difficult sites pp20–1
Shrubs for shade p79
Climbers for shade pp80–1
Shrubs for ground cover p87
Mulches p122

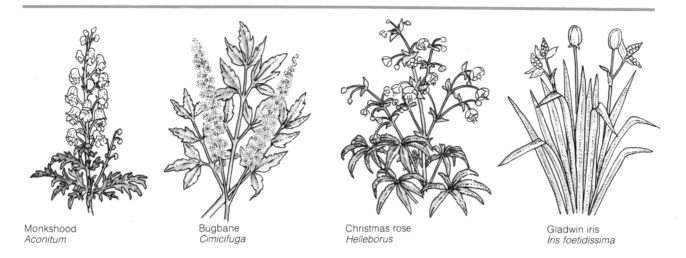

| Monkshood *Aconitum* | Bugbane *Cimicifuga* | Christmas rose *Helleborus* | Gladwin iris *Iris foetidissima* |

in partial or full shade. Most of the Christmas roses, such as *H. niger*, enjoy some shade. Growing 12 inches tall, it has white and rose flushed flowers which bloom late into the fall.

Lamium maculatum, Dead nettle Zones 3 to 9. This ground cover doesn't require good soil, it is drought-tolerant, and does well in partial shade. The flowers can be white, pink, rose, or purple. Beacon Silver has pink flowers and requires full shade.

Pachysandra Zones 4 to 8. A valuable ground cover for shady areas, pachysandra will even thrive under shrubs. *P. terminalis* Variegata has a nice silver edge.

Primula, Primrose This is a very large family, most of which like partial shade. All prefer moist, rich soil.

And what about poor soil? The simplest answer is to improve the soil. The plants that are more tolerant of poor soil include the lamiums, campanulas, and pachysandra. Dry, shady soils are even harder to deal with, but generous applications of organic matter will be beneficial.

Plants from the list that are fairly tolerant of dryness include alchemilla, digitalis, geranium, helleborus, and lamium.

tall and weak individuals should not be planted among much lower-growing species. Finally, it explains why dead flowering stems must be promptly removed from the plant.

Despite all this, you will still want to support many of the taller flowering perennials. This is often done with stakes or canes made of wood, bamboo, or metal. The plants should be tied to the stakes or canes with a soft material that won't injure the stems. You can also surround the plants (or groups of them) with chicken wire or stakes surrounded with twine. Another option is to buy manufactured supports that are made of metal rings or tripods; some of these have adjustable heights and diameters.

Get the supports in place early in the season; don't wait until the stems have fallen and are weakened or damaged by wind or rain.

 How important is mulching for herbaceous perennials?

Extremely. Not only will it keep weeds down and add to the aesthetic appeal of your garden, it will help retain moisture in the soil. Even the species mentioned earlier as being tolerant of fairly dry conditions will benefit from the improved moisture retention in the soil. An important rule with mulching is to remember that a surface mulch will maintain the soil in its existing condition — mulch a dry soil, and it will remain dry. So always mulch after a good rain or after heavy watering.

Spring is generally the best time to apply a mulch, for it will help to conserve moisture during the summer, although a mulch like straw in autumn has the benefit of protecting the crowns of perennials from the penetrating winter cold. Don't apply a winter mulch until the ground has frozen to a depth of 2 inches. If it is applied earlier, rodents may make a home in it and feed on the roots and crowns of your plants. It will also delay dormancy and plants will be more susceptible to low temperatures.

Good materials to use for mulching are well-rotted manure, compost, and leaf mold. Pulverized bark is aesthetically pleasing, although somewhat more expensive. Peat moss also looks good, but it tends to crust on top and become less permeable to water.

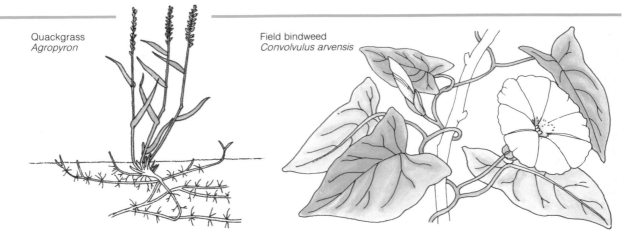

Quackgrass
Agropyron

Field bindweed
Convolvulus arvensis

How can I clean up a bed that is overrun with quackgrass, bermudagrass, or bindweed?

These are several common, deep-rooted, and tenacious perennial weeds that are very difficult to eradicate, particularly from established beds. Bermudagrass is more problematic in the South and West; quackgrass and bindweed are more of a problem in the northern two-thirds of the country.

If these weeds are present before you plant, there are several things you can do. If your problem is quackgrass or bindweed, and you don't mind waiting a year to plant, cultivate the area every couple of weeks throughout the season. By continuously taking off the tops of the weeds, the root reserves will gradually become depleted. You might complete this process by planting a weed-smothering crop, such as buckwheat, and/or a quick-growing cover crop, such as rye, which could be turned in before the next season. In a small area, you can mulch with a heavy layer of black plastic for the season.

What about using an herbicide? In a really badly infested area, you might try a nonselective chemical that will eradicate a great amount of plant life. After the chemical is applied, however, you may have a problem with residual roots that will still have to be removed with a fork.

With weeds that have invaded an established bed, some gardeners report success with mulching around perennials with a very thick layer of newspaper, topped with a mulch, such as wood chips. After a couple of seasons of this treatment, many perennial weeds will be largely eradicated.

Most horticulturalists agree that applying nonselective or even selective herbicides to an established bed risks causing damage to the perennials. So if all else fails, and you can't keep up with the weeding by hand, the best solution might be to dig up your perennials during the dormant season and move them to a new spot — permanently or until you can clear out the weeds in the old spot. Be careful not to transplant tenacious bits of roots along with your plants.

What do I need to know to grow succulents outdoors?

Succulents store water in their juicy leaves, stems, and roots in order to withstand drought. Although we usually think of cacti growing in the desert when we talk about succulents, there are many different kinds adapted to different growing conditions. Even in the coldest parts of the United States, there are succulents that are adapted to survive the climate, although most can survive outdoors year-round only in warm and arid regions.

There is a common misconception that succulents do best in full sun, sand, and with no watering. Actually, the amount of light succulents need varies greatly, so check with the nursery before buying a particular plant. With too much light, the sunny side of the plant may develop bleached or blackened areas. If there is too little light, the plant will become pale and the stem will thin out. Pay particular attention to light requirements when moving a plant from the house to the outside, and only gradually increase the intensity of light received by the plant.

Succulents should be raised in well-drained soil. A mix of two-thirds soil and one-third coarse sand is good. Generally, you should water your plants thoroughly when the soil dries out, although agaves and yuccas can get along with less water, and cacti prefer less still.

As for temperatures, most succulents prefer warm weather, but some can tolerate some cold if they are hardened-off. Opuntia, sedum, and sempervivum are the most cold hardy and can succeed in most parts of the United States. If your succulents are tender to frost, help them to go dormant and be less susceptible by cutting back on nitrogen fertilizer and water. You can also cover them for added protection — a good idea particularly in colder climates. Don't water succulents in the winter.

Because succulents grow slowly, most don't need additional fertilizer, although cacti, in particular, benefit from fertilizing from April through September for good growth and fruit and flower formation.

See also:
Minimal maintenance garden p26
Dividing perennials p55
Herbaceous perennial beds pp54–5
Foliage plants pp64–5
Naturalizing bulbs p68

What plants will give all-season color in a minimum maintenance bed?

It is an essential feature of any good flower bed that it gives continuity of color; the minimum maintenance aspect means using plants that require the least amount of staking and deadheading to produce the longest possible season of flowers.

In order to limit the time spent on weeding, it is important to provide good ground coverage with weed-suppressing foliage. For this reason, dahlias are included in our plan: although they need to be planted out at the beginning of each season and lifted at the end, they do provide good weed suppression. Similarly, although peonies have a fairly short flowering season, their large and attractive foliage lasts until the killing frost and provides an excellent foil for other plants.

The suggested plan is for a one-sided border against a wall or fence, but it could be doubled up, back to back, for an island bed. It requires an area of about 18 square yards, but larger or smaller beds could be planted by adjusting the number of plants. Where individual varieties are suggested, they have been chosen on the basis of our experiences, but other similar varieties would work as well.

Below is a key to plants in this minimal maintenance bed which would require about 18sqyds.

1 *Bergenia cordifolia* Perfecta; 2 *Cimicifuga racemosa*; 3 *Lilium henryi*; 4 *Echinops humilis*; 5 *Aconitum napellus* Bressingham Spire; 6 *Delphinium* Pacific Hybrids; 7 *Digitalis*, foxglove; 8 *Achillea filipendulina* Gold Plate; 9 *Paeonia*, peony; 10 *Chrysanthemum maximum* Snow Cap, shasta daisy; 11 Dahlias; 12 *Helenium autumnale*; 13 *Helleborus orientalis* Hybrids; 14 *Euphorbia polychroma*; 15 *Hosta* Krossa Regal; 16 *Geranium* Claridge Druce; 17 *Doronicum caucasicum*; 18 Gladioli; 19 *Phlox* Pinnafore Pink; 20 *Ceratostigma plumbaginoides*; 21 *Polygonum affine*; 22 *Sedum spectabile* Autumn Joy; 23 *Geranium sanguineum* Album; 24 *Lavandula angustifolia* Nana; 25 *Aster alpinus*; 26 *Hosta sieboldiana elegans*; 27 *Geranium grandiflorum*; 28 *Calamantha nepetoides*; 29 *Aurinia (= Alyssum) saxatile compactum*

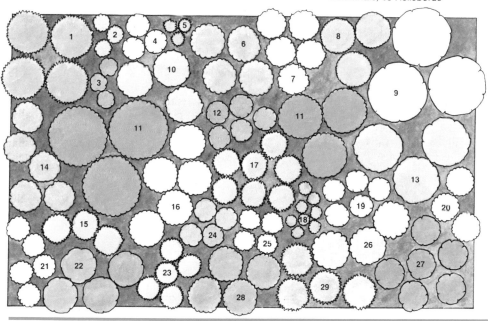

When should chrysanthemums be planted, divided, and pinched?

Since chrysanthemums bloom so beautifully in the fall (August through November or December) when many other flowers have stopped blooming, they are commonly offered for sale by nurseries at that time. However, they are more likely to winter over successfully if planted in the spring. If planted in the fall, most mums in zones 4 to 9 will winter over; but in the coldest areas, they should be covered with a mulch of hay after the ground freezes or be planted close together in a cold frame. They have most trouble wintering in wet soil.

Divide chrysanthemums each spring. Lift the entire plant. Then replant the stronger outside shoots and discard the center.

For more compact bushy plants, pinch back the tips of all the stems when they are 6 inches tall and keep this up until mid-July. (Skip this step with the smallest types, such as the cushion mums.) If you want fewer, larger flowers, disbud by removing all but four or five stems on each plant and pinch off all but the top bud on each. Provide support for taller varieties if they need it.

How can I have a successful perennial herb garden?

For a combination of function, beauty, and relatively low maintenance, nothing beats a perennial herb garden. Once established, a perennial herb garden will give you years of flowers, fragrance, and herbs to dry for culinary and medicinal purposes — for very little effort.

When planning where to locate an herb garden, remember that it should be accessible for frequent harvesting. Choose a site that gets at least six hours of sun every day. Plan the garden so small plants have plenty of room to spread. But with those herbs that spread prolifically, such as mint and comfrey, you may want to plant them in underground clay pots to contain them. If space is limited, consider raising some of the herbs you want in pots or tubs. Generally, herbs do best in well-drained and moderately rich, loose soil, although some herbs, like mint, prefer light shade and moist soil.

Which herbs to select is really a matter of personal preference. For a basic herb garden, you might include some mints, chives, fennel, lavender, lemon balm, oregano, rosemary, sage, winter savory, French tarragon, various thymes, bergamot, chamomile, salad burnet, and tansy. You may also want to interplant some annuals or biennials, such as sweet basil, borage, dill, and parsley.

Once established, herb gardens need little attention except for weeding and watering during dry spells. Herb gardens generally don't need much fertilizing, although the plants will respond to an application of a balanced fertilizer (such as 5–10–5 or compost) in the spring. Don't give them too much nitrogen as this could result in lush foliage that has a reduced concentration of fragrant oils.

If the herbs outgrow their bounds, or if you want more plants, you can divide most herbs easily — the best time is in the spring or fall. Herbs with spreading root systems, like mints, can be divided by taking just a small section from the parent and replanting.

Herbs can be harvested for using fresh all season long. The young leaves are best. To extend the foliage production, pick off flowers from tender plants, such as basil. For dried herbs, harvest just when the flower buds begin to open for the best concentrations of oils. Mints, oregano, and thyme are exceptions to this rule: their essential oils are at their peak when the plant is in full flower.

At the end of the season, cut the herbs near to the ground. Although herb gardens do not generally need winter protection, a light, airy mulch applied after the ground freezes can be beneficial in areas with severe winters. In cold climates, evergreens, such as rosemary, should be brought in for the winter.

 ## Which herbaceous perennials should I plant to use as dried flowers?

There are many perennials that make nice dried flowers, just as there are many annuals. To dry these flowers, follow the same methods as those outlined for annuals on page 52.

Achillea, Yarrow Zones 3 to 9. Yarrow has fernlike foliage and blooms in July and August with yellow, white, pink, and crimson flowers. It can tolerate dry weather and poor soils. Coronation Gold dries particularly well.
Anaphalis margaritacea, Pearly everlasting Hardy to zone 3. Often found growing wild, it has dry, white

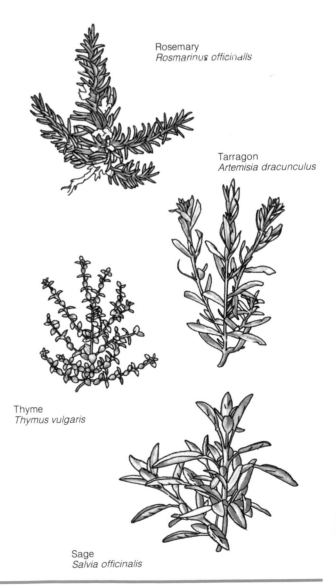

Rosemary
Rosmarinus officinalis

Tarragon
Artemisia dracunculus

Thyme
Thymus vulgaris

Sage
Salvia officinalis

clumps of round flowers. Pick them before they are fully open.

Artemesia Artemesia is a large genus of plants grown mainly for their foliage, which is often silvery and usually fragrant. They are tolerant of poor, dry soils.

Gypsophila paniculata, Baby's breath This is very popular in dried flower arrangements. It does well in full sun with well-drained soil. There are white and pink types and they bloom in July and August.

Liatris scariosa, Gay feather Zones 3 to 8. This plant usually produces purple flowers on spikes that grow up to 4 feet tall. It thrives in light soils with either sun or light shade.

Limonium latifolium, Perennial statice or sea lavender The perennial statice produces bright blue, pink, and purple flowers that don't fade if picked when the flowers are in full bloom.

Santolina chamaecyparissus, Lavender cotton Hardy to zone 6. This deciduous dwarf shrub grows only 8 to 10 inches tall and has silvery gray foliage and small, yellow, daisylike flowers.

Stachys lanata, Lamb's ears Zones 4 to 9. This low-growing plant has soft, silvery leaves and sends up tall spikes with tiny purple flowers.

In addition to those plants that are often cultivated in the garden, there are a great number of perennials growing wild that can be added to dried arrangements. Some of these include goldenrod, loosestrife, meadow-sweet, and hare's foot clover.

I want to attract hummingbirds to my garden. Which perennial plants should I choose?

Hummingbirds add an exciting dash of color to the garden. They are easy to attract once you understand their basic needs.

First, because they have such a high metabolism, they need a frequent nectar supply. They are particularly attracted to brightly colored tube-shaped flowers, especially to reds and oranges. However, vivid contrasts are as important as color; in the Southwest where the landscape is often brown, hummingbirds will go for greenish flowers. As the birds feed, they act as pollinators for some of the flowers. In fact, many brightly colored flowers have evolved to rely on hummingbirds, rather than insects, to pollinate them.

To attract hummingbirds, try planting salvia, cardinal flowers, trumpet vine, columbine, phlox, delphinium, and morning glories. In the South, also try lantana and mimosa; in the West, century plant, *Agave americana*, is another likely choice.

In order to assure constant visitors, plant species with overlapping bloom periods. Also, avoid insecticides because the birds eat insects and because the insecticide can get into the flowers and be ingested with the nectar.

Trumpetvine *Campsis*

The hummingbird's long beak is designed to dip into tube-shaped flowers in search of nectar.

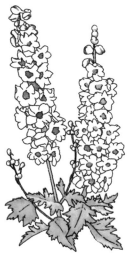
Delphinium *Delphinium elatum*

Columbine *Aquilegia*

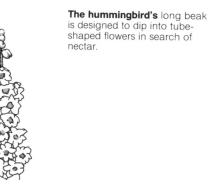

What kind of care do ferns require and what types are good in a garden?

Ferns need slightly acid, woodsy soil that is high in organic matter, although there are some species that prefer rockier areas and a more neutral pH. Generally, partial shade and constant moisture are necessary.

Once established, ferns need little care. Occasionally thin out the more vigorous ones and top dress with organic matter; other fertilization is not necessary. It is a good idea to divide ferns in the spring to avoid overcrowding. In the winter, mulching with leaves or hay to protect the crowns from the cold can be beneficial.

A few good choices for planting in the garden follow.

Adiantum pedatum, Maidenhair fern A very airy, graceful fern, maidenhair grows 12 to 26 inches tall. It prefers loose, well-drained soil.

Athyrium spp., Lady fern If the soil remains moist, this fern can tolerate a fair amount of sun. *A. felix femina* is delicate and lacy, with 36-inch fronds that turn dark green as the summer progresses.

Dryopteris spp., Wood fern or shield fern Most hardy to zone 3. This large group of ferns includes many types that are very easy to grow. They all need rich soil and light shade. The crested wood fern, *D. cristata*, has 30-inch fronds that are evergreen in some of the warmer climates.

Matteuccia struthiopteris, Ostrich fern Zones 2 to 8. This is a good fern for holding the soil; it does well in shade or sun. The outer, lacy fronds are shaped like the tail feathers of an ostrich. It can grow over 5 feet tall.

Osmunda cinnamomea Cinnamon fern Zones 3 to 8. This fern has large, upright, coarsely cut leaves. The name comes from the sterile frond that resembles a cinnamon stick. It needs moisture and will thrive in wet swampy land as well as in moist shade. It can tolerate some sun. A very sturdy plant, it can grow to 4 feet tall.

Cinnamon fern
Osmunda cinnamomea

Lady fern
Athyrium felix-femina

Toothed wood fern
Dryopteris spinulosa

Ostrich fern
Matteuccia struthiopteris

Are daylilies as easy to grow as I have heard?

Probably. They are very hardy and tolerant of extremes in the weather, and they multiply freely. Daylilies can be grown in all parts of this country and numerous varieties are available. They are evergreen in many climates, and partially so in the colder ones.

Daylilies prefer a fertile, well-drained soil with full sun or partial shade. Unless the soil is unusually poor, extra fertilizing is not necessary. They can be planted almost any time when the ground isn't frozen. In the North, however, the evergreen types (specified in catalogs) do better when planted in the spring. Set the plants 1 to 2 feet apart.

One routine chore these prolific plants require is dividing every four or five years. To divide, dig up a clump of daylilies, cut the roots back by about half, and cut the foliage to several inches. Separate the clumps with a knife, leaving four to six shoots per clump. Then replant.

Cut back dead foliage in the fall. In cold climates, mulching may be beneficial in the winter.

The varieties are too numerous to list, so browse through catalogs to get an idea of what is available. Many of those listed in catalogs are tetraploids, which have twice the number of chromosomes and, it is advertised, larger flowers with more intense colors.

See also:
Annuals that reseed p51
Perennials for shade pp60–1
Foliage plants p64

I'd like to grow perennial native wildflowers in my garden. What do I need to know?

The first thing to know is that wildflowers should not be dug up from their natural settings. Many of our wild plants are already in danger of extinction from development. We must not add to that the pressure of overcollection. Even species that seem abundant in your area may be bordering on extinction elsewhere and should not be collected. Besides, many wildflowers have convoluted root systems, which help them accommodate natural barriers but make root damage inevitable and transplanting risky.

There are, however, many catalogs that offer seeds and native plants — but make sure the nursery either propagates its own stock or collects only to save plants from sites that are being bulldozed for development.

When deciding which plants to buy, research each individual plant's normal growth habits to determine if you can provide similar conditions in terms of soil, moisture, light, temperatures, and so on. But don't forget the many climatic factors that may affect success — including the amount of sun, wind, and snow cover.

If your plants arrive bare-rooted, which they often do, it is a good idea temporarily to pot them in a light potting mix until there is some leaf growth. Then transplant them into a permanent spot.

Once your plants are established, many can be propagated by seed, although you may get some variations. Gather the seeds when the seed pod is plump, hard, and dark. Generally, seeds should be collected within a month after flowering. Since most of our wild plants have evolved in areas of cold winters, most of the seeds will need a period of cold before they can germinate. So plant seeds in the fall, winter, or very early spring in flats that can be left out in a cold frame or garage. Then transplant the seedlings when they are several inches tall. Many can also be propagated by cuttings or division.

Many, many wildflowers can be successful in gardens. Here is a sample listing.

Anemone patens, Pasque flower The pasque flower prefers well-drained soil in full sun. The purple or white flowers resemble crocuses, while the foliage is finely cut. It is propagated by seed or division in the spring.

Cornus canadensis, Bunchberry The flowers of the bunchberry look like miniature dogwood blossoms growing on a 3-inch whorl of oval leaves in late spring. It forms clusters of red berries in the fall. The plant prefers cool, moist, acid soils in full shade.

Cypripedium calceolus, Yellow lady's slipper If you have a shady site, you may want to start with yellow lady's slipper, the easiest cultivated native orchid. It will do well in many different climates if you provide well-drained, humusy soil. A spring-blooming plant, it

should be propagated by division in the spring.

Delphinium tricorne, Wild larkspur The first of the delphiniums, this blooms in the spring with small violet, white, or blue flowers on 1-foot to 2-foot stems. It prefers well-drained neutral soil with at least half sun.

Lilium canadense, Canada lily The Canada lily produces nodding yellow or reddish bell-shaped flowers in early summer. It prefers rich soil, partial sun, and plenty of moisture.

Lobelia cardinalis, Cardinal flower or red lobelia. This is another suitable plant for a shady site. It is easy to grow from seed and blooms with brilliant red flowers in late summer. Cardinal flowers prefer moist, well-drained soil in partial shade.

Sanguinaria canadensis, Bloodroot One of the earliest spring wild flowers, bloodroot has large white flowers with yellow stamens. The 8-inch silvery leaves are uniquely shaped. The plants prefer rich soil and summer shade, with some sun at blooming time.

Yellow lady's slipper
*Cypripedium calceolus
pubescans*

Can you suggest some foliage plants to give a range of colors and leaf shapes in the garden?

Although the value of foliage plants in the house is widely acknowledged, they are generally not given the recognition they deserve in the garden. There is, nonetheless, a wide variety to choose from and some nurseries even specialize in them. Don't forget to include ferns in your consideration of foliage plants. Details about raising ferns can be found on page 62.

Most foliage plants produce flowers too, and sometimes these are appealing in their own right. In some instances, attractively leaved varieties can be chosen of what are basically flowering plants. The following list, however, was compiled only with leaf color, form, shape, and availability in mind.

Artemesia Zones 5 to 9. This is a large genus of lovely silvery foliage plants. *A. ludoviciana albula* (Silver King) has fragrant silvery foliage that dries nicely. It grows from 1 to 4 feet and prefers sun or light shade.

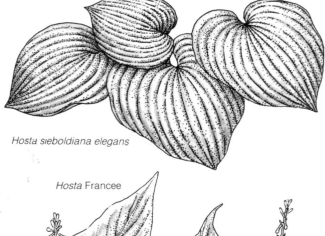

Hosta sieboldiana elegans

Hosta Francee

Hosta lancifolia

Bergenia Zones 3 to 9. These plants are known for their shade tolerance. They require sandy soil. Bergenia have thick rosettes of fleshy, rounded leaves. *B. cordifolia* has heart-shaped, glossy leaves with clusters of pink flowers that start blooming in May.

Hosta There is a tremendous range of hostas, and most have purple or white flowers. Although usually considered plants for a moist bed, they will put up with a surprising level of dryness. The list that follows is representative of the main types. *H. fortunei* has bluish green leaves, no variegation; *H. marginata* has oval leaves with a white margin; *H.* × Piedmont Gold has yellow leaves; *H. sieboldiana elegans* is a larger plant with bluish-green leaves; *H.* Francee has dark green leaves with striking white margins; *H. undulata* has wavy leaves; *H. lancifolia* has waxy, narrow leaves; and *H.* × Love Pat has puckered leaves.

Lamium Because the cultivated lamiums are relatives of the dead nettle, many gardeners scorn them, but they make an attractive ground cover. *L. maculatum* Album has dark green leaves splotched with silvery white.

Mentha Many of the mints have attractive foliage and, although invasive, they can be contained by growing them in large pots sunk to the rim. A good one for its foliage is *M. rotundifolia* Variegata, which has green and white variegated leaves.

Ophiopogon Zones 6 to 10. The variety *O. planiscapus* Nigrescens is a grasslike member of the lily family. It is not to everyone's taste, but it is invaluable for its rare blackish leaves. This 6-inch ground cover has small pink flowers.

Sedums These fleshy-leaved plants thrive in poor soils and drought conditions. Actually they do well in many climates. Some varieties have interesting flowers; some are evergreen.

Sempervivum tectorum, Hens and chickens Hardy to zone 4. Ideal for rock gardens, these plants produce a fleshy rosette of leaves and multiply by forming new plants at the base of the old. They prefer a hot, dry location.

Plants with interesting foliage add variety of form and color to a bed. Clockwise from the top are: *Fatsia japonica*; bearded iris; hosta; oenothera; lavender; dead nettle; cinnamon fern and peony.

See also:
Perennials for shade pp60–1
Ferns p61
Bamboos p81
Propagation of shrubs, climbers, ground covers p83

Yucca Yuccas have an assertive presence and look good in a large tub or pot as well as in a bed. The foliage is spiky and swordlike, sometimes viciously so. *Y. filamentosa* is the species seen most often since it is hardy even in the North (to zone 4), and there are variegated types now available.

Don't forget to consider grasses and bamboos (they both belong to the same family; bamboos are woody). A danger with these plants is that many types are invasive, but they do add unique colors and shapes to a garden planting scheme.

Interesting grasses include *Molinia caerulea* Variegata, which forms dense clumps of narrow, 2-foot-tall leaves with cream margins (hardy to zone 5) and *Festuca ovina glauca*, sheep's fescue, (hardy to zone 4), which has dense tufted mounds of 12-inch bluish foliage.

Among the bamboos, don't overlook *Arundinaria viridistriata* (hardy to zone 7). This is one of the best variegated bamboos, although it can look a little ragged toward the end of the season. It grows a little over 3 feet tall with pale green canes and white stripes on the leaves. *Bambusa multiplex* varieties often have yellow or striped leaves. *Shibataea kumasaca* (hardy to zone 8) is a very compact plant, with leaves a more or less uniform pale green.

If I'm not ready to divide my perennials, can I take cuttings to propagate them?

Yes. Many perennials can be propagated by stem cuttings or basal cuttings, a few can be propagated by root cuttings, and very few (sedums mainly) by leaf cuttings. Grasses and members of the lily family cannot be propagated from cuttings.

Several hours before taking a stem cutting, water the plant well. If the plant is old, take the cutting from younger growth. Cut the stem off cleanly just below where the leaf joins the stem. Fill a pot with a light soil mix — one part sand to one part peat. Most stem cuttings should be planted immediately, but ones with sticky sap, like geraniums, should be allowed to dry for an hour or two to avoid rot. Plant the stem with the bottom end 1 inch below the surface of the soil. Fashion a mini-greenhouse with a piece of plastic over the cutting or put the cutting in a closed cold frame out of the direct sun. You can also plant the cutting right in the garden covered by a mini-greenhouse. The ideal rooting temperature is 65 degrees F. to 75 degrees F., although most perennials will root at lower temperatures. Pull gently to determine if the cutting has rooted. Once it has established a good set of roots, transplant to the garden. Chrysanthemums are one of the easiest perennials to root with stem cuttings. Delphiniums, pinks, petunias, and dahlias also can be successfully propagated in this way.

Basal cuttings are just short, young shoots severed near the base. They are treated in the same manner as a stem cutting.

Some perennials, like oriental poppies and phlox, can be easily propagated with root cuttings. This is best done in early spring. You should select roots that are somewhat thicker than a pencil.

A simple "mini-greenhouse" can be used to create the warm and moist conditions necessary for rooting herbaceous cuttings. Don't allow the plastic to lie directly on the leaves.

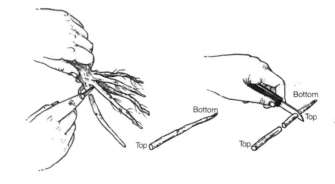

When taking root cuttings, cut the roots into 2-in to 4-in sections. Set the sections upright in a pot containing a light mix of sand and peat or loamy soil, making sure to orient them correctly. Cover the cuttings with ½in of soil. Keep the pot shaded and moist until shoots emerge; plant out when roots and plant seem sturdy.

BULBS, CORMS AND TUBERS

Flowers from
underground storage

How deeply should bulbs be planted?

There are so many different types of bulbous plants that no single rule fits every situation. It is usually suggested that you plant your bulbs and corms at a depth equal to two and a half times the average diameter. This system works reasonably well with most, but not all, bulbs and corms.

Lilium candidum, Madonna lily, is an outstanding example of a bulb that must be planted close to the surface of the soil and will perish if buried deeply. It is the only lily that requires shallow planting. On the other hand, *Iris reticulata* must be planted deeper than the general rule suggests. To plant this bulb at two and a half times its diameter would place the base at only 2 inches deep or so. Although the bulb may flower for one season at this depth, it may well be washed or pulled from the soil or produce only leaves in future years. It is commonly suggested that *I. reticulata* be planted at least 4 inches deep.

In light sandy soils, you may want to plant slightly deeper, and in heavy clay, slightly shallower, than the general rule. Some people feel that planting deeper regardless of the soil type can help to delay flowering, which may be desirable. A better course of action might be to plant the bulbs in a northern exposure.

The chart depicts the best general planting depths for some common bulb species.

1 *Lilium candidum*; **2** *Cyclamen persicum*; **3** Puschkinia; **4** Muscari; **5** *Scilla hispanica*; **6** *Acidanthera bicolor*; **7** *Galanthus nivalis*; **8** *Narcissus* spp.; **9** *Iris reticulata*; **10** *Lilium auratum*; **11** *Fritillaria imperialis*

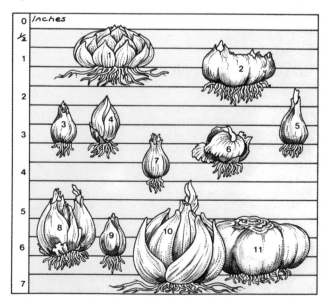

See also:
Naturalizing bulbs in grass p68
Treating bulbs before planting p71
Irises p73
Cutting foliage after flowering p74

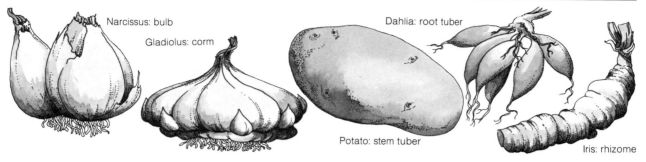

Narcissus: bulb

Gladiolus: corm

Dahlia: root tuber

Potato: stem tuber

Iris: rhizome

What is the difference between a bulb and a corm?

We often mention bulbs and corms together because both give rise to the same types of plant, generally require the same treatment, and serve a similar purpose in the plants that produce them. But bulbs and corms are quite different botanically.

A bulb is a specialized form of shoot in which the leaves are closely folded over each other and swollen in order to store food reserves for the young plant. The stem on which the leaves are borne is reduced in size and shape to a flattened plate at the base, and from this modified stem the roots arise. So even though no roots may be present when you plant the bulbs, place this flat plate downward in the soil.

Some bulbs (onions, narcissi, and tulips, for example) have swollen leaves closely covering the entire structure, with the outermost leaves reduced to paper scales. In other bulb types, of which lilies are the best-known example, the swollen scales are more loosely overlapping and have no papery outer layer. At the base of the parent bulb, small buds form, and from these, the daughter bulbs develop. In narcissi, for instance, the old and new bulbs remain attached, and eventually a large mass develops. In other plants, the old parent bulb dies, leaving one or two slightly smaller offspring.

Structurally more simple than a bulb, a corm is a solid, swollen stem that serves the purpose of storing food. Superficially, some corms, such as those of crocus, look like bulbs, but they have a bud at the top, not within. One or more — as with gladioli — daughter corms are formed below the parent during growth. These should be carefully separated if the corms are lifted at the end of the season.

Some plants, such as potatoes, produce swollen storage organs that are neither bulbs nor corms but stem tubers. And these must be distinguished from root tubers, of which dahlias are the best-known example. Stem tubers bear buds over a large part of the surface (potato eyes are buds), whereas root tubers have buds only at the top.

Finally, among the bulbous plants in your gardening catalogs will be lilies-of-the-valley and irises. Although some irises do produce genuine bulbs, all of the large, familar bearded forms, as well as lilies-of-the-valley, develop swollen rhizomes — fleshy stems that creep horizontally below the surface of the soil.

In this chapter, we will be referring to all plants that produce swollen food storage structures as bulbous plants, whether or not the storage organ is a bulb in the botanical sense.

What soil preparation is needed before planting bulbs?

Because their food reserves are already contained within the swollen storage tissues, bulbous plants will give a good display of flowers in the season after planting, with the absolute minimum of soil preparation. But after flowering, that food reserve will be depleted. If the plants are to repeat their show the following year, they must have a fertile soil.

Before planting, make sure the soil is well drained to minimize the likelihood of the soft fleshy tissues succumbing to rot. It is a good idea to incorporate plenty of organic matter into the soil to fertilize and lighten it at the same time.

If the soil has a tendency to become waterlogged, place the individual bulbs on a bed of sand mixed with bonemeal. With the most rot-susceptible bulbs — those with overlapping scale leaves like lilies and fritillarias — you can pack sand around the bulbs as well as underneath them.

When you plant, make sure that no manure comes into direct contact with the bulbs, for this will encourage rotting. Manure can, however, be worked in below the planting depth to add to the fertility of the soil. A general light application of bonemeal, well worked into the soil or mixed into each planting hole, will aid in root development.

A bulb planter can be a useful tool for planting single bulbs in grass or moist soil. Push the planter into the ground to the required depth to remove a core of earth; place the bulb in the hole and replace the soil and grass neatly.

What are the best bulbs for naturalizing in grass?

Masses of bulbs among grass look spectacular and add interest to areas under trees that are otherwise pretty bleak early in the season. And bulbs grown amid grass do not occupy bedding space needed for other plants when their flowering season is over. Also, the dying foliage of bulbs that have already flowered does not look nearly as unsightly in grass as it does in a bed.

The chief consideration in selecting species and varieties is to look for bulbs that will not be in competition with the grass. Many of the bulbs that naturalize successfully are fairly large and favor being planted quite deeply, below the level at which the grass roots deplete the nutrients in the soil. Second, since planting into established grass is laborious and something you will want to do only once, the bulbs should be capable of flowering for many years without needing to be replanted. Daffodils and narcissi are the most obvious choices for naturalizing, but some varieties will be more successful than others when grown this way.

In addition to daffodils and narcissi, there are many other bulbous plants that look excellent in grass. The lilac-colored autumn-flowering *Colchicum autumnale* (often wrongly called crocus) produces its 8-inch flowers after the leaves have died down. Some of the genuine autumn crocuses also naturalize well.

Many of the spring-flowering crocuses naturalize exceedingly well in short grass. Among the large-flowered Dutch types, consider Jeanne d'Arc (white), Queen of the Blues (silvery lilac), Yellow Giant (egg yellow), and Striped Beauty (white, streaked purple). They can be interplanted with another good plant for turf, the golden-yellow winter aconite, *Eranthis hyemalis*. The tiny hoop-petticoat daffodil *Narcissus bulbocodium* is another delightful plant that looks excellent in short grass. Cyclamen always look pretty (both in flower and leaf) in short grass beneath trees; *C. hederifolium* is a nice and readily available autumn-flowering type. To bring a touch of class to your grass planting,

try *Fritillaria meleagris*, the checkered flower. These are checkerboard, bell-shaped flowers that come in a range of colors on 10-inch stems and prefer cool, shady spots.

Generally, plant small bulbs in short turf, and trim carefully around the foliage. After the plant flowers, allow the foliage of the lower-growing bulbs to die down naturally. The foliage of all bulbs should be mown only when the plants are dormant below the ground — for daffodils and narcissi this usually means six weeks after flowering finishes.

There may be some competition between the bulbs and the grass, so consider applying a balanced liquid fertilizer after they have finished flowering. On the other hand, if you fertilize your lawn in the fall, this probably will not be necessary. In fact, naturalized bulbs sometimes fail to flower because the extra nitrogen from the fall lawn fertilization causes late growth and prevents hardening-off.

Sometimes naturalized plantings will become overcrowded, producing much foliage and few flowers. Since bulbs like daffodils are continually forming offsets that become new bulbs, even naturalized plantings may have to be dug and divided every few years.

Dig the bulbs once the foliage has yellowed and leave them to dry in the sun for a few days so the offsets will separate easily. Then replant immediately or store in a cool, airy place for the summer and replant in the autumn.

GOOD VARIETIES FOR NATURALIZING

The following daffodils and narcissi can be relied on to naturalize well and to give a good range of flowering season and colour.

Variety	Color
King Alfred	golden yellow
Mount Hood	white
Spellbinder	greenish-yellow
Barrett Browning	red and white, small cup
Duke of Windsor	cream cup/white frill
Green Island	greenish-white cup/white frill
Mrs R. O. Backhouse	pale apricot cup/white frill
Ice Follies	pale yellow-white cup/white frill
Irene Copeland	double; creamy white-apricot
White Lion	double; white-cream
Actaea	yellow eye, edged red/white frill

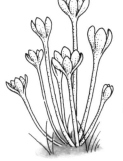

Colchicum autumnale Album

Cyclamen hederifolium

Snake's head fritillary
Fritillaria meleagris

See also:
Bringing plants indoors p19
Naturalized bulbs for minimal
   attention p26
Lifting dahlia tubers p77

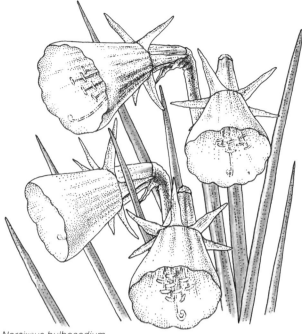

Narcissus bulbocodium
conspicuus

Winter aconite
Eranthis hyemalis

Should bulbs be lifted every year or can they be left from season to season?

Most bulbs — naturalized in grass or planted in beds — will survive and proliferate if left more or less indefinitely. While some gardeners routinely lift almost all their bulbs each season, it seems doubtful whether the time and effort spent is worth it — except with a few nonhardy plants.

The two most common candidates for annual lifting are lilies and tulips. However, given a good surface mulching with leaf mold and well-drained soil, most lilies will survive and multiply for many years without lifting. Tulips are often lifted since, in the process of multiplying, they tend to produce smaller and less uniform flowers. Gardeners may lift and discard all or the smallest of the offsets and replant. Planting tulips more deeply encourages them to multiply less and to continue to produce large flowers for a longer time.

Some nonhardy bulbs, such as amaryllis, can be left in the ground in the warmest climates, since their roots resent disturbance. There are some nonhardy bulbs, though, that either lose roots or multiply so rapidly — as do gladioli — that they are generally replanted annually, regardless of the climate. With tender, nonhardy bulbs, such as cannas, glads, and tuberous begonias, lift the bulbs after all the foliage has died down completely.

If you want to lift and separate a group of bulbs, do it at the beginning of the dormant period, just after the foliage has died down. After separating, return the bulbs to the ground so that the roots can start developing.

The small, deep yellow hoop-petticoat *Narcissus bulbocodium conspicuus* blooms in late winter. Its narrow, cylindrical leaves and flaring trumpet show to best advantage when it is grown in short grass. The stems of winter aconite,

Eranthis hyemalis, are bare, with only a collar of pale green leaves around the base of the cup-shaped golden-yellow flowers. Plant them in drifts with snowdrops and early-flowering crocuses for a stunning effect in early spring.

Sweetly scented *Crocus laevigatus* is completely hardy and can often be seen poking up through the snow. Its flowers

range from white to pale blue-lavender, with deep purple veining and bright orange centers and stamens.

Is it possible to have bulbs flowering in succession right through the year?

Unless you live in zones 9 or 10, you won't be able to plan on having bulbs bloom all year-round *outdoors* — but if you include forcing bulbs indoors during the winter, it is possible to have bulbs in flower throughout the year.

Where you live, and the dates of your last spring frost and first fall frost, will determine the types of bulbs you can plant and the length of blooming. Planning for blooms is reasonably simple since most bulbs have predictable flowering habits and bloom in a predictable order within a season, regardless of the location. For example, in zone 4, the early spring bulb season runs from late March to late May, while the same bulbs in zone 8 will bloom from mid-February to mid-April.

To plan for a long bloom season, be aware that some summer and fall bulbous plants will blossom until the frost, while hardy bulbs tend to have a shorter set bloom period. But while a single bulb might bloom for only a week, varieties within the genus might bloom at slightly different times, so by planting a combination of varieties, you can often stretch the bloom season. Some bulbs, such as gladioli, can be planted successively throughout the season for a long bloom period.

In addition to planting different varieties to extend the season of bloom, there are certain planting techniques that can affect the blooming time. For instance, the type of soil in which the bulbs are planted will make a difference. As might be expected, bulbs planted in clay will bloom later than those planted in light, sandy soils.

The early spring bulbs include snowdrops, winter aconites, and dwarf irises. These are followed by such flowers as crocuses, daffodils, hyacinths, and fritillarias. While most of these early spring bulbs prefer cool climates, they can be planted to begin flowering in January and February in most of the warmer climates. In the coldest parts of the United States, blooming will begin in early April.

Summer-flowering bulbs include allium, cannas, callas, lilies, and gladioli. Some summer bulbs, such as tuberous begonias, can be started indoors in northern areas and moved outside later.

In the fall-flowering group, there are dahlias, colchicums, nerines, cyclamens, and autumn-flowering crocuses. The most long-lasting in this group are the dahlias, which will bloom from mid-summer until freezing weather sets in.

Unless you live in a very warm zone, winter flowering is mainly confined to forcing bulbs indoors. Suitable bulbs include narcissi, hyacinths, and other spring-flowering bulbs, as well as amaryllis and tender tropical bulbs, such as gloxinia, which are almost always treated as houseplants. Not all bulbs are suitable for forcing, so purchase recommended varieties.

If you live where amaryllis can be grown outdoors all year, you can have early spring bulbs blooming in January and February. But in zone 10, spring-flowering bulbs are rarely grown.

Crocus cancellatus
September

Crocus longiflorus
November

Crocus speciosus
October

Crocus tomasinianus albus
March

Crocus laevigatus
December, January

Crocus sieberi
February

AN EXTENDED SEASON OF NARCISSUS

Dates are for sample zone 8; dates will change but order of bloom remains the same for other zones.

Average bloom	Variety	Color
March 1	van Scion	yellow
March 3	Pretty Miss	white/yellow
March 9	Quail	yellow
March 12	Ice Follies	white
March 17	Magnet	white/yellow
March 20	Flower Record	white/orange
March 23	Goblet	white/yellow
March 28	Mount Hood	white/yellow
April 1	Bridal Crown	white/yellow
April 3	Mary Copeland	white/orange
April 8	Geranium	white/orange
April 10	Cheerfulness	white/yellow

See also:
Bulbs, corms and tubers p67
Soil preparation for
    planting bulbs p67
Potting mixes p15

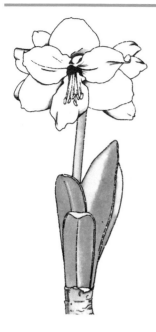

Amaryllises, *Hippeastrum* spp., can bloom for many years indoors to provide a splash of color. They are planted from October to March for blooms from December through April.

 ## What is the difference between a daffodil and a narcissus?

All the plants we call daffodils and narcissi are either species, varieties, or hybrids belonging to the genus *Narcissus*. For horticultural purposes, the genus is divided into several groups, depending on the species from which the particular plant was derived, its flower type, and its flower color.

The name daffodil has no strict scientific meaning, but it tends to be applied to those plants whose flowers have markedly elongated trumpets, irrespective of size. And some bulb nurseries habitually refer to any member of the genus *Narcissus* as a daffodil.

 ## Why do some of my bulbs refuse to flower but produce leaves?

Although it is difficult to generalize, since there are so many different types of bulbous plants, there are several common reasons for an obstinate refusal to flower.

The most common is simply that too much has been expected of the plants, and they have been crowded or have not been fed and given the wherewithal to replenish food reserves exhausted during the first season's growth. This is especially true in poor soil or where no advance cultivation and fertilizing is carried out before planting. If the foliage is cut down too soon in the previous season, the plant may not have been able to manufacture and store enough food to flower. Or, if sun-loving bulbs are grown in the shade, they may not be able to manufacture enough food for flower production.

A second reason for a failure to flower is that the bulbs have been attacked by a pest or disease — a bulb rot or maggots of the narcissus fly, for example. Some of these problems will be more serious in certain seasons than others, but three general precautions can be taken. *Never* plant bulbs on waterlogged or poorly drained soil. If the soil is wet, you can soak the bulbs in a fungicide before planting. If the problem is insects, you can apply an approved insecticide to discourage soil pests. Finally, don't replant healthy bulbs in an infected or infested area.

Another reason bulbs fail to flower is a build-up of virus contamination in the plants, which sometimes occurs after several years. There is no way to determine with certainty that this has indeed happened, and no cure. If feeding the plants fails to achieve results, but there is no sign of rot or pest attack on the bulbs, virus should be suspected and fresh stock planted.

 ## What is the process of forcing bulbs?

Quite simply it is manipulating conditions so the plant will bloom at a time other than its normal flowering season.

Hardy bulbs, such as hyacinths, tulips, and daffodils, should have about six to ten weeks of temperatures between 35 degrees F. and 45 degrees F. (although most will flower with less) — outdoors, in a cold garage, or in the refrigerator — before they will flower. Then move the bulbs to a shaded spot for several days, then to a sunny window where the temperature stays between 50 degrees F. and 65 degrees F. Water the soil when dry. When buds appear, move to indirect light.

Tender bulbs, such as freesias, should be potted in the autumn and grown in a cool (50 degrees F.) shady spot inside. Keep the soil damp. When roots start to develop (tug on the bulbs to check), move to provide temperatures of 55 degrees F. to 60 degrees F. and more light. When the buds open, move back into the shade. Rest the bulbs in dry soil for the summer.

Many of the spring bulbs, particularly hyacinths and crocuses, as well as tender narcissus, can be grown in pebbles and water or in water alone. With paperwhites, bury the bottom of the bulb in a container of pebbles, keeping its base just above the water line. When the shoots are several inches tall, move the container to a window. Alternatively, you can plant both tender and hardy bulbs in a well-drained soil mix so that the top of the bulb pokes through the soil.

All bulbs have adequate nutrients to produce good flowers, but if you want to save these indoor bulbs for replanting, you will have to fertilize them after they have finished flowering.

71

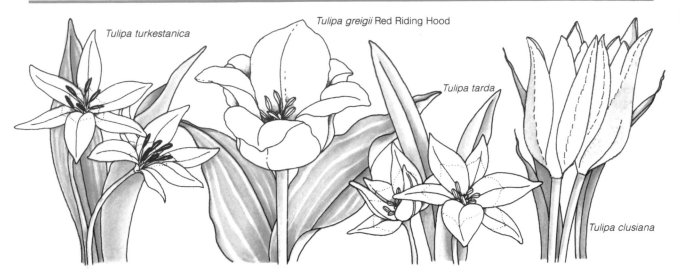

Tulipa turkestanica

Tulipa greigii Red Riding Hood

Tulipa tarda

Tulipa clusiana

What are species tulips and how do they differ from normal garden tulips?

All plants that grow wild and have not been specially selected, crossed, or otherwise bred by horticulturists are natural species. When these unaltered plants are grown in gardens, gardeners use the word species as a prefix to distinguish them from hybrids. Thus, species tulips, often called botanical tulips, are wild tulips, principally from the western parts of Asia, whereas the Darwins, Parrot-flowered, and other familar garden tulips are all hybrids, derived over many years of breeding from one or more of the species.

Recently, species tulips have again become popular and widely available as their merits as garden plants have become more widely recognized. They have several appealing features. Most are lower growing and have smaller flowers than the hybrids and so are excellent in small beds and rock gardens. They occur in a wide range of flower shapes and colors. By choosing the right ones, you can manage to have them blooming for a six-week period. In addition, despite their increased popularity, they still have the appeal of novelty.

About twenty pure species are frequently seen in catalogs and garden centers, together with a small selection of varieties of a few of them and a range of hybrids obtained by crossing *Tulipa kaufmanniana* with *T. greigii* or *T. fosteriana*. It is sometimes suggested that the bulbs be lifted every year, but this is not necessary, although the flower size and quality of some of the *kaufmanniana* hybrids may diminish in time. The selection given in the table is made largely on the basis of variety in form and flowering season.

VARIETIES OF SPECIES TULIPS (TULIPA)

Species	Color	Height inches	Flowers
acuminata	green and red twisted petals	18	May
aucheriana	pink with yellow base	4	April
batalinii Bronze Charm	bronze apricot	5	May
biflora	white, two or three per stem	6	March
clusiana	white with red stripe	12	April
eichleri	scarlet with yellow and black center	9	May
fosteriana Red Emperor	scarlet with black and yellow base	18	March/April
fosteriana White Emperor	white with yellow center	20	March/April
greigii	scarlet (with spotted leaves)	8	April
greigii Red Riding Hood	scarlet with black base (spotted leaves)	8	April
kaufmanniana	yellow/pink with white center	8	March
kolpakowskiana	red with golden center	12	March/April
marjoletti	soft primrose border with rose-red petals	20	May
maximowiczii	scarlet	5	April
praestans Fusilier	scarlet-orange, up to five per stem	8	April
pulchella violacea	purple with black or yellow center	4	February/March
sylvestris	yellow	16	April
tarda	cream with yellow center	6	April
turkestanica	white with yellow center, up to nine per stem	9	February/March
urumiensis	bronze with golden center	6	March/April

KAUFMANNIANA HYBRIDS

Cherry Orchard	scarlet red	8	March
Heart's Delight	pink with white, red/yellow center	8	March
Joy Bells	salmon orange with mottled leaves	8	March
Tartini	bright crimson, edged with cream	8	March

See also:
Waterside plants pp35, 36, 40
Planting depths for bulbs p66
Bulbs, corms and tubers p67
F1 hybrids pp118–19

I am confused by the many types of iris; how do they differ?

The genus *Iris* is a large one with more than 200 species. Although the iris is immediately recognizable from its flowers, the plants vary widely in other respects, and this often leads to confusion. Some irises have large creeping rhizomes, others tubers, and yet others bulbs. They also cover a wide range in size, from tiny rock garden species to giant waterside plants. Botanically, the genus is divided into a number of groups. For basic garden planning, here are a number of useful subdivisions.

Bearded iris Hardy to zone 3. The most familiar garden iris, bearded irises come in many varieties, heights, colors, and range of blooming times. The central portion, the beard, is fuzzy. Bearded irises produce thick, fleshy rhizomes that should be planted at the soil surface, with only the fibrous roots buried. They require a sunny well-drained site. They bloom for a two-week to three-week period in April, May, or June.

Small bulbous irises Many of these are early flowering and make nice additions to rock gardens. Among the earliest to bloom and most frequently seen are the blue *I. reticulata* and its varieties, the blue *I. histrioides* and the yellow *I. danfordiae*.

Large bulbous irises These are the varieties usually known as English, Dutch, and Spanish irises and are derived principally from the species *Iris xiphium* and its relatives. They reach a height of about 2 feet and prefer deep, well-drained soil in full sun. They flower from mid-May (the Spanish varieties) through to July (the English varieties). They are available in a wide range of colors and make excellent garden flowers. Since they produce their leaves early in the autumn before flowering, the best time to lift, move, and divide is in late summer. The tall, delicate Dutch irises are commonly offered by florists as cut flowers.

Marsh and pond irises There are a number of species that are adapted to boggy areas and shallow water and prefer full sun. Many can also be grown in continually moist garden soil. One of the best-known species, *I. pseudacorus*, yellow flag, is a tall, hardy plant with lovely flowers. It is found naturalized throughout most of the country.

Gladwyn iris, *Iris foetidissima*, is an evergreen iris that does well in dry shade. Although its flowers are unexciting, its vivid red seeds, which remain attached within the split pod, are extremely striking and good for flower arrangements.

Japanese iris, *Iris kaempferi* Zones 4 to 9. Another easy-to-grow, showy iris (grows 2 feet tall), Japanese irises bloom from late June to July. They come in a limited color range of white, blue, lavender, and rose, but have very beautiful veination and mottling. These irises prefer a slightly acid, moist soil, but cannot tolerate standing water.

Louisiana irises Zones 4 to 9. This category consists of several different native species and their hybrid forms. They have been bred to have a neat appearance and well formed flowers and they make excellent cut flowers. There is a wide range of sizes, colors and growth habits. These irises grow best in a moist, rich, slightly acid soil in full sun.

Pacific Coast hybrids This is a group of beautiful irises, all only about 18 inches tall, in a wide range of subtle colors. Although sometimes said to require an acid soil, they will tolerate a small amount of lime, as well as light shade. They spread by rhizomes.

Siberian iris Zones 3 to 9. These reliable garden perennials are hardy, require a minimum of attention, and grow 2 to 3 feet tall. They produce narrow, grassy leaves and bloom in many colors in late spring or early summer for at least two weeks.

Bearded irises have large rhizomes that lie on the surface of the ground. They prefer a rich, well-drained soil and need plenty of sunshine. Before planting, cut back the leaves to about 6in. Dig an oblong hole, lay the rhizome at one end and spread out the roots. Do not cover the top of the rhizome but press soil down firmly around the roots, banking up more to cover them if they become exposed.

Iris danfordiae

Iris reticulata

Lilium henryi

Lily bulbs are expensive to buy. Can I increase my stock by saving seed from my plants?

Lilies certainly are among the more expensive bulbs, so buy them with care. Examine potential purchases from garden centers to be sure the bulbs have been carefully packed and that they are plump. If you buy by mail order, avoid cut-price offers and ascertain when delivery will be made. It is important that lily bulbs are replanted soon after they have been lifted in the autumn, before the roots have dried and shriveled.

Since the bulbs are expensive, you are unlikely to buy many at one time. So propagating by seed is an attractive option. The illustration to the right shows other methods of propagation, some of which take years until the plants will flower.

Do not bother to save seed from any of the hybrid lilies; it is unlikely the seed will produce plants resembling those from which it was collected. This is, however, the simplest way to raise large numbers of species lilies, although some seeds may take a long time to germinate, and the rapidity with which plants reach flowering size varies: *Lilium regale* may flower within two years, *L. martagon* may take seven.

Sow the seed in a soil-based seedling mix or in the nursery section of your garden as soon as possible after collecting. Sow thinly, for some lilies suffer root damage when disturbed, and the less thinning out needed, the better. Place the seedbox in a cold frame and be prepared to wait two weeks to a year for germination.

Should I cut off the leaves of bulbs when they have finished flowering?

Resist the temptation to tidy up the garden and cut off the foliage of any bulbous plant as soon as the plant has lost its appeal, for healthy foliage is the key to flowering in future seasons. The bulb must be given the opportunity to replenish its depleted food reserves, and it is the leaves that enable it to do this. Extensive tests with daffodils have proved that a period of six weeks after the end of flowering should elapse before the foliage is cut off or mown, and this should be taken as the rule for all other bulbs.

All, that is, except tulips, which really should be left longer. Larger hybrid garden tulips can be lifted and temporarily replanted elsewhere to make room in the bed for summer flowers. The smaller species tulips usually can be left in place, although their leaves should be removed carefully as they die off to prevent the soil

See also:
Dividing herbaceous plants p55
Bulbs, corms and tubers p67
Lawn weedkillers p104
F1 hybrids pp118–19

Lily bulbs are composed of overlapping scales, which may be removed and used to produce new plants. Press each piece, with the tip up, into a container of potting mix or in a nursery bed and keep warm while the plants develop. As soon as the first leaf appears, remove and pot up each plant. Plants started in this way will flower in 3 to 4 years.

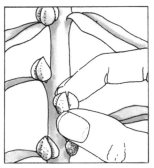

Bulbils are tiny dark bulbs produced on the stem by some species of lily. Remove them after the flowers have faded and before the bulbils drop to the ground when they'll be difficult to find. Sow bulbils with their tips just below the surface in potting mix or in a nursery bed in partial shade. Sow thinly to avoid transplanting before they're established. They should flower in 3 to 4 years.

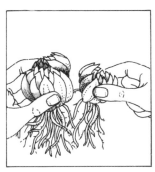

The bulbs of a mature lily that has been in position for a few years should proliferate to produce a fairly large clump. This may be lifted and carefully divided in the autumn and the separated bulbs replanted. Quite often these bulbs will produce flowering plants the next year.

What conditions do lilies need for good growth?

Lilies are best grown in zones 3 to 8 because they prefer cooler temperatures and because the bulbs need a chilling period before they will send up new shoots. In warmer climates, you can refrigerate your bulbs for eight to twelve weeks each year before planting.

Lilies won't do well in poorly drained soil. A deep soil of 12 to 18 inches is preferred. Select a site that provides good air circulation and a fairly cool environment. Half sun or three-quarters sun is best, although full sun is okay. In hot climates, where the temperature is often above 90 degrees F., it is a good idea to provide shading during the hottest part of the day.

Generally, plant the bulbs two or three times as deep as the width of the bulb; if you have light sandy soil, plant the bulbs about half as deep again. Apply a dusting of bonemeal in the hole.

As the plants grow, be sure they have adequate water. Some may require staking. Mulch with an organic material like leaf mold to help keep the ground cool and control weeds. Ground covers, such as pachysandra or periwinkle, *Vinca*, can sometimes serve as a living mulch, but watch out for overcrowding. After the plants flower and the leaves turn yellow, cut the stalks to just above the bulbs. In cold climates, provide a mulch cover for the winter.

Some lilies increase slowly and can be left untouched for years; others may need dividing every three to four years. It is time to divide when the lilies are growing in a crowded group with few or poor blooms. It is best to replant in the fall, after the plants have faded.

from becoming contaminated with a damaging fungus disease that develops on old foliage.

Although some tidying up of the foliage of daffodils by carefully tying the leaves together with light twine is permissible after flowering, actually knotting them damages the leaves so that they cease to function properly. One way to disguise dying foliage is to plant fast-growing annuals to block the view.

Is it safe to use weedkillers on an area planted with bulbs when they are dormant?

If it is a weedkiller that is active when absorbed by green plant tissue but not persistent in the soil, then it is likely the bulbs will not be harmed. If it has some residual soil action, damage may well result. It is generally considered safe, therefore, to use lawn weedkillers on grass during the summer after all the above ground growth of the bulb has disappeared but before any early-flowering species have begun to produce new shoots below ground.

Similarly, in beds, foliar-absorbed weedkillers are probably safe to use while the bulbs are dormant. Many products, however, can harm your bulbs in the soil. When in doubt, contact your local Extension office for specific information.

Which of the less-familiar bulbs are easily grown outdoors?

The increase in the range of bulbous plants for sale has been one of the most welcome features of gardening in recent years. Contributing to this growth has been the rapidity with which newly discovered wild plants are brought into cultivation, multiplied, and made widely available. Here are some plants you might enjoy trying.

Allium This is the genus that includes onion, garlic, and chives, as well as other highly ornamental species. Two points to watch when choosing alliums are that some have a fairly strong onion smell (although usually only when the foliage is bruised), and one or two can get out of hand, for they produce large numbers of rapidly dispersed bulbils. The taller species all need staking.

Among the best are *A. ostrowskianum*, which is hardy to zone 2. It produces deep rose pink flowers about 6 inches high, in late spring. The bulbs should be planted close together so that the flower stems provide support for each other. *A. caeruleum* (hardy to zone 2) produces deep blue flowers on 2-foot stems in June; *A. moly* (hardy to zone 2), a rapidly spreading, but not unruly, yellow-flowered species, has flower stems about 10 inches tall in June and July; *A. christophii* (hardy to zone 4) is a striking plant with large violet flower heads on

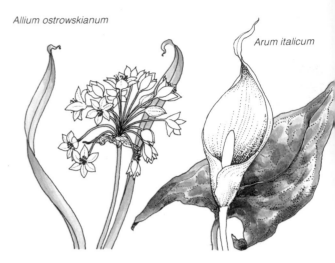

Allium ostrowskianum

Arum italicum

2-foot to 3-foot stems in June. For the back of the herbaceous border, *A. giganteum* (hardy to zone 5) is an imposing, June-flowering species with large pale lilac flower heads on stems up to 5 feet tall.

Canna These plants produce tall (2-foot to 5-foot) flower spikes with many blossoms from early summer until the frost. The blooms may be white, pink, scarlet, or yellow. The foliage also varies from green to blue-green to bronze. In zones 7 to 10, the plant can be started outdoors; but in colder climates, the plant should be started indoors and then set out.

Chionodoxa, Glory-of-the-snow Hardy to zone 4. A March-flowering genus, chionodoxas look a little like bluebells, but with the flowers directed upward and only about 6 inches tall. *C. luciliae* and the larger flowered *C. gigantea* are most frequently seen.

Erythronium, Dogtooth violet or adder's tongue Hardy in all but the hottest climates. This is a genus of beautiful plants for moist, shady sites. They have broad, lush, often variegated leaves and almost lilylike spring flowers on stems up to 10 inches tall. The bulbs tend to be expensive, but among the best and most frequently

Erythronium tuolumnense

Erythronium dens-canis
Dogtooth violet

See also:
Lifting dahlia tubers p19
Bulbs for naturalizing p68
Succession of bulbs p70
Forcing bulbs p71
Species tulips p72

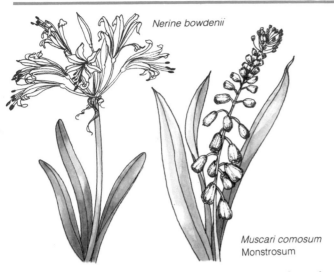

Nerine bowdenii

Muscari comosum
Monstrosum

Muscari, Grape hyacinths Hardy to zone 4. Muscaris have a reputation for rapidly becoming garden weeds, but their ability to spread rapidly is useful in wilder parts of the garden. A somewhat different and pretty species is the tassel hyacinth, *M. comosum plumosum*, which has fine feathery plumes of violet filaments in the spring.

Nerine Nerines are autumn-flowering bulbs with long-lasting, onionlike, pink flowers on 1-foot to 2-foot leafless stalks. They can be grown outdoors only in the warmest climates, with *N. bowdenii* being the hardiest in zones 8 to 10. They can be grown in containers and brought inside in other zones. They prefer light shade.

Scilla, Squill Hardy. With a rich blue flower, scillas are invaluable for late spring. They naturalize well. The best form of the common *S. sibirica* is Spring Beauty, with strong color and an 8-inch flowering stem.

Zephyranthes, Zephyr lily Hardy to zones 8 to 10. Generally autumn-flowering, these plants are hardy only where the ground doesn't freeze. In other areas, they can be planted in the spring and lifted in the fall after blooming. They produce crocuslike flowers, about 8 inches tall.

offered are *E. dens-canis* in a range of white, pink, and purple varieties; *E. revolutum* White Beauty, which has large white flowers with yellow centers, and *E. tuolumnense* Pagoda, with flowers of sulfur yellow.

Leucojum, Snowflake Hardy to zone 4. Best described as large, late-flowering snowdrops, snowflakes, especially *L. aestivum*, can extend the snowdrop season into late April or May, when they make a very attractive blend with the blue of muscaris and scillas.

My dahlias are always spindly and have small flowers; what am I doing wrong?

The key to success with dahlias is to start with strong, healthy stock and then to provide adequate water and nutrients. Although you may be able to obtain reasonable flowers from tubers in the first year if you plant in an unsuitable and inadequately prepared bed, it will be difficult to achieve even one season's success with root cuttings unless the site is prepared in advance.

Dahlias thrive in a sunny location with a deep, moist, but freely draining soil. Adding well-rotted manure or compost in the autumn always benefits dahlias, for it improves the moisture retention in well-drained soil, it opens up heavy soil, and provides a modest supply of nutrients for both. Incorporating bonemeal for good root development is another recommended practice.

Although dahlias are surprisingly tolerant of dry spells, the plants will become spindly and develop poor flowers if watering is neglected for long. Applying a mulch of well-rotted manure after a period of rain will help to maintain the soil in a moist condition. Routine liquid feeding during the summer will also help to produce good plants during the season and ensure that sound tubers are built up for the following year.

Unless you are growing the flowers for exhibition, no disbudding or pinching-off of side shoots is necessary. Leave dahlias in the ground until the foliage is killed by the first frosts. Then lift the plants with a fork, taking care to avoid spearing the tubers. Cut the stems down to about 6 inches and allow the roots to dry. You can dust the roots with a fungicide before putting them in storage for the winter.

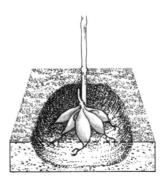

Dahlia tubers should be planted around the time of the last frost, about 6in deep. Insert a strong stake close to the tuber now, since it can be damaged by a cane pushed in later. Allow 15–36in between plants, depending on the variety.

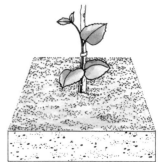

Rooted cuttings should be planted only after all danger of frost has passed. They, too, should be staked and lightly tied. As plants grow, you can add more ties, being careful not to damage the stems.

SHRUBS, CLIMBERS, AND GROUND COVERS

Year-round interest

for every garden

What roles can shrubs, climbers, and ground covers play in my landscape?

Within these broad categories, you will find plants that can add color, fragrance, and texture to your landscape, as well as disguise or conceal unattractive areas, such as fences, compost piles, sheds, or hard-to-cultivate slopes.

Shrubs often provide the permanent framework around which the annuals and other perennials are woven. They come in all shapes and growth habits, including rounded, spreading, weeping, upright. Often they define and delineate the garden space; English boxwood, *Buxus sempervirens*, can be used to make an excellent boundary hedge. Sometimes shrubs are planted as windbreaks; the bayberry, *Myrica pensylvanica*, has a suitable upright growth habit for this purpose.

Deciduous shrubs change with the seasons, often providing flowers, berries, and leaves that change color. In the North, evergreen shrubs with needles are frequently planted, to provide winter color and because they often thrive in shady areas. In the South, broadleaf evergreens are more common.

Vines and climbers can be planted to conceal unattractive areas or soften rough features, add fragrance and grace (as with honeysuckle), utilize a vertical space, and provide shade and noise reduction. These plants can also be planted to provide visual interest through their flowers (honeysuckle, clematis, wisteria), their bright berries (Chinese bittersweet), or their foliage (English ivy, winter creeper).

Before selecting a vine or climber, be aware of the plant's growth habit. Some vines, such as English ivy, cling to surfaces by their rootlets; others, such as wisteria, twine around structures.

Ground covers can be shrubs, vines, or herbaceous perennials; they can be evergreen or deciduous. Despite the foliage or flowers they may produce, they are generally selected because of their low and dense growth habits. Ground covers can be planted to add texture, cover problem spots (old bulb foliage, for example), discourage weeds, and prevent sloping ground from eroding.

Ground covers also vary tremendously in their growth habits. Some, like *Sedum*, spread very quickly; others may take years to provide thick cover, depending on how closely they are planted. Plants that spread via root runners, such as crown vetch, are the best for holding banks. Shade-tolerant pachysandra does well under trees.

See also:
Windbreaks p25
Minimal attention garden p26
Illusion of garden size p27
Arbor for climbers p30
Perennials for shade pp56–7

Climbers for a shady wall p80
Flowering shrubs for a small area p80
Trees for autumn color p111

What attractive shrubs will grow in a shady spot?

Shady areas, especially dry, shady areas, always present problems for shrubs, and the choice of plants is fairly limited. The species list given here offers suggestions for shrubs that will provide at least some color all year-round. Most of the plants are available in a range of varieties.

What are some good shrubs for autumn color?

Just as trees can provide spectacular fall foliage, so can shrubs. Leaf color will be better in some years than others, depending on the weather.

Acer, Maple Although almost all *Acers* are really trees, some are small and others so slow growing that in many gardens they seldom reach more than shrub size. *A. pulmatum dissectum* in its several varieties is the most widely grown of these small forms and is a good species for red autumn color.

Berberis, Barberry Most have attractive fall foliage, but many species have been restricted in much of the United States because they are alternate hosts for a wheat rust. Japanese barberry, *B. thunbergii*, is popular; many varieties have purple foliage, which turns fiery red.

Cornus, Dogwood Many of the dwarf dogwoods are valuable, but none more so than the varieties of *C. florida* (hardy to zone 4), which has scarlet-orange fall foliage.

Cotinus coggygria, Smoke tree Hardy to zone 5. Many gardeners think that the fiery autumn colors of the smoke tree are unrivaled among shrubs.

Cotoneaster Several cotoneasters have a good autumn color, but there are few reds more vivid than that of *C. horizontalis*.

Euonymus Hardy to zone 4. *E. alata* is the one most prized for its scarlet autumn color. Compacta is a nice variety with a well-rounded outline.

Hamamelis, Witch hazel Hardy to zones 4 to 5. Most have yellow autumn color, but the popular hybrid *H. × intermedia* has bright red and yellow fall foliage.

Roses Shrubs roses put on a superb display of hips and complement this with some glorious leaf colors. The yellows of the many varieties of *Rosa rugosa* are probably the most appealing.

Viburnum Hardy to zone 3. This is a large genus with many deciduous and evergreen species. One of the most commonly seen deciduous viburnums, with good red autumn color, is *V. opulus*.

SHRUBS FOR A SHADY SITE

Plant	Zone	Noteworthy features
Aucuba japonica	7	Gold dust plant. Variegated and female (berried) forms are best
Euonymus fortunei	5	Wintercreeper. Low growing; some good variegated varieties are available.
Fatsia japonica	7	Large, glossy leaves.
Ilex altaclarensis	6	A large-leaved holly; many beautifully variegated forms exist
Ilex aquifolium	6	Common holly; numerous varieties with variously colored leaves and berries
Lonicera nitida	7	A relative of honeysuckle; stands clipping and is good for low, shaded hedges
Mahonia aquifolium	5	Yellow flowers in early spring; tolerates dense shade
Osmanthus heterophyllus	6	Holly-like with scented flowers in autumn; variegated forms are best
Phillyrea decora	6	Hardy small shrub; fragrant white flowers in spring
Prunus laurocerasus		Cherry laurel; hardy big shrub with large, glossy leaves
Rhododendron (some)	4–10	Enormous range of varieties; the hardy hybrids are among the best for shade
Ribes alpinum (deciduous)	2	Underrated small, dense shrub with pretty yellow flowers and red berries
Skimmia japonica	7	Choose female clones with attractive red berries
Tsuga canadensis	4	A graceful evergreen hedge or specimen.
Viburnum davidii	7	Low growing, with large, glossy leaves; plant several to ensure that berries form

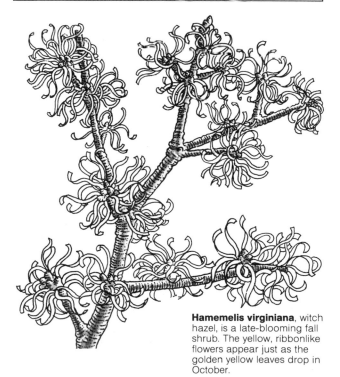

Hamamelis virginiana, witch hazel, is a late-blooming fall shrub. The yellow, ribbonlike flowers appear just as the golden yellow leaves drop in October.

79

Which flowering shrubs can I plant in a very small area?

There are many dwarf or slow-growing shrubs that are suitable for small areas or containers. Many are dwarf varieties of old garden favorites. Some examples follow.

Berberis circumserrata, Cutleaf barberry Hardy to zone 5. This small shrub (3 feet tall with a 3-foot spread) has clusters of small, yellow flowers in late spring. During the fall, the bright red foliage contrasts with yellow berries. Full sun is preferred but it will tolerate partial shade.

Caryopteris × clandonensis, Hybrid bluebeard Hardy to zone 5. This small shrub bears blue flower spikes that bloom in late August. Blue Mist and Heavenly Blue are two popular varieties; they grow 2 to 4 feet tall and have a compact growth habit.

Daphne The rosy purple blooms resemble lilacs, but are smaller. *D. mezereum*, (February daphne), grows to 3 feet and is hardy to zone 4. It flowers in early spring before the leaves open and then produces brilliant red berries. Plant daphne in partial shade for best results.

Erica carnea, Spring heath Hardy to zone 5. Grows to 1 foot in height. Pink blossoms will appear between mid-winter and late spring, depending on the temperature. Although most heaths are acid-loving plants, *E. carnea* can tolerate slightly alkaline conditions. It can be grown either in full sun or partial shade.

Forsythia viridissima Hardy to zone 5. This dwarf form of an old garden favorite grows 2 feet tall with a 2-foot spread. It blooms with small yellow flowers around mid-April.

Potentilla fruticosa Princess

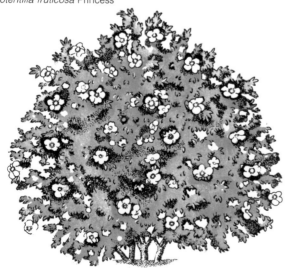

Fothergilla gardenii, Dwarf fothergilla Hardy to zone 5. These lovely, low-growing shrubs grow to 3 to 4 feet high and provide two main seasons of interest. In the spring, they bear masses of white, feathery, pussy-willow-like flowers and in the fall, their dark green foliage turns to a magnificent reddish-orange. They prefer sun or light shade.

Potentilla fruticosa, Bush cinquefoil Hardy to zone 2. This sun-loving shrub will bloom on and off all summer with bright yellow or white flowers. It is easily kept at 2 to 3 feet and has very few pest or disease problems. Try Tangerine which, if grown in partial shade, will have orange flowers.

Rhododendron spp. Many rhododendron hybrids and species are small flowering shrubs. They require a rich, moist, acid soil for good growth. The compact hybrid Windbeam (hardy to zone 5) has flowers that change from apricot yellow in bud to pink then to white as they open.

Spiraea Hardy to zone 4. There are some nice hybrid dwarfs, including the fairly recent *S. × bumalda* Alpina, which is a beautiful mounded dwarf with light pink flower clusters. It grows under 1 foot tall.

Syringa meyeri, Meyer's lilac Hardy to zone 5. Growing to a maximum of 6 feet, this lilac prefers a sunny location and produces profuse violet-purple blooms with small foliage.

What climbers are suitable for growing on a shady wall?

One of the few flowering climbers that may do well in such a situation is the climbing hydrangea, *Hydrangea petiolaris*, which is hardy to zone 4. It is a self-clinging climber with large green leaves and large clusters of greenish-white flowers in June. It is very vigorous and attractive when flowering, but doesn't have much winter interest.

If you have a low shady wall that offers cool shade at the bottom but more light at the top, it might be just the place for a large-flowered hybrid clematis, since they do need cool roots. There are numerous varieties; Nellie Moser, which has rose blooms with pink centers, is one of the best known.

If the absence of attractive flowers is of no concern, the various species of *Parthenocissus* thrive in the shade and more than make up for the lack of bloom with their autumn colors. *P. quinquefolia* is the Virginia creeper, although that name is sometimes applied incorrectly to *P. tricuspidata*, Boston ivy. Both are self-clinging, as is the even more beautiful *P. henryana*. But if you have a wall with old bricks and mortar and are concerned about damage that might result from a self-clinging plant, try *P. inserta*, which has many of the features of its relatives but needs a wire support since it climbs by means of tendrils.

See also:
Invasive plants p24
Illusion of garden size p27
Perennials for shade pp56–7
Foliage plants pp64–5
Shrubs to grow in shade p79

Are there any small shrub-like bamboos that won't spread uncontrollably in my yard?

Although bamboos are actually grasses, they often serve the same ornamental purpose as shrubs in a yard. Most bamboos inhabit tropical, subtropical, and warm climate areas, but there are some that are hardy enough to manage as far north as zone 5. They require a humid spot with protection from drying winds, particularly in the North.

There are two broad groupings of bamboos. Running bamboos propagate by sending out vigorous underground rhizomes. Although among the hardiest, these bamboos are the most likely to spread uncontrollably. If you plant to plant them in a small area, sink metal strips or concrete at least 2 feet deep into the soil to contain the spread. Clump bamboos tend to be less hardy, but they are very graceful and their growth is more easily contained.

Various examples of shrub-like bamboos are given in the table. Some of the dwarf varieties can even be grown as ground covers.

☐ *Arundinaria viridi-striata* Hardy to zone 7, but this and many of the others in this table can be hardy in colder zones if heavily mulched. Running type. Beautiful 3-foot dwarf. Tolerates partial shade. Leaves are brilliantly green and yellow striped in spring.

☐ *Arundinaria variegata* Hardy to zone 6. Running type. Green and white variegations make this a lovely maximum 4 feet tall dwarf.

☐ *Bambusa multiplex*, Golden goddess bamboo Hardy to zone 8. Clump type with graceful, arching culms. Stays under 10 feet tall.

☐ *Bambusa multiplex* Rivierorum, Chinese goddess bamboo Hardy to zone 8. Clump type. Fernlike appearance. Tiny, delicate leaves and a maximum of 5 feet tall.

☐ *Sinarundaria nitida*, Hardy blue bamboo Hardy to zone 4. A clump type with purplish culms. Will grow 12 feet in cool climates and lower where it's hot.

Although we would never recommend ivy, *Hedera* spp., for old walls, it is perfectly safe on sound, modern bricks and mortar, and there are now dozens of attractively leafed forms. *H. helix* Cavendishii has leaf margins variegated with white to yellow; Maculata has leaves spotted or striped with yellowish-white; Conglomerata has small (1½-inch) leaves on stiff, upright stems.

If a young ivy plant refuses to climb (as Goldheart in particular is prone to do), don't try to force it by pinning it to the wall. Allow it to form a clump at the base of the wall for the first year or two. It will then usually take off of its own volition.

Although it is a twining vine that may need some structure or trellis, *Aristolochia durior*, Dutchman's pipe, is one that prefers some shade. Its small, pipe-shaped flowers are largely hidden by the large, rounded leaves (sometimes 1 foot long). Hardy to zone 4, it grows vigorously and should be given plenty of space.

Another suitable twining vine is the five-leaf akebia, *Akebia quinata*, which is hardy to zone 4, being deciduous in cold climates but evergreen in the South. The leaflets are arranged like fingers on a hand. The plant produces small purple flowers in mid-May. It propagates by means of long, vigorous runners, so give it plenty of room to spread out.

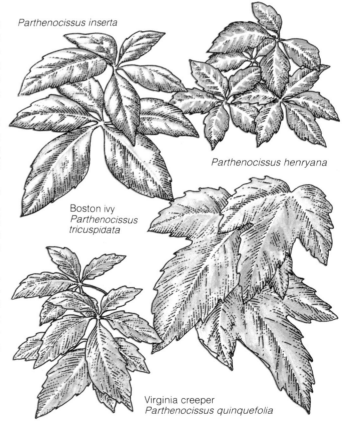

Parthenocissus inserta

Parthenocissus henryana

Boston ivy
Parthenocissus tricuspidata

Virginia creeper
Parthenocissus quinquefolia

Do dwarf conifers need special conditions? What varieties can be recommended?

There has been a phenomenal growth of interest in dwarf conifers in the past few decades, and nurseries specializing in these plants now offer a large range of varieties. Some of these conifers may not be true dwarfs, but they have such a slow growth rate that they stay small for years. Dwarfs remain much more compact than their large counterparts and require little or no pruning.

With such a large selection available, it is not surprising that there are varieties tolerant of a wide range of soils and situations. Although most prefer a well-drained, slightly acid soil, they will grow well in all except the most alkaline conditions. Most also prefer a sunny location, but they may be browned by exposure to cold wind.

Many dwarf conifers will thrive in pots and tubs, where a soil-based or soil-less potting mix can be used. If you are growing your conifers in pots, add a thick mulch of pulverized bark to help retain moisture — having the roots dry out can be a problem for container-grown conifers.

The table on the right contains a short list of recommended varieties. But a visit to a specialist supplier is recommended so you can get an idea of the real potential offered by dwarf conifers.

A VARIETY OF DWARF CONIFERS

Firs (Abies)	A. koreana This species is not truly miniature, but is so slow growing it can be regarded as such. It has green needles with silvery undersides and is especially valuable for producing its appealing bluish cones when still young. 6½ft. A. nordmanniana Golden Spreader A slow-growing, compact, rather irregularly shaped bush with rich golden needles. 20in.
Cedars (Cedrus)	C. deodara Golden Horizon This variety forms a low-growing mound of weeping, green-gold foliage. 30in.
Cypresses (Chamaecyparis)	C. lawsoniana Ellwoodii A slow-growing, compact, pillar-shaped plant with blue-green foliage. Popular and widely available. 30in. C. lawsoniana Minima Aurea A compact, bushy plant with golden-yellow foliage. 24in.
Junipers (Juniperus)	J. communis Compressa A columnar plant with blue-green foliage that sometimes appears too perfect to be real; more like a green chess-piece than a shrub. 18in. J. horizontalis Jade Spreader A prostrate variety; excellent green ground cover. 6½ft. J. × media Plumosa Aurea A compact, semi-prostrate variety with green-gold foliage. 4ft × 5ft spread. J. squamata Blue Carpet Almost prostrate, good silvery blue ground cover. 12in × 6½ft spread.
Spruces (Picea)	P. glauca Albertiana Conica A neat, compact, conical shrub with bright green needles. 4ft × 2½ft spread.
Pines (Pinus)	P. strobus Nana A compact form of one of the long-needled pines, with dense, blue-green foliage. 3¼ft.
Yews (Taxus)	T. cuspidata, Japanese Yew The hardiest of the dwarf yews. Nana is a dwarf with uniform dark green foliage. 3ft wide and high.
Red Cedars (Thuja)	T. orientalis Aurea Nana A vivid golden-green, rounded shrub, with the foliage appearing like the pages of a half-open book. 30in.

Heights are for plants growing in good conditions after 10 years.

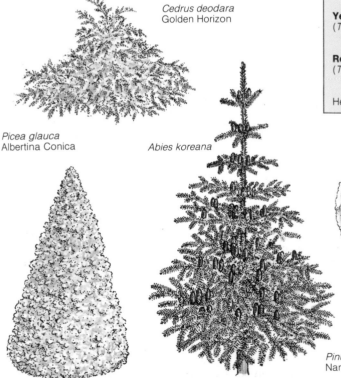

Cedrus deodara
Golden Horizon

Picea glauca
Albertina Conica

Abies koreana

Juniperus compressa
Compressa

Chamaecyparis
lawsoniana
Minima Aurea

Thuja orientalis
Aurea Nana

Pinus stroba
Nana

See also:
Herbaceous beds p54
Propagation of herbaceous
perennials p65
Trees from cuttings p110
Dwarf hedges p116

Simple layering is an easy way to propagate many shrubs, climbers and ground covers. A low branch is bent over, nicked on the bottom to stimulate rooting and covered in the middle with soil. Plants that are layered in the spring should be well rooted by the fall, but in areas with cold winters, it's best to wait until the following spring to cut away the new plant.

Compound layering works best on plants with long, flexible stems, such as clematis. It is based on the same principle as simple layering, but many new plants can be formed at once.

Make sure to have at least one bud per section.

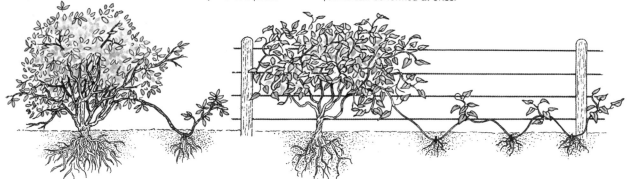

I'd like to increase my stock of shrubs, vines, and ground covers? How can I propagate them?

There are numerous ways to propagate these plants vegetatively. Some methods require more care, skill, or materials to be successful, and some will be more successful with certain plants than others. When in doubt, check with your local Extension office.

With many plants, such as lilacs, **propagating by suckers** is easiest. Dig up and transplant the suckers in the spring so they have time to become established before the winter. When replanting the sucker, prune back the top by about one-third to balance the leaf growth with the new roots. Plant in fertile soil, water well, and keep weeded until the new plant is well established.

Layering is a process whereby roots are encouraged to form on a low-growing outside branch or stem, after which it is separated to form a new plant. This method is useful for shrubs such as cotoneasters, dwarf viburnums, and shrub roses.

In the early spring, select a branch that grows close to the ground and is about ¼ inch in diameter. Bend the branch over, remove the leaves from the middle, and bury a 3-inch to 5-inch section. To encourage faster rooting, cut away a portion of the bark on the bottom and dust with a rooting hormone. Try to keep the tip upright for best growth. As soon as the branch roots, cut apart and transplant.

Many vines (clematis, honeysuckle, wisteria) and ground covers will root along many spots on the branches. You can bury several sections, as long as each section is near an above ground bud or shoot. Then allow to root as above. This is called **compound layering**.

Stool layering is similar. Cut the plant back to 2 inches above the ground; new sprouts will pop up. When the new sprouts are 6 inches tall, bury them with light soil. When they have rooted, clip off the rooted pieces and transplant. This method works with some lilacs and some viburnums.

Many flowering shrubs and small fruits can be propagated by **softwood cuttings**, but it is a slow process; it may be one to two years before you will have a new plant to set out. Providing a covered propagating box with bottom heat will help guarantee success.

Start the process in late spring or early summer. Select a cutting from the soft-growing part of a woody plant; generally this means selecting new growth. Take the cutting when the plant is wet. Cut at an angle to provide a large area for rooting. Make the cutting 6 to 12 inches long and cut above or below but close to a node, depending on the plant — there is no hard and fast rule for this. Dip the cutting in a commercial rooting powder and set in a pot containing a light potting mix. Cover the container with plastic or glass. Provide warmth and humidity and keep the pot out of direct sun. After the cutting has rooted, it can be hardened-off and planted outside in a bed.

Propagating by **semi-hardwood cuttings** is similar to propagating by softwood cuttings, but the cutting is taken after the new growth is somewhat mature in late summer. The cutting may not be ready to plant out until the following spring. As with softwood cuttings, harden them off before setting them out. This method is suitable for forsythia and broadleaf evergreens.

Propagating by **hardwood cuttings** is one of the easiest methods for home gardeners, as moisture conditions are not that critical. Sometime between late fall and late winter when the plant is dormant, take 6-inch to 12-inch cuttings from the healthy wood of the previous summer. Cut the tops and bottoms on a slant. Bundle the cuttings and plant them in a soil mix or sand, tip side up. Keep the soil barely moist and store in a cool area for the winter.

Plant the cuttings 4 to 6 inches apart in a partially shaded bed or nursery in the spring, after the bottoms have started to callus over. Provide water and fertilizer. They will root and start to grow. Transplant to a permanent spot in the fall in warm climates, or wait until the following spring. Grapes, spireas, honeysuckle, and privet can be successfully propagated this way.

Is it possible to move a mature shrub without harming it?

Yes, but with certain reservations. A mature large shrub will be more difficult to move than a small one. And the ease with which any big plant is moved is influenced by the position in which it is growing, the soil type, and the proximity of other trees and shrubs. The species of plant is also a consideration; deep-rooted shrubs will present more difficulties than shallow-rooted ones, and evergreens more problems than deciduous plants.

Certain general rules apply. Perform the operation so as to cause a minimum of root disturbance. Move the plant with as much soil as possible still adhering to the roots and don't let them dry out. Move the plant at a time of year when it will suffer the least interruption to its growth. A deciduous plant can be moved any time during its dormant, leafless period, as long as the ground isn't frozen.

Evergreens present an additional complication because they retain their leaves throughout the winter and will continue to lose water through them at a time when the roots may be unable to replenish it. For this reason, moving evergreens in the spring, particularly in the North, before the season's growth has started, is the best plan.

Well in advance of the moving operation, water the plant and the surrounding soil thoroughly. Have on hand a supply of burlap, plastic bags, or chicken wire if the shrub is really large. The idea is to gather the soil and roots into a large ball with the help of these materials. You will also need some extra pairs of helping hands; moving anything larger than a very small shrub requires at least two people.

Before moving the plant, prepare the new planting hole. Be sure it is well watered and liberally dosed with bonemeal.

To remove the plant, dig around, but well away from, the plant; the distance will vary with the size of the root system — plan to dig a hole with a diameter of 3 to 4 feet for a large shrub. As you dig, gradually ease the burlap, plastic bags, or chicken wire underneath the plant to form a large bag; tie it at the top to hold the soil and roots together.

Over a short distance, the shrub can be dragged, but for more than a few yards, it must be lifted. Don't underestimate the weight! Even more pairs of hands may be needed at this stage. Once the plant is in position in the new hole, cut away the burlap or plastic. Leave the chicken wire in place; new roots will grow through — trying to remove the wire could cause considerable damage.

If a stake is needed, drive it in at this stage, while you can see exactly where it is going. Firm the soil thoroughly to be sure you haven't left any hollows in the soil at the base of the stem where water might accumulate. Water well and continue to do so until the plant is well established.

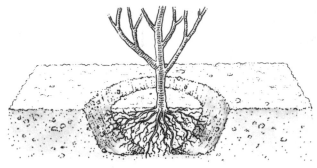

When moving a shrub, the objective is to leave a ball of soil around the roots. So, some time ahead, water the plant and the surrounding earth thoroughly. Dig well away from the plant; the size of the hole depends on the size of the shrub's root system.

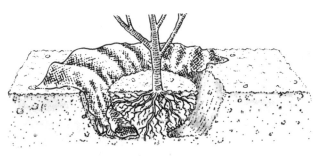

Ease burlap, a sheet of plastic or, with a large shrub, chicken wire into the hole and underneath the shrub. Keep the root ball as intact as possible.

Gather the burlap or plastic, tie it firmly around the stem of the shrub and carefully lift it out of the hole. This is a job for two people if you want to avoid damaging the plant.

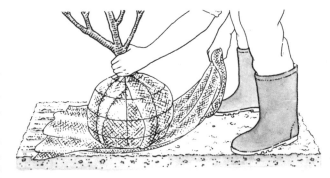

Drag the root-balled shrub on a sheet of plastic to its new position if this is nearby. Otherwise lift the shrub or move it to its new hole on a wheelbarrow; cut away any burlap or plastic.

See also:
Transplanting trees pp108–9
Pruning fruit trees p132
Training and pruning grapevines p137

When should I prune garden shrubs?

Many books have been written on pruning, and the best give detailed instructions for the whole range of common garden ornamentals. Rather than duplicate that advice, we will explain some of the guiding principles behind pruning to enable you to make judgments about particular species.

First, don't assume that a shrub must be pruned simply because it is there. Pruning should be done only when necessary to improve the growth of the plant. This means you will want to prune away any dead or diseased wood and any branches or shoots that have become so tangled together they restrict the penetration of light and air into the plant. You should also remove dead flowering shoots — to prevent them from becoming diseased or to improve the appearance of the plant. By removing some of this growth, you will stimulate the production of new leaflets or flowering shoots to enhance the attractiveness of the plant.

When should pruning be carried out? It depends on when the plant flowers. Some shrubs flower on wood produced in the previous year and tend to bloom early in the season, before the current year's shoots have developed. These can be pruned as soon as the flowers fade. Shrubs that flower on wood of the current year can be pruned between late autumn and late winter or early spring, the later the better. Dead or diseased wood can be pruned at any time. If you follow this rule of thumb, you are unlikely to do much harm or prune away all the next crop of flower buds.

Relatively few early-blooming shrubs require a great deal of regular pruning, apart from the removal of old flower shoots and a little shaping. Some of the later-blooming group require more severe and regular treatment to give their best, but don't prune severely until you are certain it is appropriate. *Buddleia davidii* (but not other buddleias), *Hypericum calycinum*, St John's wort, *Indigofera*, *Lespedeza*, and *Rhus typhina*, staghorn sumac, when grown solely for its foliage, are among the few shrubs you should prune to within a few buds of the base in late winter.

You'll find comments on pruning other plants elsewhere, but a word should be added about clematis, for their treatment often causes confusion. Clematis can be divided into three groups for the purpose of pruning. The first group comprises the early-flowering species *alpina*, *macropetala* and their varieties, and *montana* and its varieties. Prune these immediately after flowering, simply to remove dead shoots and to keep the plant within its alloted space.

The second group comprises the early, large-flowered varieties, such as Nellie Moser, Elsa Spaeth, Mrs Cholmondeley, and Niobe, together with the Jackmanii group and the mid-season large-flowered varieties, such as W. E. Gladstone. Remove any dead or weak shoots in late winter and cut back other shoots to a pair of strong buds.

The final group of clematis includes the *viticella* varieties and all the late-flowering species, such as *flammula*, *orientalis*, *rehderiana*, *tangutica*, and *texensis*. Severely prune these in February or March, cutting back the previous season's growth to a strong pair of buds just above the base. Although this sounds complicated, it is really just following the guidelines relating pruning to flowering time — with only some plants needing a severe late-winter pruning.

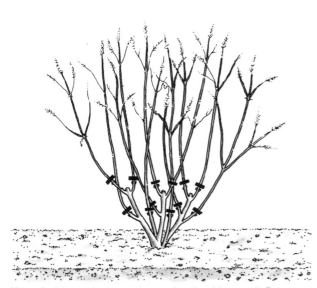

Many deciduous shrubs, such as *Buddleia davidii*, that flower on the current year's wood, must be pruned back almost to the base in late winter to ensure that they bloom well. Prune shrubs that bloom on the previous year's growth as soon as the flowers fade.

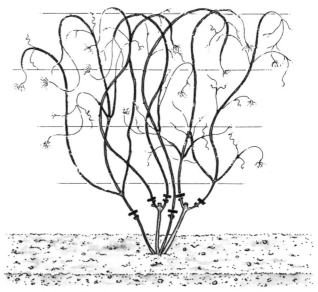

Prune late-flowering clematis to the lowest pair of strong buds on the previous season's growth in February, *above*. At the same time, merely cut out dead or weak shoots on early and mid-season bloomers.

How can I use ground covers to stabilize a sloping area?

There are a number of ground covers you can plant that will help to hold the soil on a bank. Many of them have stems that root easily or have rapidly spreading prostrate roots.

There are a few tricks to planting on a slope so that your plants don't wash away before they have a chance to become established. First, when you plant, stagger the rows so that water can't run straight down and wash away the soil. If the slope is very steep, you can build small flat terraces or set the plants in saucerlike platforms to catch water. You can also press boards, sod, or galvanized metal strips 1 to 2 feet apart crosswise between rows of plants and leave them there until the plants are well rooted. This will hold the soil and prevent erosion. In any case, you may want to cover the area with a layer of straw held in place with netting or a network of string. The straw will help shed water, hold the soil, and allow the plants to become established.

How close to space any ground cover plants varies with the type of plant and your budget. Obviously, the closer they are planted, the more quickly they will fill in. Plants such as English ivy and pachysandra can be planted 6 to 8 inches apart for fairly rapid coverage. You can set the plants 12 inches or farther apart, but it may take more than a season for them to fill in.

Junipers and euonymus are often planted on 3-foot centers. Larger ground covers, such as trailing roses and virginia creeper, should be spaced even farther apart. Since they can spread a great deal, setting plants like juniper too close together can result in overcrowding. So if you want an immediate effect, be prepared to take some plants out later.

Here is a list of some ground covers that are particularly suitable for sloping areas.

Arctostaphylos uva-ursi, Bearberry Hardy to zone 2. This is planted widely in many areas; it thrives in poor sandy soils and sun. The foliage turns bronze in the fall.
Baccharis pilularis, Coyote bush Hardy to zone 7. This evergreen is for warm climates only. It is not especially attractive, but it is good for dry slopes in full sun.
Coronilla varia, Crown vetch Hardy to zone 3. This is commonly used for banks, but it can be a problem if allowed too close to the garden. The plant spreads rapidly by underground stems. It produces pinkish-white pealike flowers.
Cotoneaster Some species, such as C. dammeri (zone 5), can make good ground covers for slopes. This one will root along its 12-inch stems.
Hedera helix, English ivy Ivy makes a good stabilizing ground cover because it roots along its stem and is easily grown.
Hypericum calycinum, Aaronsbeard, St John's wort Hardy to zone 6. The prostrate branches root rapidly, and the plant can tolerate sandy soils. It produces bright yellow flowers in late July and purple autumn foliage.

Juniperus, Juniper There are a number of creeping and prostrate types of juniper that make good ground covers for slopes, including J. horizontalis. J. h. Douglassi has steel blue foliage that changes to a pinkish-purple in the winter.
Rosa wichuraiana procumbent, Memorial rose Hardy to zone 5. This grows vigorous roots wherever the stems touch the ground. It produces small white flowers in late summer.

Juniperus horizontalis
Blue Rug

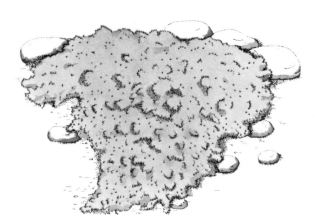

Should ground covers be mulched?

While mulching an established ground cover planting is not generally necessary, applying mulch to a new planting can be very beneficial. Aside from the obvious help in reducing weed competition and providing organic matter, an organic mulch of a couple of inches will keep the soil moist so that above ground runners and stems will have moist soil in which to root. The mulch also helps to maintain more even soil temperatures, which in turn aids in rooting.

If you have established ground cover, you can apply a mulch after the ground is frozen in winter to avoid damage from alternate freezing and thawing.

See also:
Mulching herbaceous perennials p57
Dwarf conifers p82
Winter protection for roses p97
Ground covers for lawns pp106–7
Mulches p122

My euonymus lost most of its leaves by mid-summer. What might be the cause?

This sounds like a case of euonymous scale. There are many species of scale insects, but the euonymus scale is the most common and is particularly damaging. It attacks the evergreen varieties and many other ornamentals. You can tell if this is the problem by checking the stems and undersides of leaves for flattened white and brown scaly bumps. These bumps can easily go unnoticed until the insect has done serious damage, so check susceptible plants periodically.

To control euonymus scale, cut off and burn any infected branches. Check other ornamentals that are growing nearby, such as bittersweet, pachysandra, and English ivy, for they may also be infested. To prevent a repeat infestation, apply a commercial dormant oil spray in early spring or late winter before growth starts. This should smother the scales. You could also use an oil spray that is combined with a chemical insecticide.

Can low-growing shrubs be used to suppress weed growth?

Anything that can be done to make weed control easier is to be encouraged. While mulching is both effective and fairly inexpensive, in some situations plants themselves can be put to work. The basic requirements for an efficient weed-suppressing plant are that it should grow strongly and compete with the weeds for nutrients, moisture, and light.

A good ground cover plant need not be prostrate. Many of the best, such as some of the spreading junipers, work more on the principle of casting shade, rather than smothering. Others in this category include several species of cotoneaster, some of the brooms, such as *Cytisus kewensis*, and the hypericums.

Among the smothering types are the low-growing roses, such as *Rosa nitida*; heathers; *Pachysandra terminalis*; and the extremely useful vincas. But be careful that the plants used for weed smothering are not grown where they can become a menace by invading beds and borders.

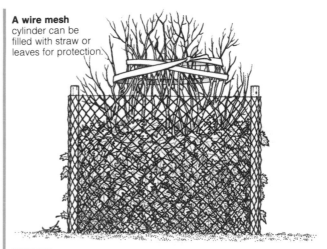

A wire mesh cylinder can be filled with straw or leaves for protection.

What should I do for winter protection for my shrubs?

If the shrubs have been planted in a sheltered position, protected from winds and frost pockets, not much protection will be required unless the shrubs are marginally hardy for your area. Shrubs that are marginally hardy can be protected by taking a few simple precautions.

First assure sufficient water in the autumn, so the plant doesn't suffer dehydration; this is particularly important for evergreens. So that the plant doesn't suffer from alternate freezing and thawing, mulch the ground with pine boughs or straw after the ground freezes. Wrap evergreen and tender shrubs with burlap, boughs, or straw to protect them from drying winds and winter sun. Wall shrubs and vines can be protected by mats made of straw-covered chicken wire.

Finally, don't allow heavy loads of snow to fall or build up on the branches of your shrubs, particularly the evergreens.

Weeds are suppressed by shading by *Juniperus horizontalis* Jade Spreader, *right*, and by smothering by the creeping *Pachysandra terminalis*, *below*

ROSES

Cultivating the garden favorites

Some terms describe the various types, or groupings, of roses, such as hybrid teas, floribundas, and so on. Other terms describe the different forms, or growth habits, of roses, such as shrub, bush, tree, climbing. So one type of rose can be referred to in various ways. For instance, a hybrid tea is usually a bush rose, but it may be a tree rose. So first, we will describe the forms that roses take or can be trained to take with respect to their growth habits. Then we will describe the common types.

FORMS OF ROSES

Shrubs A shrub rose can be almost any size, but the name generally describes a plant that retains its size and shape without heavy pruning. Many are native species; others have been bred to the form.

Bush A bush rose may be the same size and form as a shrub, but without annual pruning it will lose both its shape and its flowering efficiency. Most modern roses, such as hybrid teas, floribundas, and grandifloras, are generally grown as bushes.

Tree (Standard) This is a rose budded onto the top of a bare stem, 18 inches to 5 feet in length, so that the flower head is raised.

Climbers and Ramblers These roses produce long, pliable shoots that require support. In the garden, they are trained up trellises and walls.

TYPES OF ROSE

OLD GARDEN ROSES (sometimes called old-fashioned roses) are varieties that were grown extensively until early this century. Most are shrub roses, usually with a short flowering season, but many of the categories include some climbing varieties.

Alba Roses These very old roses are early flowering, disease-resistant, and extremely hardy. The flowers are medium-sized and often fragrant. Two popular varieties are Félicité Parmentier and *Rosa alba semiplena*, or the White Rose of York.

Bourbon Roses These nineteenth-century, repeat-flowering plants have medium-size double flowers in shades of pink to red. Popular varieties include Honorine de Brabant, Mme Isaac Pereire (vigorous shrub), and Souvenir de la Malmaison.

Centifolia Roses These are very old, often extremely prickly, loose-growing shrubs, with large, scented, usually double flowers, in pink with deep centers. They grow 4 to 6 feet tall. Vièrge de Clery is a popular white variety. *R. centifolia cristata* (moss rose) varieties have mossy green hairs on the stalks.

China Roses These mid-nineteenth century roses have a long flowering season for the small semi-double blooms. Most are fairly small shrubs, but there are some good climbers. Old Blush is a commonly found variety with light pink blooms. *R. chinensis* Mutabilis can grow to 6 feet and is sometimes recommended as wall rose.

See also:
Species tulips p88
Distinction between climbers and
ramblers p90

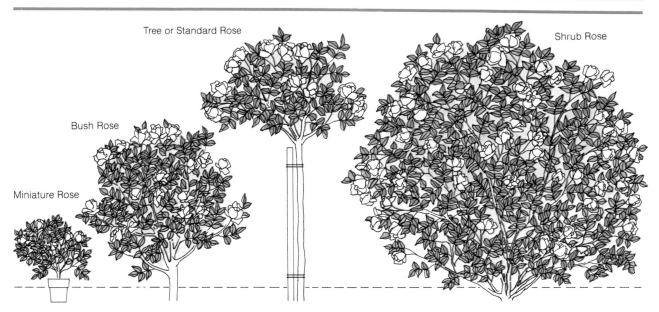

Miniature Rose

Bush Rose

Tree or Standard Rose

Shrub Rose

Damask Roses These date from the sixteenth century, possibly earlier. All are fragrant, hardy, disease-resistant, summer-flowering or repeat-flowering shrubs. Mme Hardy (white flowers with green centers) is a well-known variety.

Gallica Roses Probably the oldest of all garden roses, these are often thornless shrubs with scented, deep red, purple, or pink flowers — sometimes with white highlights. The most renowned is *R. gallica officinalis*, the Apothecary Rose. This has large, flat, medium-size rose-red flowers.

Hybrid Musk Roses Disease-free, free-flowering, repeat-blooming, usually scented shrubs, these produce flowers in large clusters, reminiscent of floribunda roses. Buff Beauty grows 5 to 7 feet tall with apricot buds and cream flowers.

Hybrid Perpetual Roses These hardy, vigorous, often repeat-flowering shrubs are usually scented; they were popular in Victorian times. Recommended varieties include Ferdinand Pichard, Frau Karl Druschki, and Reine des Violettes.

Miniature Roses Increasingly popular in recent years, most bloom continuously, often with little scent. They come in a wide range of colors and forms and range from 3 to 12 inches tall. Baby Darling has an apricot double flower.

Noisette Roses These are fairly vigorous climbers but usually not hardy. They bloom with large clusters in pastel colors. Mme Alfred Carrière is among the hardiest, growing 12 to 20 feet. It can be a large shrub or a climber.

Polyantha Pompons These are low-growing, continuously blooming plants with large clusters of small flowers. Fairy is known for its vigor, spreading growth, and hardiness. It grows 24 to 42 inches tall.

Rugosa Roses These are thorny, disease-resistant, hardy plants with large flowers, hips, and nice autumn foliage. Frau Dagmar Hastrup is a well-known variety, growing to 4 feet, with single pink flowers. It tolerates poor conditions.

Sweet Briar Roses These are vigorous shrubs, producing arching prickly branches that grow 8 to 12 feet, with scented foliage. The variety Duplex has double pink flowers.

Tea Roses Often slightly tender, these roses are similar to China roses with a scent that is supposed to be reminiscent of tea chests. Duchesse de Brabant grows 3 to 5 feet tall and is one of the first to bloom in the spring in warmer climates. It has double pink flowers.

Wichuraiana Roses These are typical rambler roses, usually flowering only once in early summer and needing a great deal of pruning. They are vigorous growers and can tolerate less than ideal conditions, but they are susceptible to mildew. Dorothy Perkins makes a good cover for fences, but should be planted in an open area to avoid mildew.

MODERN ROSES have been developed in this century. It is a loose term, but relates especially to those shrub roses bred over the last 80 years or so.

Hybrid Tea Roses These originated late in the nineteenth century from crossing hybrid perpetuals with tea roses; today there are thousands of varieties. They vary in size from 2 to 6 feet and require regular pruning. The flowers bloom continuously in a wide range of colors and are borne singly on long stems or in small clusters. Most are fragrant. If they are well protected in cold regions, they can be grown practically throughout the United States.

Floribunda Roses These were derived early this century by crossing hybrid teas with hybrid polyanthas to produce a group bearing its sometimes fragrant flowers in clusters, with many blooms open at the same time and with a long flowering season. They need careful pruning but are neat and colorful all summer. Most are disease-resistant, often hardy, medium to low growing, and can generally tolerate lower temperatures than the hybrid tea roses.

Grandiflora A sub-group intermediate between the hybrid teas and the floribundas.

What is the difference between a climbing and a rambling rose?

Despite what is popularly believed, the distinction between climbing and rambling roses is not a rigid one. The typical rambler has long, pliable shoots and a vigor that enables it to grow in a spreading and almost smothering fashion. It also has crowded, flat flower clusters. Most ramblers derive these attributes from the Japanese species known as *Rosa wichuraiana*. There is no such plant as a typical climber, for the group includes roses ranging from the climbing types of hybrid teas (large-flowered roses), such as Climbing Golden Dawn, through the old bourbon roses, such as Zéphirine Drouhin.

The most significant difference lies with the pruning. Almost all ramblers, like their ancestor *R. wichuraiana*, flower on previous seasons' growth. Most gardeners remove these canes once they have flowered in the second year, although if pruned back to within two buds of the main stem after flowering, they will usually bloom again the following year. But the quality of flowers will diminish in successive years, so removing the old, less productive growth is recommended.

The flowering habits of most climbing roses differ and so do the recommended pruning practices. Although it is impossible to give hard and fast rules for such a diverse group, there are three general pruning principles to follow. Old or diseased wood should be removed, overcrowded shoots thinned out, and the bush cut back to maintain it in a manageable size and shape. For the really vigorous species and for climbers that may be growing over an old building or through a tree, pruning of any sort is scarcely practicable or necessary.

Many of the climbers and some of the newer rambler types will bloom recurrently, so you can have a long season of blooms. The following is a small selection of climbers to show the range of colors available.

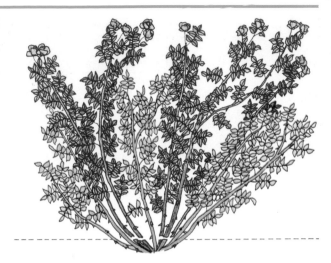

Ramblers bloom during the summer on long shoots produced in previous years.

These shoots are typically pruned back to about 12in from the base soon after flowering.

Albéric Barbier (Rambler)

Mermaid (Old Climber)

CLIMBERS FOR ALL-SEASON COLOR

Modern Climbers

America	salmon (scented)
Coral Dawn	coral pink
Blaze	scarlet
Golden Showers	yellow/cream
Handel	white/pink edge
Climbing Talisman	red/yellow (scented)
Don Juan	dark red

Old Climbers

Dorothy Perkins	pink
Gloire de Dijon	apricot and pink (scented)
Mermaid	yellow
Climbing Paul's Scarlet	scarlet
Rève d'Or	yellow/cream (scented)
Climbing Souvenir de la Malmaison	white/pink (scented)

See also:
Hanging baskets p50–1
Rose terminology p90
Edible hedges p114

What roses can be used to make a hedge?

Many varieties make excellent hedges, requiring a minimum of attention. The best hedge roses have dense leaf coverage to the ground and resistance to most diseases, bloom all season, and offer added interest from the hips. They can grow to almost any height you choose, depending on the variety, and will provide an almost impenetrable barrier to people and animals.

Although a few modern varieties make good hedges, most of the better ones are old varieties or species. Plant them about 3½ feet apart. Some of the hybrid musk roses, such as Penelope, can make a sturdy hedge, but they need more training and deadheading. The following make good hedges.

Blanc Double de Coubert	Roseraie de l'Hay
Nevada	Scabrosa
Reine des Violettes	*R. rubrifolia*
Frau Dagmar Hastrup	*R. rugosa alba*
Great Maiden's Blush	

Are there miniature roses that I can plant in a hanging basket?

Yes, many of the miniatures are climbing types that will cascade nicely in hanging baskets. Miniature roses tend to bloom profusely, offer long seasons of color, and are easily pruned.

There are a number of catalogs devoted solely to the sale of miniature roses. Some good varieties include:

Red Cascade Growing 9 to 12 inches high, this bears crimson flowers in abundant clusters. It is a fairly vigorous grower that must be kept pruned back.
Green Ice This very easy-to-grow rose features apricot buds that become white blossoms in the sun and green in the shade. It is disease-resistant.
Baby Darling This plant has bushy growth and apricot-orange double flowers.
Zinger Growing compactly, Zinger has profuse blooms of brilliant red with yellow centers.
Spanish Dancer Has semi-double red blooms.

What roses can be particularly recommended for their fragrance?

Before we make any specific recommendations, be aware that some roses appear to develop a fuller fragrance when grown in certain soils, possibly with certain fertilizer treatments. It is also true that some categories of rose are inherently more scented than others — many of the old shrub roses have a stronger, heavier, and sweeter scent than most modern varieties.

No two gardeners will agree on a short list of the best scented varieties and, from the thousands available, any short list can soon become a long one. These recommendations are limited to several varieties in some of the main categories of rose.

SOME ROSES TO GROW FOR FRAGRANCE

Old Shrub Roses

Königin von Dänemark	pink
Mme Isaac Pereire	deep pink
Persian Yellow	deep yellow
Austrian Copper	yellow and red
Thérèse Bugnet	medium pink

Hybrid Teas (large-flowered roses)

Perfume Delight	pink
Granada	red/yellow blend
Friendship	deep pink
Sweet Surrender	medium pink
Double Delight	red/white blend
Mr Lincoln	dark red

Floribundas (cluster-flowered roses)

Angel Face	lavender edged with red
Apricot Nectar	pink/apricot with a gold base
Intrigue	mauve
Spartan	orange/red
Iceberg	white

Grandifloras

Camelot	salmon pink
Roundelay	medium red
Olé	orange red
Shreveport	orange blend
Buccaneer	buttercup yellow

Old Climbers

Jeanne d'Arc	pure white
Maréchal Niel	butter yellow
Lamarque	white with yellow center
Dr Van Fleet	pale, silvery pink
Gloire de Dijon	apricot and pink

Modern Climbers

Don Juan	dark red
Climbing Crimson Glory	deep crimson to purple
Royal Gold	golden yellow
Viking Queen	medium to deep pink

Is it possible to take cuttings from roses?

Yes, it is quite easy to propagate roses from cuttings — but those that are closest to their wild ancestors (such as *R. multiflora* and *R. wichuraiana*) will respond best to propagation by cuttings. Hybrid teas do not have vigorous enough roots for this method.

Generally, the hybrid teas are propagated by a process called budding, in which a bud of the desired variety is inserted into a plant with a more vigorous rootstock. There are a great many buds on a single rose plant, so budding allows a commercial grower to produce tens, if not hundreds, of new plants from one stock plant.

The best time to take cuttings is during late summer. Take cuttings from wood that is partially mature (somewhat woody but still pliable). They can be rooted indoors in a potting mix or outside in a 10-inch deep trench of loose soil.

Take rose cuttings during late summer or early autumn from well-ripened wood of the current year. Select straight shoots 12in long with a cut at the top above a bud and a cut at the bottom just below a bud.

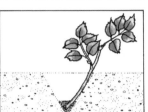

Trim off any lower leaves. Dig a narrow, V-shaped trench about 10in deep and place 1in of sand at the bottom. Dip the lower end of the cuttings in hormone rooting powder and set them into the sand about 6in apart so that they can lean against the side of the trench.

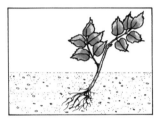

Fill the trench with soil, leaving about 3in of the cuttings exposed and water well. The cuttings should form roots within 12 months, when they can be transplanted; they should flower within 2 years.

Roses are commonly budded on the rootstocks of wild roses. Cut a young stem that has just flowered from the variety to be grafted — the scion.

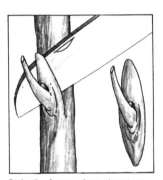

Strip the leaves from the stem and cut out a suitable bud, or eye, with a sharp knife. Shorten the leaf stalk to a stub and peel the bark away from the eye.

Just above the ground, make a T-shaped cut ¾ to 1½in long in the bark of the stock. Slide the bud under the bark right side up and trim it level.

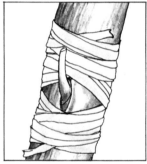

Bind the wound with tape or a special budding tie. The following spring, cut off the top of the rootstock before growth

What is the general method of pruning roses?

Different types of roses will require different pruning treatments. Sometimes it makes sense to remove some of the dead wood before winter to reduce the possibility of disease and to reduce the number of limbs that may be whipped by the wind. Some types of roses prefer more drastic pruning than others. Here are some general guidelines.

☐ Always use sharp clippers and make cuts at an angle sloping away from the bud, about ¼ inch above a bud.

☐ Try to keep the center open to a vase shape to encourage good air flow and discourage diseases.

☐ If the prunings are at all diseased, remove and destroy the wood.

☐ Start by removing all dead, injured, or diseased canes down to the nearest healthy dormant bud.

☐ Remove any suckers.

☐ Take out any twiggy, weak growth. Shape by removing crowded and older canes and by cutting the plant back to the desired shape.

In general, roses that flower on new wood, such as hybrid teas, floribundas, and grandifloras, should be pruned in late winter or early spring, just before the end of the dormant season and before the buds swell. Timing is important here; in cold climates, you don't want to prune too early and expose the plant to possible winterkill. The best time might range from January in warmer climates to April in very cold zones. If you prune too early, new growth, which will be stimulated

See also:
Propagating shrubs p83
Pruning climbers and ramblers
pp90–1
Staking trees p109
Pruning hedges pp116–17

Why do my roses always work loose in the ground?

There are several contributing factors that lead to this common complaint. Not surprisingly, the most important factor is wind; a rose garden on a windy site will always experience this problem. The effects of the wind are usually compounded if the roses are planted in light, loose soil; if they are inadequately staked; and if they have been inadequately pruned — especially if some superfluous top growth has not been removed before winter sets in.

Your roses will also be vulnerable if they have not been adequately fed and watered — because they won't have developed a deep and secure root system — or if they weren't planted deeply enough initially. You can correct most of these problems easily. It is essential to plant roses correctly, for many of the other problems will almost certainly follow incorrect planting.

How deeply to plant roses is a critical question. Most roses that you buy from a nursery or garden center will have been grafted onto a rootstock of a different variety. If you examine the base of the plant carefully, you will see the swelling where the graft union has formed. At what height to set the graft bud when planting is sometimes a controversial point. Generally, the rule of thumb is to set it 2 inches below the soil level in areas with cold winters. In mild climates, some experts advocate placing the graft at or above the soil level to reduce suckering and make control easier.

This advice applies to bush and shrub roses, but not to standards or half-standards, where the graft union is at the top of a tall stem arising from the root stock. Standards (tree roses) and bush roses on their own roots should have a good 4 inches of soil over the uppermost roots, and standards require staking in the same way that trees do.

to begin early, could be damaged by late frosts.

Prune climbers and ramblers according to their category, pruning ramblers and once-flowering climbers as soon as they are done flowering. By removing this old wood after the plant has flowered, you can make room for the new growth which will flower the following season.

There are differences of opinion regarding how far back to prune bush roses. Usually, severe pruning produces fewer, larger blooms, while light pruning produces a profusion of smaller flowers on larger bushes. In northern areas with much winterkill, there may not be a choice since there may be a great deal of die back. A very general rule is to cut back about one-third to one-half of last year's growth in the South and two-thirds to three-quarters of last year's growth in the North. To play it safe, cut back to where the wood is white in the center, not tan.

How important is deadheading for keeping roses healthy and attractive?

Deadheading is the removal of dead flowers from a garden plant. It is one of the more leisurely of garden tasks — an ideal accompaniment to a stroll around the garden on a summer afternoon with a good pair of pruning shears in one hand and a basket in the other.

Since dead flower heads are unsightly, deadheading has obvious aesthetic appeal. But the practice is important for more than just looks — removing the dead shoots stimulates the production of new flower and leaf buds elsewhere on the plant, and it also removes a potential point at which diseases can become established. Dead tissues of any sort, especially when they become wet, will attract the fungi of decay, which can easily spread to affect the open blossoms or even the shoots themselves. So deadheading is a valuable part of overall garden hygiene.

How much of the shoot should be cut away when the dead head is removed? There is no rule; many experts recommend cutting back to the first leaf that has five leaflets to assure that you will cut into strong wood with a strong bud.

There is one instance where deadheading should not be practiced. Most old rose varieties have only one flush of flowers, and removing the dead heads will not encourage more flowers to form. More important, many old varieties will not produce their extremely attractive hips in the autumn if the dead heads have been removed. Indeed a few old rose varieties and rose species are well worth growing for their hips alone. These include *Rosa moyesii*, which has deep orange-red fruits, *Rosa rubrifolia*, and many of the rugosa roses, such as *Rosa rugosa Alba*, which produces large brick-red hips.

Deadhead roses by cutting back to the first outward-facing leaf with five leaflets, thus ensuring that you cut into strong wood with a strong bud.

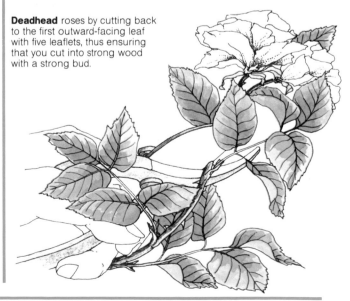

Is there a way to prevent suckers growing from the roots of roses?

 ## What are some of the common pests and diseases of roses?

The simplest way to prevent suckers is to grow your roses on their own roots so that every shoot appearing will be of the chosen variety. But this is not really a practical solution, since any rose plants you buy will certainly be budded onto a different rootstock and so will be prone to produce suckers.

To remove suckers, cut them away cleanly, as close as possible to their point of origin below ground level. You will need a sharp pair of pruning shears — but don't use your best pair, since the inevitable slicing into the soil will blunt them and may even cause damage to the blades.

Can selective weedkillers be used? Not really; for while some of the contact chemicals will kill off suckers, there is always the risk of spraying the chemical on the bush itself, and you will still be left with a dead sucker to remove. Similarly, systemic weedkillers will kill suckers, but with these you stand a much greater chance of damaging the whole plant and, once again, you will still have to remove the dead stem.

To remove a sucker from a Bush Rose, dig away the soil to find the junction with the rootstock, and cut off the sucker with clippers.

Suckers sometimes form on the stem of a Tree Rose below the grafting point; they should be cut off, close to the stem.

While numerous insects and diseases can cause trouble for roses, only a few are actually widespread problems. Rose varieties differ in their resistance to diseases and pests. So if you know that a problem exists in your area, plant resistant varieties. Described below are some of the more common rose problems.

Blackspot A more severe problem in areas where the summers are warm and moist, blackspot is manifested by circular black areas on the leaves that later turn yellow and drop.

Canker Canker generally enters through wounds during wet weather and produces sunken lesions on canes, causing poor growth or death in the canes.

Crown gall Large corky growths appear at the base of the plants, which usually lose their vigor and may produce abnormal flowers and become stunted.

Powdery mildew Affected leaves will be covered with a white or grayish powder; the leaves will shrivel and new growth will be stunted. Mildew may also affect the flowers. It occurs under all conditions, but is most likely in cool, dry conditions.

Rust Rust appears as orange spots on the undersides of leaves, with yellow-brown spots on the upper surface. Infected leaves are twisted and dry, and severely infected plants lack vigor. Rust can be found everywhere, but it thrives in cool, moist summers (as in the Northwest).

Aphids When aphids attack, you will find clusters of soft-bodied insects on young growth. The flower buds may be deformed and fail to open properly. Aphids do little damage in small numbers, but they are very prolific.

Caterpillars Many moth and butterfly larvae feed on rose leaves, buds, and flowers. The adult moths or butterflies lay their eggs with the onset of warm spring weather. Then the larvae feed for two to six weeks.

Japanese beetles These red, green, brownish, or metallic ½-inch beetles eat holes in flowers and buds; the flowers may be eaten or deformed. The beetles are found in late spring and summer.

Rose chafers (rose bugs) These beetles chew into the foliage, flowers, and stems. They are particularly common in areas with sandy soils.

Spider mites The minute pests suck the juices from the undersides of leaves, which become stippled and curled and drop off. Their webs are sometimes obvious on leaves. They are more common in hot, dry weather.

Thrips These small (¹⁄₁₆ inch long) sliverlike insects feed on the tender parts of flowers, which turn brown at the edges and may fail to open.

See also:
Aphids on annuals p52
Tree suckers p116
Suckers on fruit trees pp132–3
Disease and pest prevention in
  greenhouses p143

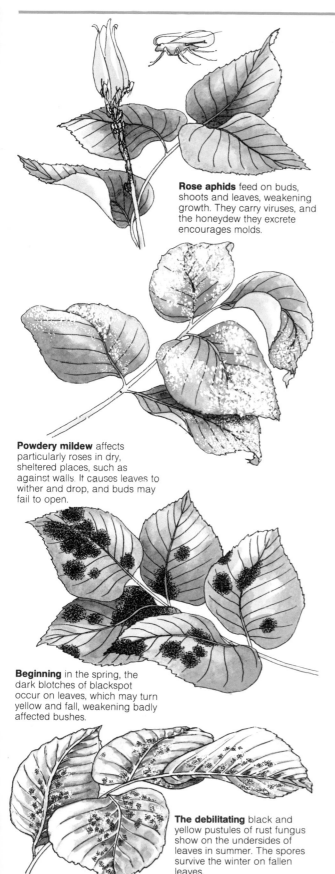

Rose aphids feed on buds, shoots and leaves, weakening growth. They carry viruses, and the honeydew they excrete encourages molds.

Powdery mildew affects particularly roses in dry, sheltered places, such as against walls. It causes leaves to wither and drop, and buds may fail to open.

Beginning in the spring, the dark blotches of blackspot occur on leaves, which may turn yellow and fall, weakening badly affected bushes.

The debilitating black and yellow pustules of rust fungus show on the undersides of leaves in summer. The spores survive the winter on fallen leaves.

Can I control these pests and diseases without relying on noxious chemicals?

As usual, an ounce of prevention is worth a pound of cure. Keeping your plants healthy and vigorous is the best way to avoid pests and diseases.

Start with healthy-looking plants. When possible, choose resistant varieties (although the degree of resistance varies with the environment and with your cultural practices). Plant in healthy, rich soil, but avoid excessive application of high nitrogen fertilizers since lush growth is more vulnerable to pests and diseases. Make sure the plants are well spaced (particularly in humid areas) so that there is good air circulation.

When you water, try to avoid wetting the foliage and keeping it wet, since many diseases are transmitted rapidly on wet foliage. Apply a heavy mulch to avoid spattering soil when watering, since the most devastating rose disease, blackspot, can be spread this way.

When you prune, keep the centers of the plants open to promote good air circulation. Prune out infected canes as soon as they appear, and prune infected plants heavily in the fall to avoid overwintering pests and diseases. Always sterilize your pruning tools between cuts with rubbing alcohol or bleach when pruning infected plants.

If you keep an eye out for early signs of trouble, you can often deal with it without resorting to chemicals. Before the problem gets too severe, many of the insect pests can be controlled by hand-picking or spraying off with water or an insecticidal soap. Caterpillars, if caught early, can be controlled with the bacterial insecticide, Bacillus thuringiensis, which is harmless to all else.

Mildew can be arrested with streams of water on the leaves, but since this practice encourages rust and blackspot, it should be done in sunny weather or be followed with the application of an approved fungicide (there are some safe ones available) that will control blackspot.

More elaborate methods of nonchemical pest control include introducing beneficial insects to keep populations under control.

How can I persuade a climbing rose to flower at the base as well as at the top?

Climbing roses with bare lower branches are common, especially on a north or east wall — and frustrating, too. Why does this happen?

Part of the reason is that the lower parts of the plant are shaded and suppressed. More important, the plant is expressing a phenomenon known as apical dominance, in which the tendency is for the buds at the tips of the shoots to grow, while the lower buds remain dormant. This same effect can be seen on apple trees — leaves and fruit will form only at the tips of the shoots if the branch leaders and laterals are not cut back in winter. In the same way, apical dominance in roses can be remedied by shortening the long shoots.

But you can't simply cut down the long shoots. If they are pruned too hard, the lower buds will form more long shoots, still leaving the base bare. A better plan is to force some of the buds lower down to break without drastic pruning by putting them in a position where they are no longer subject to apical dominance.

Untie the rose from the wall and pull down some of the long growths until their tips are horizontal or slightly lower. If you don't have space for this, bend the long shoots at right angles, so they have a kink some way up. Then retie them.

Why do some flower buds on my roses fail to open properly?

This is common in some seasons and on some varieties. The problem is known as balling — half-opened blooms become rounded, rather wet, brown masses. The condition tends to be more frequent on varieties with thin petals and normally occurs in rainy weather or toward the end of the season when you have cool nights with heavy morning dews and dark, damp days.

Incorrect feeding predisposes blooms to balling, so use a balanced rose fertilizer twice each season, first after the late winter pruning and then again in early summer after the first flush of flowers.

A severe infestation of aphids on young buds also appears to cause sufficient damage to prevent the flowers from opening properly, enabling the gray mold, *Botrytis*, to cause browning and decay. Although routine fungicide spraying may lessen the problem, once the young blooms are balled and wet, little can be done to revive them.

Incorrect feeding and aphid damage can cause rosebuds to form balls prone to mold.

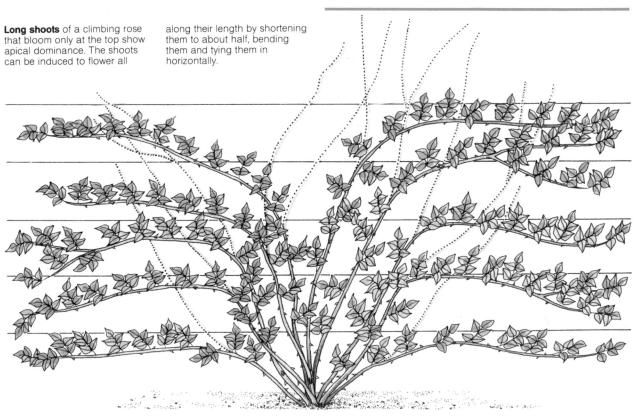

Long shoots of a climbing rose that bloom only at the top show apical dominance. The shoots can be induced to flower all along their length by shortening them to about half, bending them and tying them in horizontally.

See also:
Ground cover plants p26, 87
Foliage plants pp64–5
Winter protection for shrubs p87
Pruning climbers and ramblers
pp90–1

What plants can I grow between roses to improve the appearance of the bed?

While there is nothing wrong with leaving a rose bed to roses, some gardeners do prefer to cover up the bare soil and mask the twiggy look the roses have when dormant. If you do want other plants, choose them carefully; almost any plant that flowers while the roses are in bloom will detract from them.

A good plan would be to use small plants that flower when the roses are still dormant and then disappear. Small bulbs are the obvious choice, but be generous when planting them. You may find that discrete clumps of small bulbs will not look as effective as, say, an extravagant carpet of scillas.

If you prefer a plant that will remain during the summer, consider a foliage plant with gray or silver leaves. Dwarf lavenders, such as *Lavandula nana atropurpurea*, which grows to about 2 feet, look most attractive. Avoid crowding the bed and reducing air circulation, which would encourage disease. Where bush roses are planted with plenty of space between them, and sunshine can penetrate, you might consider using a low-growing herb such as silver thyme.

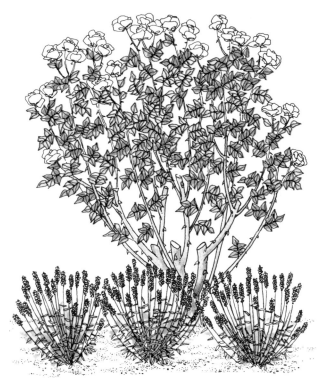

Dwarf lavender planted around the base of a large shrub rose will mask the bare, woody stem.

What kind of winter protection should I provide for my roses?

There is some controversy as to whether protection is necessary. In warmer areas, it is probably not needed and could, in fact, cause problems. In very cold areas and in transitional zones where the temperatures can reach 10 degrees F. or colder, some protection is needed from the extreme cold and strong winds.

It is not just the severe temperatures that can harm the plants; rapid drops in temperature can be extremely damaging. The protection is applied to maintain a constant temperature, particularly at the base of the plant.

The condition of the plant is also an important factor in winter hardiness. A plant that is healthy — has not been weakened by pests or disease, underfertilized or underwatered — will have a better chance of surviving the winter. Overvigorous, tender new growth is also particularly susceptible to winterkill. Do not over-fertilize and avoid fertilizing late in the fall.

In cold areas, hill the soil up 9 or 10 inches around the base of the plant sometime before the first frost. If the crown is planted below the soil surface, the soil mound can be applied after the second hard freeze. Use soil, not compost or manure, since they tend to hold too much water and can promote disease. This will help to prevent drying by the sun and wind, as well as conducting heat through the soil to the plant.

An insulating mulch of loose, dry material, such as straw, can be applied on top of the soil for the greatest effect. (If your plants could be in contact with road salt, cover the soil with plastic before you apply the mulch.) In extremely cold areas, surround the entire plant with a wooden frame stuffed with mulch.

Climbers tend to be hardier than bush roses; they are often afforded ample protection by their supporting structure. To further protect climbers, retie them to a pole and wrap them with burlap, or lay the plants down and bury them with soil. If you bury them, they will be more tender, so be careful when removing the soil cover in the spring, and cover up if there is any danger of frost.

LAWNS

Growing the perfect
patch of green

How should I prepare the ground to establish a new lawn?

Begin with the grading and drainage work. Fill in low spots and level hills, distributing the soil so that any slopes are gradual. If there is a grade, it is best if it is inclined away from the house so water won't drain toward the foundation. If you plan to lay sod, make the level of the soil 1 inch lower than the walks. If you are trying to establish a lawn on heavy clay soil or hardpan, some type of drainage tile may have to be installed (check with an expert in this area).

Lawn grasses prefer a rich, loamy soil with plenty of organic matter in the top 6 to 8 inches. The soil should be rich in phosphate to get the lawn off to a good start. Also, the pH should be about 6.0 to 7.0. Be sure your soil amendments and fertilizers are mixed thoroughly with the topsoil a week or two before planting.

If time allows, prepare the site, then let it sit for a month to allow time to destroy emerging weeds several times over. The final cultivating and raking should be done just before planting or laying sod, with the aim of making the surface soil as smooth and fine as possible.

If you have a large area with very poor soil and adding enough organic matter is not feasible, consider growing a green manure crop — such as winter rye, field peas, clover, or buckwheat — which will later be tilled in. The extensive root systems and foliage will decay and contribute considerably to the humus content of the soil. Ideally you should leave about six weeks between tilling in green manure and planting a lawn.

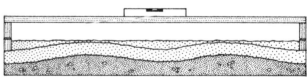

If the ground is very uneven, you will need to dig away some soil before making a lawn. At the level you want the lawn, hammer in a wooden peg, leaving 4 in of it showing.

Hammer in more pegs 6½ ft apart in a grid, using a plank and spirit level to get the tops in the same plane; stretch string between the pegs at the desired lawn level.

Take off topsoil, fill in with soil to 4 in below lawn level and replace the topsoil so that the string lies on the surface. Firm the soil and check the level again before removing the pegs.

See also:
Weeds in lawns p99
Grass mixtures p101
Lawn clippings p101
Lawn aeration p104
Non-grass lawns pp106–7

Is it better to start a new lawn from seed or turf?

Each has its advantages: seed is clearly less expensive, while turf produces faster results — although with both the work of preparing the soil is pretty much the same. There is more of a diversity of grass mixtures available in seed. On the other hand, some of the warm-season grasses, such as improved bermudagrass, are only available as sod. Sod can be easier to handle if you are planting a steep slope, and it will prevent soil erosion, which can occur before seed is established.

Although the initial time spent laying sod is greater than seeding a lawn, more time is required to get a seeded lawn off to a good start, providing consistent moisture to germinating seeds and young grass. (One way to cut down on watering is to apply a thin layer of mulch, such as peat moss or straw, after the seed has been sown. This will help to hold moisture and prevent the seed from washing away in downpours.)

You may see inexpensive seed offered for sale in bulk in unlabeled sacks. Avoid it, for you have no guarantee of its age or of how carefully it has been stored. It is best to buy seed from an established seed company that is prepared to tell you the precise composition of the seed mixtures it offers.

When buying sod, inspect it to make sure it is a uniform color and not yellowing. Either buy sod that has been certified as free from weeds, disease, and pests (some states require certification) or make sure you have a reputable dealer.

Another planting method used particularly with many warm-season grasses, mainly in the South and Southwest, is to use plugs, sprigs, or stolons. These are either small circles of sod, individual stems, or underground runners that are planted at regularly spaced points. They will spread rapidly by above ground runners or underground rhizomes and, over time, will fill in the spaces. It is best to plant them just before the warm, spring days. The results are slower than with sod, but the cost is less.

A week or two before laying a new lawn, rake the area to clear away leaves, small stones and other debris. Then rake in a phosphate rich fertilizer.

Stretch a string along one edge to make a straight line. Lay the first pieces of sod next to this, pressing them down firmly. Put a board on these pieces and stand on it to lay the next row and so on.

Stagger the sections as if you were laying bricks and fill the gaps between them with soil. Work this in with the back of a rake. The grass will eventually fill in these gaps.

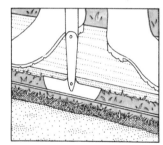

Trim the sod back neatly with an edger, making a sloping cut. Roll the lawn with a very light roller.

What causes thatch on lawns? Is it a problem?

Sometimes a thick, spongy mat of undecomposed grass stems, rhizomes, and roots accumulates at the soil level. This is called thatch. The problem is that this thatch layer can act as a barrier to water, fertilizer, and aeration and encourage the development of fungus diseases. Certain spreading grasses, such as bermudagrass, and grasses that have woody stems, such as zoysia and fine fescue, are big contributors to thatch build-up; other types of grasses create very little. Overfertilizing and overwatering can also help to cause a build-up of thatch.

Thatch build-up is not, however, a problem unless too much develops and forms a springy, impenetrable layer. On small lawns, a metal rake can often remove a great deal of thatch. If the lawn is too large or the mat too thick for a rake, you can use a vertical mower that cuts through thatch and brings it to the surface. At most, this process would have to be done once a year only on highly manicured lawns of a spreading type of grass.

For a fine lawn, choose mixtures containing a high proportion of fescues, **1**, and bentgrasses, **2**.

Deeper-rooting rye grass, **3**, is much coarser and more hard wearing for a much-used lawn.

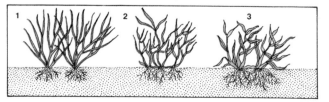

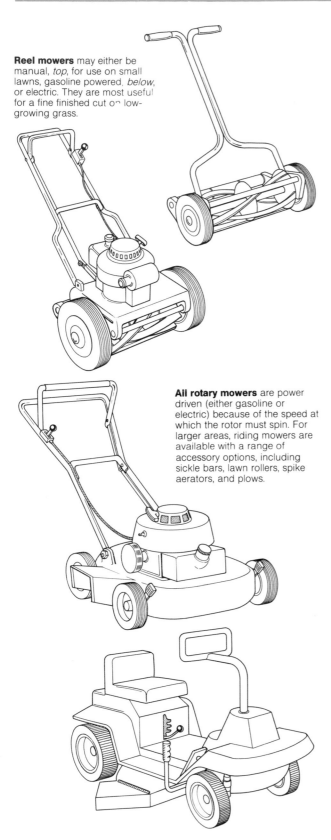

Reel mowers may either be manual, *top*, for use on small lawns, gasoline powered, *below*, or electric. They are most useful for a fine finished cut on low-growing grass.

All rotary mowers are power driven (either gasoline or electric) because of the speed at which the rotor must spin. For larger areas, riding mowers are available with a range of accessory options, including sickle bars, lawn rollers, spike aerators, and plows.

Which is the best type of lawn mower?

The type of lawn mower that is best for you depends on the size and type of your lawn, the time and effort you are prepared to expend on it, and how much you can afford.

There are two basic types of mowers — rotary and reel — with numerous variations, including push, powered, high-wheeled, electric, and rear bagging.

Reel mowers have scissor-type blades to give you a cleaner, finer cut. They are great for highly manicured lawns, but they are not very useful against high weeds or coarse grass. They are also difficult to use in hilly areas. And since a reel mower can't cope with tall grass, you will have to plan on mowing frequently. Reel mowers come in both manual and power models.

Rotary mowers are available only as power mowers; they are the workhorses of the lawn. Rotary mowers can cut much heavier grass and weeds than reel mowers, but they can't cut as low. They tend to be lower-priced and easier to handle.

Riding mowers, which are especially useful for mowing large areas, are usually rotary types. They come with numerous optional attachments, including sickle bars for cutting very tall grasses, rollers, sprayers, and disc harrows.

The final decision relates to width of cut. At a speed of 3 miles per hour and with an overlap of 2 inches, the approximate areas that can be cut in one hour are:

Width of cut	Area mown in 1 hour
12 inches	1,470 square yards
16 inches	2,000 square yards
20 inches	2,640 square yards
24 inches	2,930 square yards

Is it possible to grow grass in the shade of trees?

It is difficult to grow grass in very dense shade or under surface-rooting trees (like maples), where the tree roots compete strongly with the grass for water and nutrients, but it is possible, especially in dappled or partial shade. Since the grass will have limited root systems because of the shade or competition, give the grass every advantage by watering and fertilizing as needed and starting out with good soil structure, if possible.

Choose grasses that are shade-tolerant, such as red fescue, which is often included in seed mixes for shady sites, and St Augustine grass, which is a warm-season grass. If your shaded area is small, and if you are sowing the main lawn with a blend that already contains fescues, it is probably safe to sow the same mixture in the shaded area also, but don't expect the resulting lawn to be as good.

See also:
Grass clippings in compost p10
Alternatives to grass under trees p23
Thatch p99
Aerating lawns p104

Why do most lawn seed packages contain a mixture of grasses?

Mixtures are a guarantee that if one or another type of grass doesn't thrive in the specific conditions of your site, the others will. This is because different grasses, even different varieties of the same grass, prefer different soil and temperature conditions. The way to get around these preferences is to plant seed from a mixture of grasses.

In this way, no one disease is likely to affect them all, and you can take advantage of the different growth habits of the different species. For example, certain types of ryegrass will establish faster than other grasses. In the South, mixtures are less common because many of the warm-season grasses are only planted vegetatively and perform best as solid stands.

Warm-season grasses grow most actively in warm summer months and go dormant and brown in cold weather. Grown mainly in the South, warm-season grasses are adapted to hot temperatures. Cool-season grasses are planted in the North, where they grow most actively in cool weather. They don't do well in the hot temperatures of the South.

You will find that recommended seed mixtures vary both for different climates and for different site conditions — whether your site is shady or sunny, whether you have poor soil, fine turf, and so on. When you go to buy your lawn seed, you will also find both mixtures and blends of seed. A mixture is made up of different grasses that are fairly similar in texture, color, and growth rate; the proportions of the various grasses differ depending on the intended use. A blend, on the other hand, is a combination of several varieties of the same species. It is intermediate in adaptability between a pure stand and a mixture.

Lawn seed mixes are required to be labeled with fine-textured grasses mentioned first and coarse-textured, generally temporary, grasses mentioned last. Many of the coarse-texture grasses are very durable but less attractive. Be wary of mixes that contain more than 30 percent of the quick, temporary grasses, such as ryegrass or timothy: they are likely to give quick results, but not long-lasting quality.

The labels on the mixes should also tell you where the crop seed was raised, the percentage of viable seeds that will germinate under ideal conditions, and the percentage of weed seed and other ingredients that may be included. A high-quality mix will contain a number of named varieties, a high percentage of germinating seeds, and less than 1 percent of the total will be weed seeds. Here are some of the common types of grasses you will encounter in lawn mixtures.

Bentgrasses A good choice for a putting green, where you want to use a single species to produce very fine-textured turf; it is low growing and requires a lot of care.

Bermudagrass In the South, this is the best choice for a well-drained, sunny site, where the soil is not acidic. It is grown alone, not as part of a mixture. In the winter, it can be overseeded with a quick-growing temporary grass. Bermudagrass spreads readily and can be a problem near perennial flower beds.

Fine-leaved fescue Shade-tolerant and durable, this grass does best in cool weather and dry soils. Considered one of the best shade grasses for the North, it is also good for steep slopes.

Kentucky bluegrass Commonly recommended for cool, humid regions, this grass wears well. There are many varieties that are good for different specific conditions. In most parts of the country, except the South, Kentucky bluegrass varieties are usually the foundation for mixed lawns in primarily sunny locations.

Perennial rye The improved "turf-type" perennial ryes are quick to establish and make a tough lawn suited for high-traffic areas. The improved perennial rye is finer and more persistent than common, coarse perennial rye.

White clover This is often included in lawn mixes in small percentages. It withstands drought better than most grasses, but it doesn't wear as well.

Zoysia grass Another good choice for the South, this grass produces a dense, fine-textured lawn that is relatively free from pests and diseases and very wear-resistant. Meyer variety can be planted as far north as Massachusetts. One problem with zoysia is that it tends to build up thatch.

Should I remove the grass clippings when I mow?

There are numerous opinions, and the answer seems to depend largely on whether you are talking about a cool-season grass or a warm-season grass.

Generally cool-season grasses do not contribute significantly to the build-up of thatch and clippings can be left on the lawn if you mow often enough so that you are not taking off more than a third of the grass at a time. But in the spring when the grass is growing quickly and decomposing slowly in the cool weather, the clippings could mat and suffocate the grass below, so raking then may be advisable. Warm-season grasses, such as zoysia, have much stiffer clippings and these can contribute to thatch build-up if they aren't raked.

Compost clippings and return the compost to the lawn to replace lost nutrients; it is estimated that this can supply up to one-third of the lawn's nitrogen needs.

How and when should I fertilize my lawn?

There are many nutrients essential for good lawn growth, but nitrogen, phosphorus, and potassium will be your primary concerns (apart from calcium and magnesium for liming). Nitrogen is the most important nutrient, needed for leaf development, spreading, and greening. Nitrogen is also the nutrient most likely to be in short supply because it is quickly used up and because it is easily leached from the soil. All three nutrients are generally needed in a ratio of three parts nitrogen, one part phosphorus, and two parts potassium, so a general fertilizer with those ratios, such as 12–4–8, is usually recommended.

You can apply fertilizer in organic, soluble synthetic, or slow-release granular synthetic forms. Organic fertilizer may be in the form of dried manure, compost, bloodmeal, or a commercial organic fertilizer, such as Milorganite, which is a treated sewage sludge. (It comes in granular form and has an analysis of 6–2–0, plus iron and trace elements.) These organic fertilizers have a slow release rate so little is wasted, and the nutrients are available as needed by the grass.

Synthetically based slow-release granular fertilizers allow you to apply a heavy dose of nitrogen without any risk of burning the plants and without the need for frequent reapplications. Granular fertilizers are generally applied with a drop-type or rotary broadcast spreader. The broadcast spreader can cover a larger area than the drop type. With both there is a problem of skipping or overlapping areas. This can be avoided by dividing the fertilizer in half and applying it at half the recommended rate in two applications, instead of a single one.

Soluble synthetic fertilizers are relatively inexpensive and provide quickly available nutrients for the rapid greening-up of the grass. They will become available to the lawn before the soil has warmed up. However, they must be applied more frequently and there is more of a danger of fertilizer burn with this form. Generally, these liquids are applied with sprayers, though it may be difficult to apply them evenly.

How much fertilizer to apply varies somewhat with your climate and soil. The best idea is to base your application rate on the amount of nitrogen you need to

What are some possible reasons why my lawn has bare patches?

There are many possible reasons for the development of bare patches. Some of the more common causes are discussed here:

☐ Something noxious has been spilled on the grass: perhaps gasoline was spilled when the lawn mower was filled; or a household chemical or boiling water was dumped on the grass; or it was overdosed with lawn fertilizer; or a dog, particularly a female dog, has constantly urinated on the same spot. Although a mild dose with any of these substances may only scorch the foliage, a persisting bare patch indicates root death, and the affected areas will have to be relaid or resown.

The simplest plan is to dig out the dead turf to eliminate any chemical that may remain in the soil. Scratch the surface to prepare a new seed bed, and seed more grass. Keep the newly seeded area well watered until it becomes re-established.

If you are around at the time of the spill, you can lessen the damage by flushing the soil immediately with water if the substance is water soluble. If the substance, like gasoline, is not water soluble, try flushing the soil with a mild dish soap solution.

☐ Drought can cause bare spots. If the soil is shallow or compacted, prolonged dryness will cause the turf to die, either above the ground only, in which

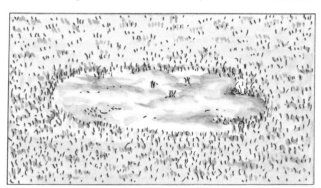

Bare patches form in grass for a number of reasons, ranging from an overdose of fertilizer to drought. The grass often yellows, dies back and the soil shows through.

Dig out the dead grass and soil from the affected patch with a trowel and then loosen the surface of the soil with a fork.

See also:
Fertilizer value of compost and
manure p11
Organic and synthetic fertilizers p12
Fertilizers pp17–18
Lawns pp104–6

provide. A good rule of thumb is to apply one pound of actual nitrogen for every 1,000 square feet of grass.

When to apply the fertilizer also varies according to climate, although liming to bring the soil pH to 6.0 or 7.0 can be done at any time. With cool-season grasses, fall is the best time to apply fertilizer since that is when the grass stores its reserves for winter. If you can't fertilize in the fall, then do so in the early spring; don't apply fertilizer in the late spring or summer.

With warm-season grasses, most of the growth occurs during the warm weather of late spring and summer, which is the best time to fertilize. For the greatest winter hardiness, the grasses should enter dormancy in the fall without stimulation from a heavy application of fertilizer. However, they can benefit from, and stay greener with, a light application at this time.

Lawns do not always need to be fertilized two or more times a year. Once may be ample. If your lawn is vigorous and healthy, don't overfertilize.

Dry fertilizer can be applied either with a broadcast spreader (hand-held or push type) or with a drop spreader. Broadcast spreaders require fewer passes for adequate coverage.

case it will regenerate, or, less frequently, below the ground too, when the roots die. Even if the entire patch of turf is not killed, it may be so weakened that lawn weeds can establish themselves in the area before the grass has a chance to grow again. Water the lawn thoroughly and, if you have a cool-season grass, raise the height of your mower. You may have to dig out the dead turf and reseed as described earlier, but see also the comments regarding end-of-summer operations on the lawn (page 106).

☐ Sod webworms may have been feeding on your grass. They are the larvae of several different evening flying moths. The moths lay eggs in the grass, and the worms feed on the blades, chewing them off at ground level, until the grass turns brown in patches. You can determine if this is your problem by drenching a small area with soapy water. If there are sod webworms present, they will be forced to the surface. You can solve the problem with either chemical or organic bacterial controls.

☐ A soil fungus could be causing the roots and stem bases of the grass to rot and die in patches. Sometimes the mold growth can be seen even on the leaves. Drenching the affected areas with a fungicide will often cure the problem, but if the soil is compacted it should be aerated.

Fill the hole with sod or by reseeding the area. Make sure to keep it well watered until the grass becomes established.

Make sure that the area replaced is level with the existing lawn.

Is aerating a lawn worthwhile?
How do I go about doing it?

All lawns suffer some degree of compaction, especially those that are well-used. The compaction will impede the free flow of water, fertilizers, and air into the soil. Aerating the lawn — which is done by drilling holes into the soil — can alleviate this problem, although most lawns manage without it.

If you have a small lawn, you can use a garden fork to aerate the soil. Even better is a hollow-tined fork designed for that purpose. For larger areas, you can use a roller type aerator, which has tines mounted on a heavy drum, or a power lawn aerating machine, which will remove cores of soil. Some places advertise spiked shoes specifically designed to aerate lawns, but generally the spikes are too short to be as effective as even the garden fork.

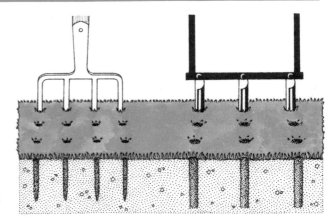

Small areas of compacted grass can be adequately aerated with a spading fork. Push the fork 4–6in into the ground, then rock it back and forth to open the holes up. Space sets of holes 6in apart.

Hollow-tined tools are available which are efficient, but hard work. When driven into the ground, they remove small cores of earth. Work backward to avoid walking on an already aerated lawn.

Weedkillers do not have much effect on my lawn; are they a waste of money?

Weedkillers tend to be very specific. They are only effective when they are used against the right weeds under the right circumstances. Your problem may be that you are not using these chemicals correctly.

First of all, there are two broad categories of weeds — broadleaf and narrow leaf, or grasslike. A weedkiller that works against one type might not harm the other. Also some chemicals are pre-emergence and others are post-emergence, meaning that some will work on the germinating weed seeds and others on the weeds once they have started to grow. If you don't use the right weedkiller at the right time, you will waste your money.

Also, some weedkillers have specifically defined weather requirements to enable them to act effectively. For example, some require a specific amount of time without rain after application in order to be absorbed by the plant. Others are affected by such factors as temperature variations and soil moisture.

So you see, almost more than with any other garden chemical, it is important to follow to the letter the advice given by the manufacturer regarding application; and don't be tempted to push your luck if conditions are only marginally correct. Remember, too, that lawn weedkillers should never be used as a substitute for good lawn care practices — a healthy lawn is the best deterrent to weed problems.

My warm-season grass turns brown in winter. Can I plant a temporary cover?

Yes. If you live in a warm climate, you can seed a cool-season grass into your dormant grass. The term winter grass applies to grass that is handled this way. The cool-season grass, either annual or perennial, will remain only through the winter. It should be seeded as the warm-season grass becomes dormant. If you seed too early, the winter grass will have trouble competing with the established grass. In the spring, as the warm-season grass starts to green up, it will grow and overtake the winter grass, which will eventually die out.

Rye grasses are often recommended as winter grasses because they are the quickest to germinate and establish under these circumstances, and new cultivars of perennial ryes are particularly well suited to the job. Other grasses, such as fine fescue and rough bluegrasses, are commonly used as well.

· In order to provide good conditions for germination, dethatch if necessary, then mow closely. Reseed the area and cover with a light organic material, such as peat moss. Keep the area well watered.

See also:
Thatch p99
Lawn mowers p100
Grass mixtures p101
Fertilizing lawns pp102–3
Watering lawns p106

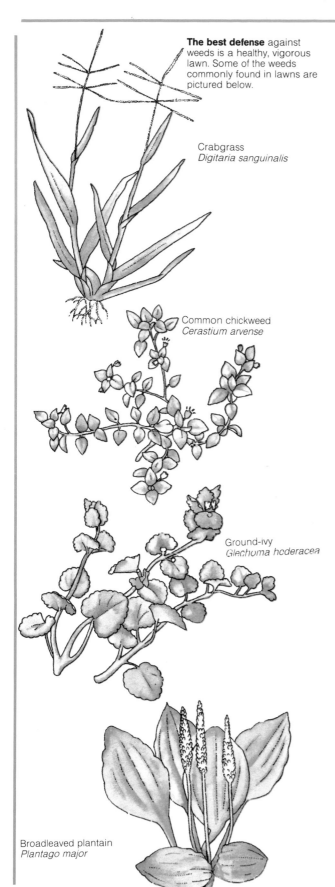

The best defense against weeds is a healthy, vigorous lawn. Some of the weeds commonly found in lawns are pictured below.

Crabgrass
Digitaria sanguinalis

Common chickweed
Cerastium arvense

Ground-ivy
Glechoma hoderacea

Broadleaved plantain
Plantago major

Is it possible to drastically reduce the use of weedkillers and maintain a healthy lawn?

A healthy lawn is the best defense against serious weed invasions. So if you want to reduce your dependence on weedkillers, you will have to start with a healthy lawn and then follow good maintenance practices. Indeed, weedkillers provide only a temporary solution. Using them leaves bare patches that invite new weeds to take hold — and it does nothing to correct the problems that led to the weed invasion in the first place.

If you are starting at a new site, you have the opportunity to prepare the site for the healthiest lawn possible. Well-drained, light soils are best. Then you will want to choose some of the new lawn grasses that have been bred for their increased vigor, which enables them to compete successfully against weeds.

If you have an already established lawn that has weeds, see if you can diagnose the cause for the weeds, then correct the problem. Often the type of weed that is growing will indicate a particular soil condition. For example, sheep sorrel indicates acid soils; knotweed indicates low fertility and soil compaction.

Mowing is a critical maintenance chore that has an impact on the development of weeds. If the grass is mowed too closely, the root development of the grass will be restricted and the plants will be weakened, allowing weeds to compete. Unless you have a grass that specifically requires low mowing, such as bent-grass, keep the mower at about 2 to 3 inches.

A little hand-weeding can go along way to reducing weeds in a lawn if you attack them before they have gone to seed. Research has indicated that, for example, if you dig up dandelions in the spring when the root reserves are low, there is a reduced chance of regrowth. Hand-weeding is most easily done when the soil is moist. If you do use weedkillers, apply them when the weed is young and growing quickly, unless the manufacturer's directions are otherwise.

Finally, you might want to learn to live with certain weeds. For example, veronica, clover, and English daisies, are often considered lawn weeds. But they are actually lovely plants in their own right (and clover fixes its own nitrogen) and are obviously well adapted to the conditions.

Judicious hand weeding can go a long way toward eliminating lawn weeds in a small area.

What can be done to revive a lawn at the end of summer?

Unless you had an exceptionally cool, rainy summer that kept the grass growing lushly and the people indoors, your lawn may well look like it needs reviving. After a really hot, dry summer, lawns often look as if they could never turn green again. But they have astonishing powers of recovery.

The end-of-summer maintenance chores can be summarized as follows:

Raking If there has been a build-up of thatch or fallen leaves, removing it will help drainage.

Mowing A close mowing just before winter will encourage basal shoots, which will thicken the grass.

Aerating If the lawn is heavily compacted, aerating it could help to rejuvenate and improve the lawn structure.

Feeding It may seem strange to apply fertilizer to a lawn at a time when it is not growing actively. But it is important, particularly for cool-season grass, to have nutrients available in the soil to start growth early in the spring. It will also encourage roots to develop laterally and deeper into the soil to build reserves for the next year. A slow-release fertilizer is best.

Seeding If there are bare spots, fall is a good time to re-seed (as happens naturally). The fall seeding usually doesn't require mulching, unless you are seeding a fairly steep slope.

Is it really harmful to water a lawn on a sunny day?

Although it is commonly said that watering on a sunny day will cause the grass blades to be scalded by the sun, it just isn't true. It is true, however, that more water will be lost to evaporation on a sunny day; on the other hand, this may actually have a positive cooling effect on the grass. Some people say that watering in the late afternoon or evening will not allow time for the water to dry and will lead to disease problems. This is somewhat controversial, and experts don't agree on this one. After all, grasses remain wet from dew throughout the night. This leaves early morning, which seems to be the safest time.

More important than when you water is how you water. Except when the grass seed is germinating, you should water your lawn only when the soil is dry, but before the grass begins to wilt; this is preceded by a cloudy, bluish cast to the foliage. Some wilting won't permanently damage the grass.

When you water, do so thoroughly; frequent shallow waterings encourage weak root growth and may favor weeds. Ideally you should water so that the soil is moistened to a depth of 6 to 8 inches.

How practical is it to establish a lawn from low-growing plants other than grasses?

Until recently, the ideal lawn was made only of grass — and with good reason. Grass is the best choice if your standard is a uniform, dense turf. Selective weedkillers made this ideal possible. But in recent years, there has developed an interest in planting mixtures of grasses

There are a few ground covers that can withstand some light traffic and light mowing. Nonflowering forms of common chamomile, *Chamaemelum nobile*, have been used in Europe as a lawn substitute. Most cannot, however, provide the uniformity, weed competition or wear and tear of a grass lawn.

See also:
Role of ground covers p78
Propagation of ground covers p83
Thatch p99
Fertilizing lawns pp102–3
Aerating lawns p104

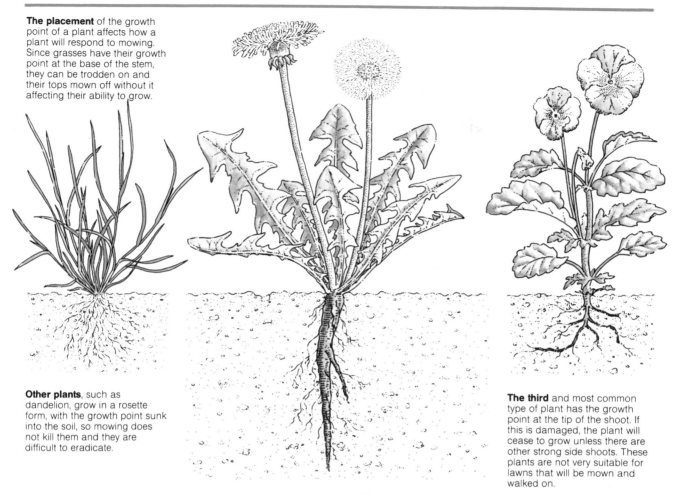

The placement of the growth point of a plant affects how a plant will respond to mowing. Since grasses have their growth point at the base of the stem, they can be trodden on and their tops mown off without it affecting their ability to grow.

Other plants, such as dandelion, grow in a rosette form, with the growth point sunk into the soil, so mowing does not kill them and they are difficult to eradicate.

The third and most common type of plant has the growth point at the tip of the shoot. If this is damaged, the plant will cease to grow unless there are other strong side shoots. These plants are not very suitable for lawns that will be mown and walked on.

and other plants (sometimes referred to as ecology lawn mixes), or in establishing pure stands of other low-growing plants. These enable lawn owners to cut back on the use of fertilizers and weedkillers, while creating more ecologically balanced systems.

If you are looking for an alternative to mowing, there are plenty of low-growing ground covers that can be planted singly or in combinations to achieve a good effect. Most require little maintenance, many produce lovely flowers, and some can withstand some traffic. Or you can plant a wildflower meadow, or a mixed flower, herb, and shrub planting.

But the term "lawn" usually refers to a planting that will be kept mowed and can withstand traffic, and for that your choices are somewhat more limited. There are a number of reasons why grass makes a good lawn. The growing point of grass is at the base of the stem, so grasses aren't easily injured by mowing. Grasses are tolerant of being walked on. And they fill in bare spots to make a uniform, dense cover.

Recent research efforts have been directed at determining which other plants, singly or in combination with grass, might be able to provide the uniform, dense coverage that grass provides, as well as being hardwearing and withstanding mowing. Some of the plants that are showing promise in this area include yarrow, strawberry clover, and birdsfoot trefoil.

Chamomile has been used for years with some success in Europe as a lawn substitute, although it will not bear heavy traffic and does not compete well against weeds. Dichondra (hardy in zone 10), with its creeping growth habit and round leaves, is commonly used in the Southwest as a lawn substitute.

Mixtures of grasses and other plants seem to be the most successful. Since grass is so competitive, grasses are chosen that will sustain themselves but lose vigor with low fertility. By cutting back on fertilizing, the grass is held in check and other plants can fill in somewhat.

These mixtures tend to vary in color and texture (which some people feel is a bonus) and do not necessarily look their peak during all seasons. The composition of plants will often change over time as the different plants find different niches. Some of the plants that are being included in these lawn mixtures, such as English daisies, were once considered weeds.

TREES AND HEDGES

The garden's living backdrop

What time of year is best for planting trees?

The answer depends somewhat on the form in which your tree was bought, the type of tree, and where you live. Although most mail order trees come bare-rooted, trees purchased at nursery centers are commonly available in containers or balled-and-burlapped. Such trees can be planted any time when the ground is not frozen and the tree can be well watered.

Deciduous bare-rooted trees are best planted in the early spring, before growth begins, or in late fall when the tree is dormant. They can be safely planted up to six weeks before the ground freezes in the fall. In the North, bare-rooted evergreens (both needle-leaved and broad-leaved) are best planted in the spring, since they have very high moisture needs and can become dried or damaged in the dry weather, wind, or severe cold of winter, particularly if planted in an exposed spot. If the site is not too exposed, and adequate winter watering can be provided, you can plant safely in early fall.

If you live where the winters are mild, there are several appropriate times to plant all types of tree. If you plant in late summer or fall, the plants will have warm soil to encourage root growth, but the shorter days will decrease moisture loss through transpiration. The plants will also have avoided most of the harsh heat of the summer and have a longer cool period in which to become established. Winter planting is often possible, although there is some danger of cold injury. It is also possible to plant in the spring before new growth begins, but this won't allow much time for root growth before demanding top growth starts.

The only time when trees should *not* be planted is in the late spring and summer when they are growing rapidly and the weather is likely to be hot.

How large a tree can be transplanted with a good chance of its surviving?

Extremely large — up to 13 feet tall or more — but not by your average gardener. Transplanting large trees is a job for an expert with specialized knowledge and equipment. Additionally, the trees to be transplanted when mature are usually grown expressly for the purpose so that they can be dug up with the minimum of disturbance to their roots.

If you truly need a large specimen and cannot wait for nature to produce it for you, call in an expert and be prepared for the bill. Don't imagine that by hiring a powerful truck and a winch you can transplant a huge tree from a friend's woodlot over the weekend and have it survive in your garden.

See also:
Relative heights of trees p24
Transplanting shrubs p84

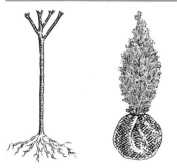

Trees may be bought from a nursery bare-rooted, or they may come with a ball of soil around the roots which is wrapped in burlap or plastic.

Increasingly, however, trees are grown in disposable containers from which they can be easily removed, with the least possible damage to the roots.

How do I go about planting a tree?

When you buy a tree it will come in one of three forms: bare-rooted, balled-and-burlapped, or potted. A bare-rooted tree is usually in a dormant stage. Most mail order trees will be shipped bare-rooted and packed in a moisture-retaining wrapping. Balled-and-burlapped trees are dug at the nursery with the root ball and soil intact and wrapped in burlap, a labor-intensive process that increases the cost of the tree. Potted trees are more expensive than bare-rooted but less so than balled-and-burlapped.

If you can't plant a bare-rooted or balled tree right away, you can hold it in a trench. Set the tree at an angle ("heeled") and entirely cover the roots with soil. Add additional soil and keep it moist.

Before planting bare-rooted trees, prune away any damaged roots and soak the roots in water while you prepare the hole. If it hasn't already been done, cut the top growth back by about a third to compensate for root loss from digging.

The most important aspect of planting a tree is preparing the planting hole. No skimping here! Your labor will be well rewarded in the long run. Dig the hole substantially larger than is needed so you can mix topsoil and ample organic matter (compost or well-rotted manure) into the bottom of the hole. Mixing in bonemeal for good early root development is sometimes recommended, but granular chemical fertilizers should not be added at this point because the roots are too tender.

Add enough of the soil mix so that the tree can be set at the same level as it grew in the field or pot. Planting a tree too deeply will smother the roots, while planting too shallowly will allow the roots to dry out. Both can kill the tree.

If the tree is in a container, carefully cut the soil from the edge of the container, and lift the tree out without losing the soil around the roots. If the tree is rootbound, loosen the matted outer roots.

Set the tree in the hole at the right planting depth, making sure it is straight and the roots are well spread out. Loosen any burlap or any plastic wrapping around the tree. Fill and tamp the hole while watering thoroughly. Leave a slight depression to hold water. Stake the tree if necessary.

If the tree settles too much, you may have to raise it and add more soil. If the tree settles only slightly, crown the soil around the tree, creating a depression with a rim at the base of the crown to hold water.

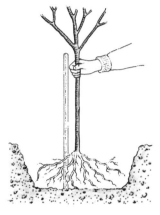

The hole for a tree should be dug wider and deeper than necessary to accomodate the roots. Loosen the soil in the bottom of the hole with a fork to aid in drainage and add a mixture of compost, leaf mold or rotted manure and bonemeal with some of the topsoil. Hammer in a stake near the center of the hole and set the tree to the same depth as it has been growing

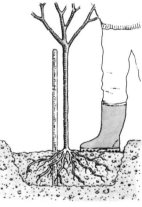

As the hole is filled in, tamp the soil and add water to avoid air pockets. Firm the soil and create a saucer-shaped area with a rim around the tree to hold water.

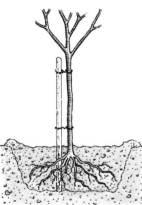

Most young trees need staking. The stake should be about 2in in diameter. Tie the tree to the stake with tree ties of rubber or other soft material. Water well and mulch around the base of the tree.

Is it worth propagating trees from cuttings or seeds?

Take semi-hard cuttings from strong shoots of the current year's growth.

Cut off the tip of the shoot, trim the lower leaves and cut the stem just below the bottom leaf node.

Propagating trees is one of those labor-intensive processes that is fun for some and too full of uncertain, slow results for others.

Many of the trees grown in gardens are hybrids and do not set viable seed, or the seed may not come true since many are grafted or budded. So be sure the seed you want to germinate is neither a hybrid nor the result of a tree grafted or budded onto different rootstock. The seeds of some trees will germinate fresh, but many require a period of some weeks or months before they will germinate, and they often need some exposure to the cold.

When possible, mimic nature by planting the seeds outdoors in a nursery bed, cold frame, or cold greenhouse, as soon as they are ripe (when they are about to fall from the tree). If this isn't possible, you can mimic these conditions with a process called stratification. Plant the seeds in slightly moistened sand, peat moss, or a mixture of both. Place the pot in a closed container in a cool spot (about 40 degrees F.); it can be buried underground or left in a cold frame, cool root cellar, or the refrigerator. Leave it there for the winter — one to four months, depending on the seed.

The next spring, plant as above, in an outdoor nursery bed, cold frame, or greenhouse. The following season, the plants may be ready to set out in a permanent spot or a nursery bed, planted 6 to 8 inches apart.

You can also experiment with softwood and semi-hardwood cuttings (see page 110). Select a shoot of the current year's growth in early to late summer. Choose a healthy 8-inch shoot with leaves and cut it close to the stem. Trim off the tip of the shoot and lower leaves, and cut the stem just below the bottom leaf node, leaving a 4-inch cutting.

Dip the end in hormone rooting powder and push it into a pot containing a mixture of peat and sand. The harder the wood, the stronger the rooting powder needs to be for good rooting. Press the mixture down and water thoroughly by spraying.

To keep the atmosphere around the cuttings moist, fashion a mini-greenhouse over the pot, using a plastic bag. Keep the cuttings in a warm place until they root — two to three weeks. Then transplant them to the outdoors.

The end of the cutting can be dipped in hormone rooting powder to encourage rooting.

To keep the atmosphere moist, create a mini-greenhouse covered with plastic. Keep the cuttings in a warm place until they root (2–3 weeks).

Some branches on my hawthorn look black and scorched and the leaves are curled. What's the problem?

It sounds like the problem could be fireblight, a bacterial disease that can be destructive to many trees and shrubs, including apples, pears, mountain ash, and some plants of the rose family. The branches of the affected tree often look as if they have been scorched by fire.

The bacteria overwinter on the infected branches and ooze out in the spring. This substance sticks to insects, which transfer it to the blossoms. The infection, which spreads quickly in warm, humid weather, can also be dispersed by rain, wind, and tools.

To treat, prune out the infected branches in the spring and fall, cutting about 15 inches below the obviously infected area, and sterilizing your pruning tools with bleach or alcohol between cuts. Protective sprays, such as copper sulfate can be applied in the spring before the buds break and again at regular intervals throughout the growing season. If fireblight is a problem in your area, consider planting a resistant variety of tree such as Washington hawthorn.

See also:
Plants to avoid p24
Germination of seeds p44
Shrubs for autumn color p79
Propagating shrubs p83

Flowering trees for a small site p112
Propagators p142

What are some good trees for attractive autumn color?

While we usually think of maples when we think of brilliant fall colors, there are plenty of other trees that change color. Eastern North America has the largest amount of native trees that produce good fall colors, but there are ornamentals for all areas that can provide fall interest, even in our warmest climates.

The degree and intensity of the color depends on a variety of factors, including soil conditions, temperature, degree of cloudiness, and occurrence of frost in the fall. The coloring is intensified by sunny, warm days and cool nights. Ground that is well drained, particularly in the fall, tends to encourage the best colors; they are less intense in areas with mild winters.

If you can't find the exact variety you want through a nursery, you may find that closely related species or varieties will provide similar coloring. But be careful, relatedness is not necessarily a guarantee of good color. For example, red oak has bright fall coloration, while the English oak has none.

SOME TREES FOR AUTUMN COLOR

Red

Acer rubrum	Red maple
Acer palmatum	Japanese maple
Amelanchier laevis	Allegany serviceberry
Cornus florida	Flowering dogwood
Crataegus crus-galli	Cockspur thorn
Liquidambar styraciflua	Sweet gum
Oxydendrum arboreum	Sourwood tree
Quercus palustris	Pin oak
Sorbus aucuparia	European mountain ash

Wine/Purple

Cornus racemosa	Gray dogwood
Fraxinus americana	White ash
Quercus alba	White oak
Viburnum lentago	Nannyberry

Yellow

Acer pensylvanicum	Striped maple
Acer platanoides	Norway maple
Acer saccharinum	Silver maple
Betula spp.	Birches
Cercis canadensis	Eastern redbud
Ginkgo biloa	Ginkgo
Liriodendron tulipifera	Tulip tree
Populus alba	White poplar
Carya spp.	Hickories

Is it true that some trees "poison" the ground?

This question clearly stems from the observation that some plants do not grow well when planted close to certain others. The truth of the observation is not in doubt, but there are few authenticated instances of one species of plant producing a poison that has an adverse effect on other plants growing close by.

The best-known example is that of the black walnut tree, which exudes a substance known as juglone into the soil. This can have the effect of retarding plant growth and may offer an explanation of the poor condition of other plants in the vicinity. Susceptible species include rhododendrons, mountain laurels, blueberries, apples, white pines, and tomato, asparagus, and other garden plants.

But the black walnut is an exception. Species that do not thrive when planted near each other are most likely in competition for nutrients and water in the soil, which is why one of the species fails to thrive. Look closely at the soil beneath a privet hedge, for example, and you should be able to see one reason why the privet is so often blamed for the poor performance of plants nearby. The ground, even in wet weather, is dry; in the summer it is likely to be really parched and dusty. Some plants simply have a root system that is so thoroughly efficient it doesn't allow for any competition.

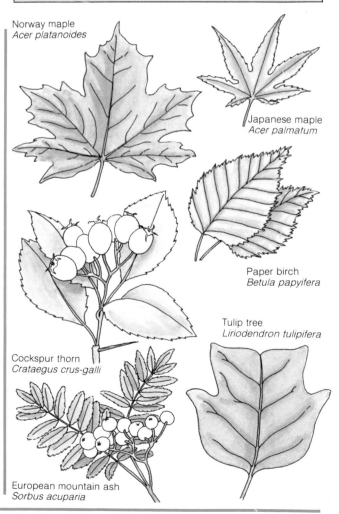

Norway maple
Acer platanoides

Japanese maple
Acer palmatum

Paper birch
Betula papyifera

Tulip tree
Liriodendron tulipifera

Cockspur thorn
Crataegus crus-galli

European mountain ash
Sorbus acuparia

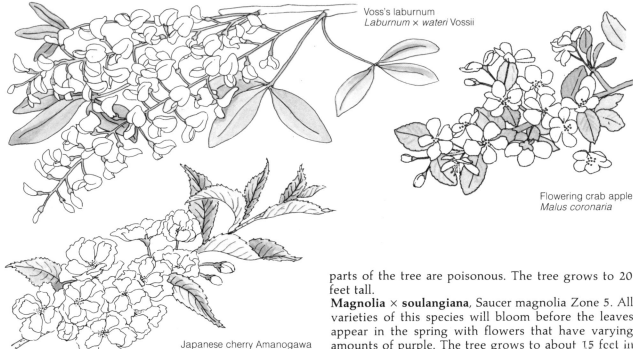

Voss's laburnum
Laburnum × wateri Vossii

Flowering crab apple
Malus coronaria

Japanese cherry Amanogawa

What flowering trees are suitable for a small space?

Trees can be spectacular when in full flower, but don't forget that the blooming season is brief. Select trees that have other attractions, such as fall foliage or ornamental fruits. Some of the trees listed below offer all of these features.

Cercis canadensis, Eastern redbud Hardy in zones 4 to 9. It is native to, and commonly grown in, the eastern half of the U.S. This tree grows 20 to 30 feet tall and has many vibrant purple-pink flowers in the spring and brilliant yellow foliage in the fall. The variety Flame has very erect branches and brilliant flowers.

Cornus florida, Flowering dogwood Hardy to zone 4. This very popular spring-flowering tree grows to 25 feet. The flowers blossom before the leaves fully unfold in the spring. The color of the blossom depends on the variety. In the fall, the leaves turn a brilliant red color and the trees produce bright red berries. Flowering dogwood are not tiny trees, but they make good ornamentals for a moderate-sized site.

Crataegus lavallei, Lavalle hawthorn Hardy to zone 4. This tree produces large flowers and showy fruits that make good preserves. The leaves turn a bronze-red in the fall. The tree grows to 21 feet.

Eucalyptus torquata, Coral gum Hardy to zone 10. This tree grows 15 to 20 feet tall and bears masses of red flowers during mid-summer, blooming for several weeks.

Laburnum × watereri Vossii, Golden chain tree Hardy to zone 5. In late spring, it blossoms with lovely yellow pealike flowers hanging in long pendulous masses. All

parts of the tree are poisonous. The tree grows to 20 feet tall.

Magnolia × soulangiana, Saucer magnolia Zone 5. All varieties of this species will bloom before the leaves appear in the spring with flowers that have varying amounts of purple. The tree grows to about 15 feet in height and width.

Malus spp., Flowering crab apples Plant resistant varieties as many varieties are susceptible to diseases such as scab, canker, and mildew. Sargent Crab is one of the smallest, shrublike varieties (grows to 8 feet) with pure white flowers; it is hardy to zone 4.

Prunus spp., Peach, plums, cherries, almonds There are many, many species of *Prunus*, and several small and dwarf varieties are excellent as ornamentals.

P. serrulata, Oriental cherry Hardy to zone 5 and grows under 25 feet in height. There are numerous varieties to chose from: Shirotae has pure white flowers with leaves that are bronze when young; Amanogawa is a more upright tree with pale pink flowers; Shiro-fugen is fairly upright with large double white flowers.

P. subhirtella Autumnalis, Higan cherry Hardy to zone 5. An autumn-flowering cherry, this grows large (30 feet), but it is wonderful for cut flowers. There may also be a flush of flowers in the spring before the buds break. Twigs can be cut at any time during the winter and can be relied on to produce flowers in the house.

P. persica, Flowering peach Hardy to zone 5. Growing about 25 feet tall, the flowering peach produces single flowers of pink, red, or white that bloom before the leaves appear in the spring. They do, however, have many insect and disease problems. An alternative to planting an ornamental variety is to plant a dwarf variety of a fruiting peach.

Sorbus vilmorinii, Vilmorin mountain ash Hardy to zone 5. This mountain ash grows to about 18 feet and produces white flowers in loose clusters in June, followed by bunches of bright fruits in September that may turn almost white as they mature.

See also:
Relative height of trees p24
Shrubs for a small area p80
Rose hedges p91
Edible hedges p114

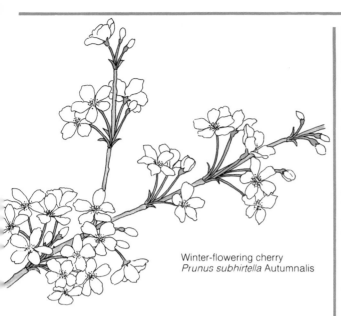

Winter-flowering cherry
Prunus subhirtella Autumnalis

 ## Are those tumor-like growths found on tree trunks harmful?

It sounds like you are describing crown gall, a disease caused by soil-inhabiting bacteria that get in through wounds in the roots, crown (trunk), or stems. The bacteria produce a substance that causes plant cells to divide and enlarge rapidly, almost like a cancer. The growths become woody and hard as they enlarge.

Eventually, the growths interfere with the plant's circulation and slow the flow of water and nutrients in the area. Infected plants become somewhat weakened; their growth may be stunted and they will be susceptible to other stresses, such as drought or winter injury.

Trees infected with crown gall can survive for many years with this condition. There is no control, but the tree will look better if the galls are pruned off — consult a professional if the galls are large and on the trunk rather than the stems.

The bacteria can be spread by infested soil, transplants, and contaminated tools. They will live in the soil for two to three years. So don't plant a new tree where one with this problem has been. And sterilize pruning shears with rubbing alcohol or bleach after you have made each cut.

 ## What are some good screening plants for windy conditions?

Although all trees and shrubs will act as screens and windbreaks to some degree, some withstand exposure better than others. Select trees or shrubs that grow fairly quickly and don't require a lot of care. If you want good screening in winter, select evergreens.

Acer ginnala, Amur maple Hardy to zone 2. Planted when it is 5 to 6 feet tall, it will grow as a shrub to a height and width of 20 feet in five to seven years. It will do well in full sun or light shade. Because it is deciduous, it does not provide good winter protection.

Cypress macrocarpa, Monterey cypress Hardy to zone 7. Although most cypresses make excellent windbreaks and screens, this is the one we picture along windswept coasts. It is a rapid grower, reaching a height of 75 feet, and is found mainly in southwestern coastal areas.

Elaeagnus angustifolia, Russian olive Hardy to zone 2. A deciduous shrub, Russian olive thrives in a variety of soils, in sunny or partially shaded areas, and withstands wind and sun. One of the best choices for a seashore planting, it has silvery shoots, gray willowlike foliage, and fragrant yellow flowers; it grows to a height of 20 feet.

Escallonia rubra Hardy to zone 9. This tree has dark green, glossy leaves and pink to red flowers. It grows to 15 feet, does well in full sun or partial shade, and is fairly drought-tolerant.

Populus nigra Italica, Lombardy popular This very hardy deciduous tree is a commonly planted quick-growing screen. It can reach a height of 90 feet. Select it for a quick, temporary screen as it is not generally long-lived. The tree is very susceptible to canker.

Although crown galls can disfigure the main trunk, trees can survive for many years with this condition.

113

What plants can I use to make an "edible hedge"?

The idea of using food-producing plants to make up a hedgerow is not a new one. Particularly in Europe, hedges of plants with edible parts have long been used as livestock barriers, garden dividers, and borders. When you select plants to act as hedges, you will want to choose those that are long-lived.

Generally, you will prune off the tops of the plants until the base of the hedge is well filled in, then you can allow the plants to grow to their full height. Many of the edible fruit-producing hedges will take longer to prune than conventional hedges, since you will probably be working branch by branch, rather than quickly shearing and shaping. The exact pruning style will depend on the type of plant, as will the cultural requirements.

Here is a list of some of the suitable plants.

Blueberry Highbush blueberries, *Vaccinium corymbosum* Hardy to zone 3. These are commonly planted in the North and grow to a height of 6 to 12 feet. Rabbiteye blueberries, *V. ashei*, (hardy to zone 7) perform better in the South and grow to a height of 4 to 18 feet. Blueberries do best in an acid soil with a pH around 5.0 and with plenty of organic matter in the soil.
Loquat, *Eriobotrya japonica* Hardy to zone 9. This subtropical tree produces attractive crops of golden, juicy fruits. It will grow to 20 feet but can be easily trained for a smaller hedge.
Natal plum, *Carissa grandiflora* Hardy to zone 9. This evergreen shrub produces fragrant white flowers and small scarlet fruits. The natal plum is thorny, which makes it a good choice for a barrier hedge. It shears nicely into a solid hedge.
Quince, *Cydonia* Hardy to zone 4. You can prune the quince to encourage multiple stems for a good hedge. The golden-yellow fruits make excellent preserves.
Rosa rugosa Hardy to zone 2. This rose produces hips, edible fruits that are very high in vitamin C and are often dried for tea. The autumn foliage is a lovely orange. Set individual plants 2 to 3 feet apart; they will spread out to become a full, thick hedge, reaching about 6 feet in height.

Consider also dwarf fruit trees — apples, pears, peaches, nectarines, citrus. They can be trained as espaliers on trellises or fencing to form a hedgerow. Dwarf fruit trees generally grow 6 to 10 feet tall and most will bear in three to five years. The many other possibilities include hazelnut, elderberry, olive, sweet bay, prickly pear, and currants (where not legally restricted as a host to white pine disease).

How can I dispose of a tree stump easily and safely?

The easiest way to dispose of a tree stump is to leave nature to her own devices. Cut the stump as low to the ground as possible — ground level or lower — then cover with soil to promote rotting. If you have a stump with a diameter of up to about 10 inches of most types of trees (oak being the most conspicuous exception), you can wait for it to become unstable after a couple of years as its roots decay. It can then be levered from the ground without too much difficulty. You can hasten the decay process in both cases by adding high nitrogen fertilizers.

If you do not want to wait, you have two options: either brace yourself and a small army of friends for a massive excavation with spades, crowbars, and levers, or call in a professional. An arborist with a chipper can render any size stump into a mountain of wood chips — an expensive undertaking for a single stump, but probably worth the cost if a small area of woodland has been cleared. If you have a 3-foot length of stump left, you can call in someone with a tractor and a winch to remove the stump, provided you can get the equipment close enough to it.

Rosa rugosa used as a hedge offers an impenetrable barrier with edible hips and orange autumn foliage.

See also:
Pruning shrubs p85
Rose hedges p91
Pruning hedges p117
Espalier and cordon fruit trees
pp132–3

One technique you should not attempt is burning. A tree stump, once ignited, can smoulder for a long time, the fire spreading into dead dry roots.

If all else fails or you are not able to afford the expense of a professional and heavy equipment, try turning the stump to good use by growing ground cover or climbing plants over it. Low-growing roses or some of the more vigorous clematis look excellent when allowed to scramble freely in this way.

When a large tree stump cannot easily be removed, practice creative landscaping and use it as a support for a climbing plant. This rose will grow rapidly over the stump, producing flowers throughout the summer.

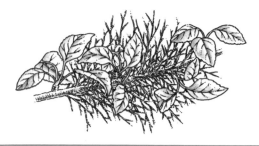

 ## What causes the large growths like birds' nests in some trees?

These growths, often seen on birches, spruce, pines, and cherry trees, are known as witches' brooms. When you see them at close quarters, they do bear a resemblance to those fairy tale vehicles witches are said to ride. Although witches' brooms are caused by parasitic organisms (fungi, bacteria, or viruses) or insects (aphids, for example), they apparently have little deleterious effect on the trees. The brooms arise when the tree's growth regulating hormones have been disturbed in some way, with the result that masses of short, twiggy growths are produced. If they are severely disfiguring, witches' brooms can be cut out and burned. Interestingly, several varieties of dwarf conifer originated as brooms cut from the parent tree and were propagated by cuttings and grafts.

 ## What can I do about the tent caterpillars I find in the crotches of my trees?

There are a number of tent-forming caterpillars found throughout the United States. The one that builds a web in crotches is the eastern tent caterpillar, which can be a problem as far west as the Rockies. They prefer wild cherry, apple, and crab apple trees, but will also feed on a number of ornamental trees. Although they weaken an infested tree, they seldom kill it — but their appearance is very unsightly.

Eastern tent caterpillars overwinter as eggs that are laid in distinctive, shiny masses on twigs. The larvae hatch in the spring, group together at a fork in the branches, and build a web. They emerge on fine days to devour foliage. Moths appear in mid to late summer.

Damage can be reduced by disposing of the egg masses during the winter and by getting rid of the tents while they are still small. Bacillus thuringiensis, a bacterial pathogen that is harmful only to certain pest larvae and harmless to humans and other wildlife, applied when the caterpillars are very young, can be effective. Some birds, including Baltimore orioles, love to eat the caterpillars.

What can be done about a tree that continually produces suckers on the lawn?

Since many tree varieties are grafted onto different rootstocks (generally of a variety whose top would be less desirable), it is not unusual to have suckers sprouting from the rootstock below where the two are grafted. Some trees, such as black locust and sumac, have a natural tendency to throw up suckers. Besides draining energy from the main trunk, the suckers are unsightly.

Sometimes it seems as though these suckers resprout as fast as they can be cut off, stimulated by the removal. If the suckers are cut off in the summer when the root reserves are at their lowest, they will be less likely to resprout. Cut the suckers as low to the ground or as close to the trunk as possible.

Sometimes suckers form higher up on the tree, and are commonly referred to as watersprouts. Often these will form when severe pruning has upset the root to branch balance. They also sap energy from the tree and should be removed.

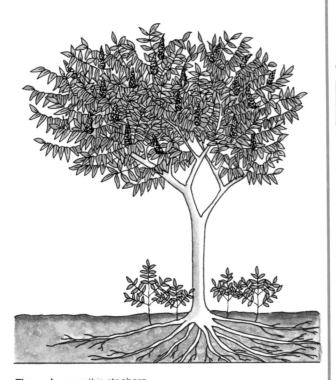

The suckers on this staghorn sumac, *Rhus typhina*, should be cut off close to where they originate as soon as they are produced.

What plants can I use for a dwarf hedge?

A dwarf hedge makes a nice border or low boundary in a garden. The important features are that the plants be small-leaved, slow-growing, and either naturally low-growing or highly responsive to being maintained in that form.

Around an herb garden what could be more natural than to use an herb or an aromatic plant? Rosemary can, with care, be kept as a low-growing hedge, but perhaps best of all is lavender. Choose the variety known as Nana, which stays under 1 foot tall at maturity and is hardy to zone 5. Cut back the dead flower shoots and gently perform any necessary shaping at the same time.

Box, a highly adaptable plant, is another good choice and there are many dwarf forms, such as *Buxus sempervirens* Suffruticosa, which is hardy to zone 5 and grows to about 3 feet. Lavender cotton — *Santolina chamaecyparissus* Nana — *Cotoneaster microphyllus*, *Hebe cupressoides*, *Berberis buxifolia* Nana, and many dwarf heaths, *Erica* spp., are all suitable.

How and when should a hedge be trimmed?

This depends on the type of hedge and the amount of time you have. If you want to keep the hedge informal, pruning once a year, unless the hedge is growing very rapidly, should be enough. Your objective is to trim just enough to prevent the hedge, from becoming overgrown with straggly shoots. A formal hedge requires pruning at least once a year; several times may be desirable to keep a highly defined shape, although vigorous growers, such as privet, might need to be cut back even more often.

The main rule for clipping hedges is to shape them so that they are narrower at the top, which enables the lower parts to get enough light. Some hedges, such as yews and privets, will do well with vertical sides. But, generally, you will want to maintain the natural shape of the plants, which is conical or rounded.

Initial training is most important to make sure the plants establish a dense growth. With hedges that have yet to attain their final height, cut new shoots back by one-third to two-thirds as you do not want the height gain to be too rapid. If the hedge is pruned hard in the first few years, it will stimulate plenty of dense growth lower down.

See also:
Dwarf conifers p82
Pruning shrubs p85
Rose suckering p94

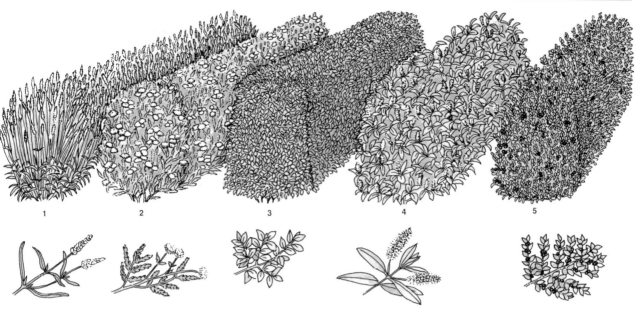

1   2   3   4   5

Lavender, *Lavandula angustifolia*, **1**, makes a very attractive dwarf hedge. The variety Nana grows 1–2ft tall and bears spikes of deep bluish-purple flowers throughout the summer.

Lavender cotton, *Santolina chamaecyparissus*, **2**, forms a dense bush about 18in high. The finely cut leaves are wooly looking and silvery and the flowers in July a bright, sharp yellow.

Dwarf box, *Buxus sempervirens* Suffriticosa, **3**, has bright green, shiny leaves that give it a neat appearance. It responds well to clipping.

Hebe cupressoides, **4**, has pale blue flowers among its tiny gray-green leaves in early summer. It grows to 5ft and must be clipped if it is to make a low hedge.

Frequently used for ground cover. *Cotoneaster microphyllus*, **5**, reaches a height of approximately 2ft. It has dark green, glossy leaves with gray undersides. The tiny white flowers are followed by masses of red berries.

Once a hedge reaches its full height, it can be trimmed to within an inch of the old growth. Over time, the hedge may grow too tall, then old growth will have to be cut. Do this carefully, since some shrubs cannot take it and will not respond well to a severe pruning. Generally, deciduous hedges can be cut to near ground level, if necessary, and will do fine.

Exactly when to prune depends on the type of shrub. The primary rule with flowering shrubs is to prune just after they flower, unless you want the berries to remain for aesthetic reasons. If the shrub is late-flowering, wait until spring to avoid stimulating new growth before winter. In the North, it is generally best to prune nonflowering shrubs early in the season so that new, stimulated shoots will mature and not winterkill.

Different species have somewhat different pruning requirements, so check with the nursery when you purchase new plants. Generally, evergreens should not be cut back too harshly. They should be well watered before pruning to avoid needle burn. It is particularly important to shape evergreens properly: if the top of the hedge is too wide, there is a greater risk of damage to the branches from heavy loads of snow.

For all hedges, both formal and informal, maintain the shape so that the hedge is narrowest at the top. This will allow light to reach all parts of the hedge and will cut down on the possibility of breakage from heavy snow. Such breakage is most likely to occur if the top of the hedge is wider than the bottom.

117

VEGETABLES

A multitude of crops
for the kitchen

How important is it to rotate vegetable crops?

A change is as good as a rest, they say. Apply this maxim to the vegetable garden, and you have the underlying reason behind crop rotation, where individual types of vegetables are grown in a different part of the garden each year. There are several reasons why this change, or rest, is good for the garden.

The first is that different species of plant utilize different amounts of nutrients from the soil, although most require more or less the same types of nutrients. For example, some brassicas (members of the cabbage family) need large amounts of nitrogen to promote their vigorous leafy growth, but peas and beans require little, as they are able to manufacture nitrogen through the activities of bacteria that live on their roots.

Similarly, fruiting crops, like tomatoes, have a much higher demand for potassium than root crops like carrots. By ensuring that the same type of crop occupies a particular area for only one season, the available nutrient resources in the soil are tapped to the full. Also, different plants have different root depths, so rotating assures that nutrients are not always depleted from the same depth.

Rotating crops has the additional benefit of improving soil structure by allowing the soil to become more uniformly cultivated overall. The rotation of crops that require deep cultivation and manuring or liming will eventually ensure that the whole garden receives this treatment.

Another reason to rotate vegetable crops is to help cut down on pest and disease problems. Many of the pests and even more of the diseases that live in the soil are fairly specific in the types of plant they will attack. In the absence of these plants, they die away. So if the length of time they are able to persist in the soil is less than the number of years before the plants are grown on the same site again, the potential problem can be kept at bay.

Could you please explain what an F_1 hybrid is?

As you look through seed catalogs, you will see more and more vegetables and flowers designated as F_1 hybrids. These F_1 hybrid seeds are usually much more expensive — but the catalogs promise larger, better flowers or fruits.

A hybrid is a cross between parents of different types, be they species, natural varieties, or artificially created varieties (cultivars). An F_1 hybrid comprises the first generation of progeny (offspring) from such a cross.

The process of hybridization has become technically complicated but, at its simplest, two parent plants with

See also:
Compost p10
Organic and synthetic fertilizers p12
Special fertilizers p17
Liquid and granular fertilizers p18

Saving seed p45
Vegetables in a limited space p121

This logic works very well in commercial enterprises because of the size of the crops and the distance between fields. There is little likelihood that a soil-inhabiting disease or pest will be readily transferred from one field to another. These arguments do not apply as well to small garden sites where the distances are much less — but there is some benefit.

The process of designing a rotation plan can become quite complicated, but it doesn't need to be. Here are some simple guidelines.

☐ Don't plant members of the same family (for example, broccoli, cauliflower, rutabagas, etc. are all in the cabbage family) in the same place two years in a row.

☐ Rotate the heavy feeders (broccoli, corn, squash, etc.) with the soil builders (peas, beans, clover) and the light feeders (onions, carrots, peppers).

☐ Consider the previous year's soil amendments. For example, don't follow with root crops on land that

has been freshly manured since it may cause them to fork. Another example: cabbage family crops require high levels of lime, so rotating them will distribute lime evenly. But don't follow with potatoes, which prefer a more acid soil.

Basically, when planning a rotation, keep in mind the nutrient needs, soil requirements, root depths, and plant families of each crop and its successor in the rotating scheme.

This is an example of a simple crop rotation plan that might be followed in a northern garden, with crops grouped together according to such factors as families and nutrient needs. Each group is planted in a different section of the garden and moved up to the adjacent bed each year. In areas with warmer climates where two or three crops are commonly planted in a single year, the rotation would be somewhat more involved. Each section would have the potential for a cool-season spring crop, a hot-weather summer crop and a cool-weather winter crop rotating through each year.

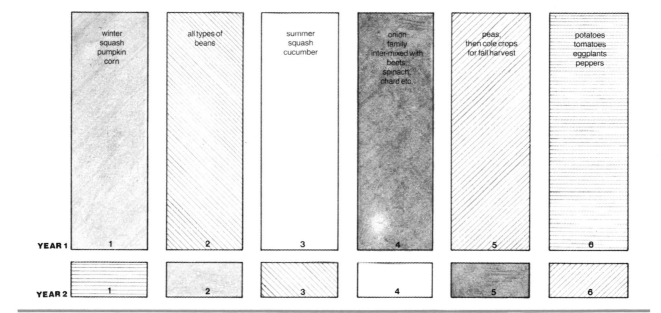

YEAR 1
1 — winter squash pumpkin corn
2 — all types of beans
3 — summer squash cucumber
4 — onion family inter-mixed with beets, spinach, chard etc.
5 — peas, then cole crops for fall harvest
6 — potatoes tomatoes eggplants peppers

YEAR 2
1
2
3
4
5
6

desirable characteristics (large flowers, good fruit quality, and so on) are each artificially fertilized with their own pollen. After eliminating those that fall short of the desired quality, carefully selected progeny plants from this fertilization are also self-fertilized.

The process is repeated many times until the desired characteristics predominate in most individuals, with the resultant plants known as an inbred line. Although these plants now have the chosen, highly appealing feature, their general vigor is low because of the repeated inbreeding.

When two inbred lines are crossed, however, the vigor returns in the hybrid, together with the selected features in concentrated form. Hence the appeal of an F_1 hybrid: it will have large, better flowers or fruit and, above all, greater uniformity. Because artificial polli-

nation is required each year, you'll have to buy a new batch of seed every season rather than save your own. When hybrid plants cross with themselves and form seeds, the seeds lose the desirable characteristics of the original hybrids.

If you seek bigger flowers and higher yielding vegetables, then an F_1 hybrid variety is probably worth the extra cost. Remember, though, that these hybrids were produced originally for the commercial market, where the uniformity of produce and of time taken to mature is important. You may not want all your tomatoes to ripen at the same time and should think carefully before rejecting older, less uniform varieties.

The wide row system of growing vegetables makes more economical use of the garden space than single row cultivation. If you have a rototiller, the wide bands can be placed far enough apart so that you can till in between them.

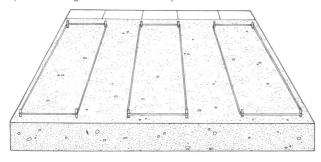

What are the advantages of planting in wide rows and raised beds?

First, let's define the terms. Both wide rows and raised beds are intensive planting methods in which plants are placed closely together.

A wide row can be as little as 10 inches wide or up to 4 feet (if you make it much wider, you will have difficulty reaching the middle of the row). You plant wide rows by sowing seeds in closely spaced rows or by broadcasting the seeds randomly — or by spacing seedlings much closer together than you would in a single row. These wide rows are, typically, spaced 2 feet apart, although if you have a rototiller, you might want to set them farther apart to allow you to cultivate between rows with it.

Raised beds are formed by simply hoeing up the soil to form a raised area or by double digging. Double digging, which is more work, involves digging out the upper portion of the soil with a spade, loosening up the remaining soil with a fork, adding organic matter, then returning the top layer of soil. A raised bed can be freestanding or have a framework, perhaps made of railroad ties. Often raised beds are permanent, which can justify the additional work required to construct them in the first instance.

The advantages of wide rows over single rows are many. First, the soil is never walked on, so there is less soil compaction and looser soil for plant growth. There is a better use of space, so overall yields are higher, although individual plants may produce less. Less weeding is required because the vegetables shade them out and successfully compete for water and nutrients. Moisture is conserved because the plants shade the soil and reduce evaporation. Fertilizer and other amendments can be more efficiently applied with wide rows.

Raised beds have all the advantages of wide rows, and then some. Generally the soil is looser in a raised bed. In the spring, the beds can be planted earlier because the soil is warmed earlier — this happens because the soil dries faster and because it is above the insulating colder air. Raised beds can help prevent water run-off and erosion.

There are a few disadvantages to raised beds. They take more effort to make. Their improved drainage may mean extra watering, particularly on sandy soils. In some cases, the greater moisture and temperature fluctuations associated with raised beds can affect the plants' growth. For example, blossom end rot on tomatoes is more likely with rapid moisture changes. However, you can overcome these problems with design modifications. For example, mulching the sides of the beds and building the beds lower will reduce the loss of moisture from the soil.

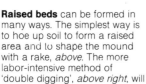

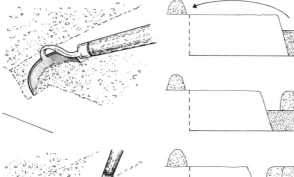

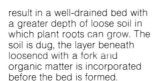

Raised beds can be formed in many ways. The simplest way is to hoe up soil to form a raised area and to shape the mound with a rake, *above*. The more labor-intensive method of 'double digging', *above right*, will result in a well-drained bed with a greater depth of loose soil in which plant roots can grow. The soil is dug, the layer beneath loosened with a fork and organic matter is incorporated before the bed is formed.

If you have a rototiller with a hiller-furrower attachment, raised beds can be easily made and later raked smooth by hand.

See also:
Organic and synthetic fertilizers p12
Clay soils p13
Special fertilizers p17
Liquid and granular fertilizers p18

Garden planning pp28–9
Unusual vegetables pp122–3
Sidedressing vegetables p128

Crops for a limited space may include those that offer a good yield for the amount of space they occupy (beans, lettuce, radishes, carrots); allow for a continual harvest (Swiss chard), or are specially developed miniature or bush varieties (bush cukes).

Which are the best vegetables to grow in limited space?

The best vegetables are probably the ones that you enjoy eating the most. Nonetheless, there are some vegetables that offer higher yields per square foot than others and some that will yield a long harvest period. And there are some vegetables that offer the maximum adaptability in growing conditions — so you can extend your garden by planting in containers and by allowing some plants to grow vertically on trellises. If space is so limited that you can grow only a very few crops, concentrate on those that are best enjoyed when freshly picked.

Those plants that have a good space/yield ratio include beans (especially pole beans), carrots, lettuce, bush summer squash, tomatoes, and radishes. Another good bet for limited space is any plant that offers a continual harvest throughout the summer, such as Swiss chard and kale.

Some plants, like broccoli, will continue to produce after the main crop is harvested. (Look for varieties, such as Deciccio, that produce abundant sideshoots.) Additionally, there are miniature, bush, or dwarf varieties of just about every vegetable — from Bush Champion cucumbers to Tiny Tim tomatoes to Baby Sweet hybrid carrots — and these will be real space savers.

You can also utilize some growing methods that will make maximum use of your limited space. Many vegetable crops can be trained to grow up on trellises rather than sprawl over precious garden space. In addition to pole beans and peas, vine crops (cucumbers, squash, melons) are excellent candidates for trellises, which will provide the added benefit of increasing your yields.

The increased yields come as a result of more leaf area being exposed to the sun, with a corresponding increase in photosynthesis. Trellises also allow for increased air circulation and decreased humidity, which could cut down on disease organisms.

Successional planting assures that the space is in constant, productive use by planting crops one after another in the same space. For example, spring peas might be followed by fall broccoli. Interplanting a quick maturing crop, such as lettuce, among a slower maturing crop, such as tomatoes, allows you to use space efficiently and to harvest the lettuce (which will benefit from the shade of the tomato plants) before there is too much competition for space.

Other space savers include planting in wide rows or raised beds. You can set the plants closely together in staggered rows so that all plants are equidistant. Most garden plants can be grown outdoors in containers and there are numerous varieties particularly adapted for this purpose. Some gardeners even report success growing potatoes in barrels of rich soil or compost. Consider, too, planting vegetable crops in areas other than your vegetable bed. For example, try treating sweetcorn as an ornamental grass and making it a feature of a mixed flower border.

Can I use one fertilizer for sidedressing all my vegetables?

Yes. You will have perfectly acceptable results using a single balanced fertilizer, such as 5-10-10, or an organic equivalent. The most important ingredient of these fertilizers is nitrogen. If you supply sufficient amounts of nitrogen, there should be adequate amounts of phosphorus and potassium too. Remember, timing is just as important as quantities (see page 128).

121

What are the benefits of mulching and what are the best mulches for a vegetable garden?

Mulches really do aid gardeners. They provide weed control and decrease rot and mold by keeping sprawling vegetables like cucumbers off the bare ground. They conserve moisture by decreasing water evaporation from wind and sun (this isn't always a plus) and form an insulating layer so the soil is less exposed to drastic temperature shifts. Organic mulches, over time, will break down to add organic matter to the soil and improve soil structure.

There are many materials that are suitable for mulching. Your choice really depends on the resources at your disposal and what you think looks best. Organic mulches tend to keep the soil cooler in the summer and warmer in the winter, while plastic mulches tend to warm the soil, which is desirable especially for heat-loving crops. Clear plastic warms the soil better than black plastic, but it allows weeds to grow.

When to apply the mulch is an important consideration. Since organic mulches insulate, don't apply them before the soil has warmed if you live in the North. In the South, you may want to apply organic mulches early to preserve the coolness in the soil for summer crops; while for winter crops, you may want to use a black plastic mulch to warm up the soil. Before applying a mulch, water the soil, but do not soak it.

When mulching new transplants with an organic mulch, leave a circle of bare soil around each seedling to reduce potential fungus or rot problems.

If you use a mulch that takes a long time to decompose, such as sawdust, you may have to add additional nitrogen to the soil to compensate for what is temporarily used up by the decomposing material.

SOME CHARACTERISTICS OF SELECTED MULCHES

Compost	Improves fertility and structure of the soil. May have weed seed, will not control weeds
Corn cobs/stalks	3–4 in. Readily available in some areas. Good weed inhibitor, but also inhibit water penetration; may be diseased. Add extra nitrogen to aid decomposition.
Cottonseed hulls	2–4 in. Readily available only in certain areas. Good fertilizer value, but very light and can be easily scattered by wind if no other mulch on top.
Grass clippings	Readily available, add organic matter. May carry weed seed and may decompose too rapidly to be effective cover.
Hay	6–8 in. Readily available. Eventually adds organic matter. First-cut hay contains many weed seeds (salt marsh hay or straw avoid this problem) and hay also tends to harbor mice.
Leaves	2–3 in. Readily available. Good food for earthworms. May inhibit water penetration and, if uncomposted, could inhibit seed germination.
Polyethylene (plastic)	Warms the soil and is reusable. Black plastic can be an effective weed control. Both types have poor water penetration, may overheat, and weeds will grow under clear plastic.
Wood chips/sawdust	2–3 in. Attractive, good for a permanent mulch. Chips may attract carpenter ants. Both decompose slowly and may tie up nitrogen if incorporated, so extra nitrogen should be added.

What are some less commonly grown vegetables that are worth trying?

Many vegetables that are considered unusual here have long been widely grown in Europe and the East. Some of these are becoming increasingly popular as more and more cooks discover their interesting tastes. Most of the vegetables listed here are available through standard seed catalogs, although the specialty catalogs tend to offer more of a variety. As with any vegetable, when possible, choose varieties that are suited to your area and growing conditions.

Florence fennel There are two common types of fennel: the herb, which is grown for its seeds and feathery foliage, and Florence fennel, which is grown for its bulbous stem base. When grown in cool weather (which is prefers), Florence fennel has a mild anise flavor. Northern gardeners can plant it in the spring, while those in warmer climates can start it in the fall or winter for a spring harvest. When the plants are about 1 foot tall, blanch the stems by hilling soil around the base to make the flavor milder. This vegetable is good raw or cooked.

Ground cherry (husk cherry) In the same family as tomatoes, ground cherries are small, round, yellow fruits enclosed in a thin, papery husk. The low-growing and spreading plant requires the same growing conditions as tomatoes, but takes three months to mature. The fruits have a sweet, somewhat acidic taste; they can be eaten raw or cooked in a savory or sweet dish.

Leeks These mild, sweet onions have been a European staple for centuries. Leeks do best in well-drained loose soils. They have a long growing season (90 to 130 days) and do well in cool weather.

In warm climates, sow seeds in the summer for fall or winter harvest. In cool climates, start the seeds indoors

See also:
Compost p10
Peat moss p15
Vegetables used ornamentally p28
Mulching p57
Vegetables in a limited space p121

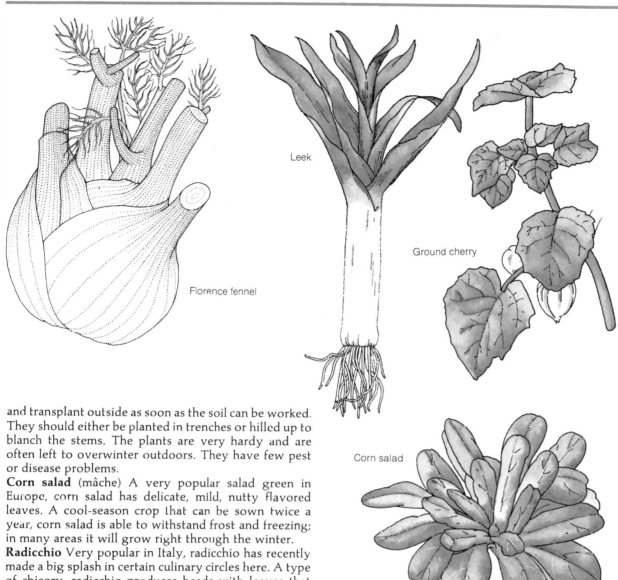

Florence fennel

Leek

Ground cherry

Corn salad

and transplant outside as soon as the soil can be worked. They should either be planted in trenches or hilled up to blanch the stems. The plants are very hardy and are often left to overwinter outdoors. They have few pest or disease problems.

Corn salad (mâche) A very popular salad green in Europe, corn salad has delicate, mild, nutty flavored leaves. A cool-season crop that can be sown twice a year, corn salad is able to withstand frost and freezing; in many areas it will grow right through the winter.

Radicchio Very popular in Italy, radicchio has recently made a big splash in certain culinary circles here. A type of chicory, radicchio produces heads with leaves that have red and pink leaves veined with white. Its slightly bitter flavor is excellent in salads when combined with milder greens, but it can also be cooked.

Depending on the area, you can sow seeds from early spring through September. It takes about five months to mature and needs a cool period at the end of its growing season to form a head.

Shungiku (edible chrysanthemum) A beautiful plant grown ornamentally in the western world, its leaves and stems have been eaten in China and Japan for years. It does best in fall, spring, or mild winter weather and tends to bolt in the heat.

Welsh onion If you have a limited amount of space but enjoy onions, this is the plant for you. It is a hardy, perennial leafy onion that will provide you with fresh onion flavor all year-round. (In the North, move the plants into a cold frame for the winter.) Divide established plants every three or four years. If you prefer a conventional onion bulb, rather than just the leaves, try the Egyptian, or tree, onion. This is another perennial, but one that produces its bulbs at the top, instead of at the bottom of the stem, in place of flowers.

In addition to this brief list, there are a number of other vegetables worth trying. Many gardeners have had very rewarding experiences with the many other oriental vegetables that are available, including celtuce (Chinese lettuce), Chinese parsley (cilantro), Chinese cabbages and broccoli, and daikon (radish). Another area to explore is the unusual varieties of common garden vegetables — the small white eggplant, blue potatoes, purple cauliflower, yard-long beans, and lemon cucumbers are a few you can find in standard and specialty seed catalogs.

123

What is the best way to support tomato plants? Should they be pruned?

Whether or not it is necessary to support and prune a tomato plant depends largely on whether it is a determinate or indeterminate variety.

Determinate, or bush, tomatoes will grow only to a predetermined height (the vine terminates with a flower cluster) and will produce a set amount of tomatoes. You can grow determinate tomatoes without support, although staking or caging can be used to provide the same advantages they do for indeterminate tomatoes. If you do stake the tomatoes, you can moderately prune them, but it isn't really necessary.

Indeterminate, or climbing, tomatoes continue to grow even after the fruit has set. They generally require some sort of staking, caging, or trellising to control their sprawling growth. Pruning is important to train the tomatoes to the support and to utilize the vertical space. It provides the additional advantage of increasing air circulation around the plants.

Regardless of which support system you use, it is best to set it up at planting time to avoid disturbance later on. Also, in tying plants, avoid using any wire or string that might cut or cause damage to the plants. Here are some of the different types of support systems you can use; each has its pros and cons.

Caging, where the plants are surrounded by wire mesh cages, generally 4 to 5 feet tall, is easy to use because the plants can be left alone and not pruned much. In hot,

Determinate bush varieties are usually sturdy plants needing no staking or pruning, although staking can be beneficial.

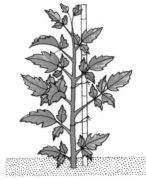

Indeterminate varieties will continue growing after fruit-set. They can be pruned and loosely tied to canes as they grow or be supported by trellises or cages.

sunny locations, the increased foliage cover can prevent the plants being scalded by the sun.

In cool or humid areas, however, you may want to prune some to increase ventilation and to allow warm air to circulate inside the cage and ripen the fruits. Caging requires more space than staking or trellising.

Staking saves space but requires extra labor, since the plants must be pruned to one or two main stems and tied to the 4-foot to 5-foot stakes. With staking you tend to get lower yields than with other supports, but the tomatoes tend to be large and clean. They are also more likely to crack and are more vulnerable to sunscald since they are more exposed. You may need to mulch around the plants to maintain moisture, since the plants do not provide much shade for the soil.

Trellising; there's no special tomato trellis, just about

What advice do you have for establishing an asparagus bed?

First, do a thorough job preparing the planting bed, as you can expect asparagus to be productive for about 20 years. Take the time to eradicate weeds by repeated tilling and by growing a cover crop before planting, and build up the soil by applying plenty of manure the previous fall.

A site with well-drained sandy loam and a pH of 6.5 is ideal, but asparagus can take great variation in soil conditions. A site that is easily waterlogged, however, could promote crown rot. It does not need full sun.

Although you can start asparagus from seeds, we recommend starting from one-year-old crowns, since asparagus takes three growing seasons to become established. Plant in the early spring as soon as the soil can be worked. Dig a trench 12 inches wide and 15 inches deep. Fill the bottom of the trench with about 4 inches of rich organic matter, some phosphorus in the form of

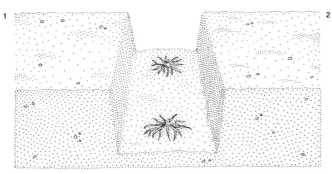
1

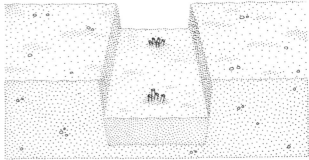
2

See also:
Eradicating perennial weeds p58

any structure will work that keeps the tomatoes off the ground. One method is to set up sturdy trellis poles and run a wire between them above your plants. Prune the plants to two or three main stems and tie them to wire with strings. As with staking, the tomatoes tend to be large and clean, but more vulnerable to sunscald and cracking. But trellising requires extra labor for setting up the trellises, as well as pruning to maintain two or three main stems. As with staked plants, trellised plants can be spaced close together.

Sprawling; leaving the tomatoes to sprawl is the least work of all — requiring no structures to set in place and no pruning. Your yields will be higher, the soil well shaded, preventing loss of moisture, and the tomatoes will be more protected from sunscald. On the other hand, more space is required, and you are likely to lose more tomatoes to rot and slugs from lying on the ground (although a mulch will help somewhat).

Pruning is necessary with staking and trellises. To prune a tomato, you pinch off those suckers (shoots) that grow at the intersection of the stem and leaf branch. When choosing additional main stems to develop, let the suckers closest to the bottom of the plant grow; they will be easier to train and have more flower blossoms.

In cool or wet areas, you may want to prune all your tomatoes — regardless of the support system — to improve ventilation and let in sunlight and warm air to ripen the fruits. But in hot areas, where sunscald is a problem, don't overprune. You might provide extra shade by letting two or four leaves of the suckers develop before you pinch off the growing tip.

Pruning a tomato plant for staking or trellising consists of pinching out the suckers (shoots) that grow at the intersection of the stems and leaf branches.

Plants that are supported by cages require a minimum of pruning. There will be decreased ventilation, so some pruning may be beneficial, particularly in cool, humid areas.

bonemeal or superphosphate (5 pounds per 100 square feet) and enough topsoil so that the final depth of the crowns will be 6 inches below ground level. Form a mound down the center of the trench and drape the crowns over the mounds, setting them about 18 inches apart. Cover with about 2 inches of rich soil and water thoroughly. As the crowns send up shoots, return the soil to the trench, an inch or two at a time, until the trench is leveled.

Fertilize in the spring and fall with a balanced fertilizer. Keep the bed free from weeds.

You can begin harvesting lightly for one to two weeks in the spring of the second year, for three to four weeks in the third year, and for about six weeks thereafter. (If you live in an area where the summer night-time temperatures average over 70 degrees F., wait an extra year to start harvesting.)

Only spears thicker than a pencil should be snapped. Allow smaller shoots and all shoots after the harvest period to grow into ferns. When they die back in the fall, cut them down and mulch over the crowns.

Dig the trench 8–15in deep, set the topsoil aside, mix in rich organic matter, bonemeal (5lb/100sqft) and topsoil so that there is a mounded planting bed 6in below ground level. Place the crowns 18in apart on this mound; carefully spread the roots on each side of it, **1**, and cover the crowns with 2in of soil, **2**, but do not fill the trench. This should be done gradually as the shoots extend during the summer so that, by autumn, the trench is level with the surface.

3. If started from crowns, asparagus can be harvested for 1–2 weeks in the spring of the second year, for 3–4 weeks in the next year, and for 6 weeks thereafter. Allow the ferns to form after harvest to nourish the plant and to build up food reserves for next season's crop. Cut ferns back in autumn and feed the crowns with a balanced fertilizer.

Is celery really a very difficult crop to grow?

It is a challenging crop, but you can have success with celery in most areas of the country. It does best where there is a long growing season and moderate temperatures, as in coastal areas. Celery can't tolerate high heat, but it can be grown in the cool summers of the North or the mild winters of the South, as long as there isn't a prolonged period with night temperatures below 55 degrees F., which could cause it to go to seed prematurely.

The plant needs 120 to 150 days to mature, so it is usually started indoors about three months before the last spring frost. In areas with a long growing season, celery can be direct seeded when the soil temperature is at least 60 degrees F.

For crisp sweet stalks, celery needs a constant supply of water. For best growth, the top few inches of soil must hold moisture and nutrients, so incorporate lots of organic matter into the soil. Celery is a heavy feeder and does best in potassium-rich soil.

Transplants can be set out about one week before the last frost, and covered with row covers if frost threatens. The plants should be spaced 8 to 10 inches apart in rows 10 inches apart. Some people plant celery in trenches, which they fill in with soil to blanch the stalks as they grow, although this can sometimes cause rot problems and make the stalks harder to clean.

We recommend planting the celery in regular rows or beds and blanching as needed by setting planks around the row or wrapping roofing paper around individual

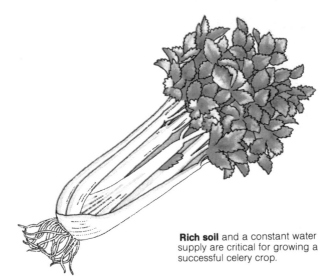

Rich soil and a constant water supply are critical for growing a successful celery crop.

plants. Many varieties are self-blanching and don't require this extra step.

Mulch with straw, or a similar material, to control weeds, retain moisture, and keep the roots cool. Water the plants regularly, but avoid overhead watering since moisture accumulating inside the stalks could invite disease. Sidedress every two to three weeks with 5-10-10 or an equivalent fertilizer (manure tea works well).

Frequent dry spells and hot temperatures can cause the stalks to be stringy and bitter. Under these conditions, the best you can do is plant in partial shade, mulch heavily with several inches of organic mulch, and harvest the outer ribs when still young and tender.

My corn ears do not always fill completely. Why?

The main reason for partially filled ears is poor pollination. In order to develop properly, every kernel must be pollinated — which happens when pollen falls onto each individual silk.

The way to assure good pollination is to plant your corn in blocks of at least three to four rows, rather than in long rows. If block planting is not possible, or if the weather prevents adequate pollination, you might also try hand-pollination. When the tassels are shedding pollen, simply shake them onto the silks.

Sometimes poor weather is the reason for poor pollination. Hot dry winds or a prolonged period of rain during pollination can prevent adequate amounts of pollen from reaching the silk. But, usually, weather-caused problems have to do with a lack of water, particularly from the time tassels appear until harvest.

Since the plants are tall and fairly exposed to the wind and heat, they can easily give off moisture faster than the roots can replenish it. Corn needs at least 1 inch of water a week. To assure good production during a dry

spell, you will have to provide the necessary water.

Insects, such as the corn earworm, feeding on the silks can damage them so that they are not receptive to pollen. You can control earworms by applying mineral oil onto the tip of each ear after the silks have wilted and started to turn brown. Apply about a half-filled medicine dropper to each ear. Or apply Bacillus thuringiensis before the caterpillars enter the ears.

Incompletely filled ears often result from poor pollination.

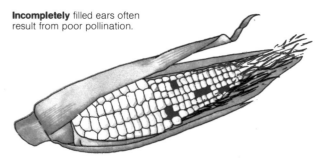

See also:
Clubroot on brassicas p14
Disinfecting contaminated soil p14
Transplanting seedlings p48
Crop rotation pp118–19
Raising transplants p142

My cauliflower heads never look like those in the supermarket. What's the trick?

Avoid discoloration from the sun by blanching cauliflower heads. Tie up the largest leaves around the heads when they are 3–4in in diameter.

There are a number of common reasons for poorly formed or discolored heads. Some situations are more easily corrected than others.

Cauliflower is particularly sensitive to checks to its growth before the heads are formed. If the young plants are stressed, they may form button, or premature, heads. For instance, buttoning may occur if the seedlings are grown too quickly, under too warm conditions, and then set outside in cool weather. Other stressful conditions are lack of nitrogen in the soil, weed competition, dry soil, and root damage when transplanting.

To avoid stress, grow seedlings indoors at temperatures of 57 to 68 degrees F. When buying transplants, buy ones planted in separate cells to minimize crowding and root damage. Assure good soil fertility with plenty of potassium and phosphorus.

As the heads are forming, the temperature should be between 60 and 65 degrees F., which is why fall crops that mature when the weather is cool tend to be much more successful. If the weather is too hot, the heads may be loose and fall apart, or the plant may not head up.

The major cause of discolored heads is failure to blanch them. Direct sunlight on enlarging heads will cause them to turn yellow or brown. To blanch cauliflower heads, simply cover them by tying or bending the large outer leaves over the heads when they are 3 to 4 inches in diameter. This should be done when the heads are dry to avoid disease problems.

Check the heads from time to time because, if left unharvested too long, they can loosen and become "ricey" in texture. There are some self-blanching varieties, such as Alert which matures early, that can save you this step. The leaves of the self-blanchers naturally wrap up around the head and protect it from sunlight.

Discolored and deformed curds also could be the result of a boron deficiency of the soil. If you suspect this, test your soil and apply the recommended amount of borax.

Various fungus and bacterial diseases can cause the heads to soften and rot. There are no controls for this. The best you can do is clean up the debris and plant your cauliflowers in a different place next season.

My garden site is mostly shaded. Is it worth trying to grow vegetables?

Although conventional wisdom holds that vegetables require at least six hours of sunlight a day, this is not a hard and fast rule that applies to all vegetables. Many greens, for example, do best in partial shade, particularly in hot weather. It is primarily the plants that are grown for their fruits — tomatoes, peppers, melons, cucumbers, and so on — that require a minimum of six hours of sun, and these will not be worth growing in a shaded site.

The quality of the shade that characterizes your garden site is most critical. A garden that is in deep shade, with very little reflected light, is not an hospitable environment for growing vegetables of any kind. A lightly shaded garden that receives only two to four hours of direct sunlight or receives indirect light for a good part of the day can provide enough light for shade-tolerant vegetables.

Shade-tolerant vegetables include those plants that are grown mainly for their leaves — lettuce, spinach, cabbage — as well as peas, and some herbs (mint, parsley). In hot weather, lettuce and other leafy greens are sweeter and less bitter when grown in partial shade. Root crops and broccoli are examples of crops that can tolerate some shade, but less than leafy greens.

Your vegetables will tend to be smaller and grow more slowly in the shade, so it is best to continue to experiment with various vegetables and varieties. Providing extra care — richer and more well-drained soil — for shaded crops can help lessen the negative impact of insufficient sun.

My onions became soft and went bad in storage. What was wrong?

It sounds like something went wrong with the growing, harvesting, or storage conditions — or it may have been due to a disease.

First, you should start with onion sets or seeds that are a good storage variety, such as Yellow Globe or Capable. These types have harder outer skins and tend to dry more quickly than nonstorage varieties. Your site should have well-drained soil. If your soil is poorly drained, the bulbs will take up so much water they won't store well.

Many fungus and bacteria problems are associated with stored onions that have a high moisture content. If you applied fertilizer late in the season, when the tops were starting to fall over, that extra nitrogen could have caused new growth that would rot rather than dry properly. Extra nitrogen at that late time is unnecessary and should be avoided.

If the onions were harvested prematurely, they wouldn't have stored well. Allow them to ripen thoroughly. When most of the tops die down, bend over the remainder and allow them to die naturally. Then pull the onions from the soil and leave them out to dry in the field for a few days. After they have dried a little, let them cure in a warm, airy place out of the sun for a week or two. Don't ever wash them!

Sort out the onions that have thick necks and plan to use them soon for cooking; they won't store well. The remainder should be stored in mesh bags or slatted crates for good ventilation. They should be kept cool (at 32 to 40 degrees F.) and dry (60 to 70 percent humidity) in order to prevent softening and sprouting.

If the onions appeared sound at harvest and were stored under optimal conditions, but they decayed anyway and developed a gray mold around the neck, just below where the leaves emerge, the problem could be onion neck rot. This fungus generally originates on the onion seed, grows slowly into the tissues of the plant while it is in the garden, and only when the mature onion has been put into store does the mold become evident. Treating the onions themselves at this stage has no effect.

Onion neck rot fungus will stay in the soil, so clean up any onion debris from the garden and rotate the crops. If you notice any of the symptoms while the onions are in the field, remove those that are affected to halt the spread of the disease. Try to keep the rest of the crop on the dry side and, if watering is necessary, keep from wetting the plants.

When should I sidedress my vegetables?

When and how often to sidedress depends on a number of factors, including soil type, the kind of fertilizer you are using, and weather factors. For instance, since sandy soils do not hold on to nutrients well, plants in sandy soils benefit from small, regular applications of fertilizer. But if you have a slow-release fertilizer, or very rich soil, you may not need to sidedress at all. Timing is also somewhat weather dependent. In cool weather, when plants are growing slowly, sidedressing may not be necessary.

Although there are no hard and fast rules for sidedressing specific vegetables, there are some general guidelines. Plants that have a long growing season, such as tomatoes and eggplants, and heavy feeders (corn) tend to benefit more from sidedressing than quick-maturing crops like lettuce. Crops, such as peas and beans, that can fix their own nitrogen don't need sidedressing at all. The table on the right gives some guidelines for sidedressing specific crops.

RECOMMENDED TIMES TO SIDEDRESS

3 times/season	
Sweet corn	3 weeks after planting; again when plants are 8–10in high; again when tassels appear
Melons	When they begin to run; a week after blossom set; again 3 weeks later
Onions	3 weeks after setting out; when tops are 6–8in tall; when bulbs start to swell
Tomatoes	2–3 weeks after transplant; before first picking; 2 weeks after first picking
1–2 times/season	
Beets	When tops are 4–5in high (light on nitrogen which encourages leafy growth)
Broccoli/cauliflower/ cabbage	3 weeks after transplant
Carrots	3 weeks after plants are well established
Celery	3 weeks after setting out; again 6 weeks later
Cucumbers	When they first start to run; when they bloom
Eggplant/peppers	3 weeks after transplant; after first fruit set
Head lettuce	3 weeks after transplant; as heads form
Potatoes	When plants bloom
Spinach	When plants are 2in high
Summer squash	When plants are 6in tall; when they bloom
Winter squash/pumpkins	When plants start to run; when they bloom
Sidedressing unnecessary Beans, Peas, Radishes	

See also:
Fertilizer value of compost and
    manure p11
Disinfection of contaminated soil p14
Special fertilizers p17

Liquid and granular fertilizers p18
Considering children in site planning
    p31
Vegetables for a limited space p121
Root crop storage p146

Onions that appear fine when
harvested but subsequently
decay in storage may be
affected with neck rot.

 ## What are the best vegetables for a child's first garden?

It's always nice to have some quick-growing vegetables like radishes and lettuce to engage the child's interest immediately. And it's exciting to include plants like peas and carrots that can be picked and eaten raw in the garden. But really, there is no limit to the types of vegetables — and flowers — that might be grown, including some that the child might not like to eat, for this experience could change his or her mind.

What is planted is much less important than what the child does in the garden. Young children can be stimulated by the various smells, colors, and textures that the garden produces. For older children, there are experiments that can be conducted with growing techniques, fertilizers, and mulches; rain gauges that can be built; records that can be kept; insects that can be inspected with a hand lens. Here are just a few examples of special activities you can share with your children.

☐ Scratch each child's name on a young pumpkin and watch it grow and stretch.
☐ Grow a cucumber in a bottle. Place the bottle over the cucumber when it is very small and shade the bottle from the sun.
☐ Collect and save seeds for planting again.
☐ Let an area of the garden become weedy and compare the vegetable growth in that patch with another cleanly cultivated area.
☐ Make a rain gauge and measure the rainfall each week to see that the garden is getting at least 1 inch of water per week.

Whatever your children do in their garden, it is important that they feel a pride in ownership and that they have the opportunity to explore and enjoy the garden on their own terms.

 ## My squash plants wilted and died very suddenly. What might the problem be?

This sounds like the work of the squash vine borer, a common pest, primarily east of the Rockies. These insects bore into the vines, causing wilt and eventually death, unless something is done to correct the problem. If squash vine borers are a problem in your area, you can spray the vines with a chemical or plant-based insecticide at intervals, beginning early in the season.

Once you notice the wilt, look for the entry hole of the borer — there may be a noticeable pile of debris underneath. Slit open the vine, remove the borer, and cover the hole and several feet of the vine with soil. It should recover and keep growing. Practice good sanitation in the garden and destroy all old vines.

An exciting experiment for a child's first garden: grow a cucumber (and make a pickle) inside of a jar! The newspaper keeps the cucumber in the bottle from overheating.

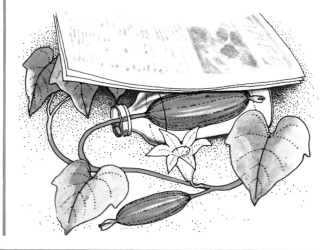

FRUITS

Succulent treats for
every taste

How much do I need to know
about rootstocks of fruit trees?

Enough to know you are getting the best tree for your needs when you buy a fruit tree. Most modern fruit trees are made up of two separate individuals grafted together to produce a single tree. The top part is the scion, which is the fruiting variety. This is grafted onto the roots of a different variety. Sometimes there will also be an interstem, which is a short piece grafted between the rootstock and the scion, often because the two are incompatible and will not graft well together.

In years gone by, apple, plum, pear, cherry, apricot, and other fruits were always grown on their own roots, but some varieties produced rather poor fruit. Although the trees were originally selected for their fruiting efficiency, they may have been so chosen that root vigor was inadvertently selected *against*. The result was a plant that was limited by its root system.

Growers gradually came to graft fruiting varieties onto more vigorous root systems, often of wild apples, pears, and plums. Eventually, it was realized that the rootstock exercised considerable influence over the final size and form the tree took. So tree breeders began to breed plants with particular types of rootstocks separately from those to improve fruiting varieties.

The breeding of rootstocks has been more adventurous and more successful with apples than with other tree fruits. Most dwarfing rootstocks for apples were originated in Britain at the Merton and East Malling research institutes. These rootstocks are identified as MM (Malling-Merton) and M (Malling). The letters are followed by numbers; rootstocks most commonly offered to gardeners are M.9, M.26, M.27, and MM.106.

Rootstocks have the greatest influence on size. A variety grafted on MM.106 will produce a tree about 10 feet tall, where those on M.26 and M.9 will produce trees 8 feet and 6½ feet tall respectively. The rootstock M.27, a very dwarfing stock, produces apple trees less than 6½ feet tall.

A dwarfing rootstock will give rise to a smaller tree, which will produce a smaller crop. But the tree will be more easily pruned and harvested, can be grown in a small space, and will generally bear fruit at a younger age than a standard-size tree. It will also require better soil.

Rootstocks also affect the way the fruit is borne, how well the tree does in particular types of soil, and how efficient it will be at using certain nutrients or adapting to certain soil deficiencies. Sometimes the interstem will provide the dwarfing influence, allowing you to select a rootstock adapted to your particular soil type.

Before buying a fruit tree, ask for information on which rootstocks or interstems have been used. The information can be critical when choosing a tree for your site.

See also:
Budding roses p92
Planting trees p109
Citrus in containers p132

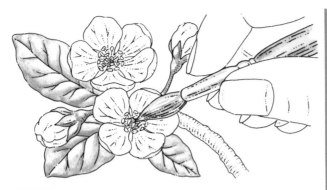

 ## Must fruit trees always be planted in twos to obtain satisfactory pollination?

No, but there are rather strict rules regarding which varieties will produce good crops when planted alone and which varieties must be planted in combination with others in order to obtain optimum pollination and fruit crop. Which trees are good pollinators for other trees depends on a variety of factors. Some trees are simply incompatible when it comes to pollinating other trees. Other trees, for reasons of their genetic make-up, require not one, but two further varieties to effect pollination; so three trees are required. Most important, the trees must all flower at the same time. Usually there are a number of possible pollinator trees for each variety. But sometimes, as with Moongold apricots, a specific pollinator variety is needed (in this case, Sungold).

Your best bet is to check with the nursery from which you will buy your fruit trees to determine which, if any, pollinator variety is needed. Generally apples, pears, and sweet cherries will need pollinators for cross-pollination. Most peach, apricot, and nectarine varieties are self-fruitful and don't need pollinators.

If you have space for only one fruit tree, you have two options. The best is to choose a self-fruitful variety. Second best is to take an inventory of your neighbor's fruit trees to see if any might act as a pollinator for your tree. The neighboring tree should be as close as possible to your own, upwind, and preferably not screened by a high boundary.

 ## What are some unusual types of citrus that I might grow?

Although unusual citrus fruits are not always available in supermarkets, there are lots of interesting fruits — beyond the familiar oranges, grapefruits, lemons, and limes — you can enjoy growing. Some are well-adapted to growing in containers, so they can be raised in climates outside of the citrus belts.

Limequats A cross between a kumquat and a lime, these attractive, graceful trees can be grown in containers. The tree resembles a lime tree, bearing a fruit that is similar to a lime, but less acidic and more cold-tolerant. Eustis is a commonly available variety.

Mandarins There is a great variety of mandarins available and the trees range in size and form. Although the foliage is hardier than that of oranges, the fruit is not and can be easily damaged. Some varieties will bear fruit for a period of seven months (November to May). Varieties with excellent flavor include Page, Encore, and Honey.

Orangequats This hybrid is a cross between the Satsuma mandarin and the Meiwa kumquat. The fruit has tart flesh and a mildly sweet rind. Kumquat hybrids, like this, are very hardy in citrus areas, quite ornamental, and will do well in containers. Nippon is the only variety.

Pummelos These are the largest fruits in the citrus family, often several times larger than grapefruit. The trees, which can be grown in most citrus-growing areas, are large and spreading, growing 15 to 18 feet high and wide. Although the largest, sweetest fruits will be produced in very hot climates, the smaller, thicker-skinned fruits that are produced in cooler climates are still good. Two of the main varieties grown here are Chandler, which has pink flesh, and Reinking, which has white flesh.

Hand-pollination is occasionally the best way to ensure that some fruit trees will produce crops. Wait until the pollen is ripe and the fine yellow grains are being shed by the stamens, **2**. Choose a warm, dry day with little wind, and using a large soft paintbrush or a small stick, transfer the pollen to the stigma, **1**. From here the pollen tube grows down to the ovule, **3**, where fertilization occurs.

What should I know about container-grown citrus trees?

There are many dwarfs that do well in containers. In the citrus belts, you can raise them outdoors year-round. Elsewhere, you can have the trees outdoors in the summer and indoors for the winter.

When your trees are inside, it is best to keep them cool (at about 55 degrees F.) so they will stay dormant, but the fruit will ripen. If it is much warmer, the plant will keep growing and you'll have to pay more attention to providing light and high humidity. When moving containers inside or out, change conditions (sunlight and so on) slowly so the plants have time to adjust.

For containers, choose one with drainage holes that holds 1 to 15 gallons — anything larger will be difficult to move. Fill it with a layer of crushed rock and rich, well-draining soil.

Citrus trees in containers require frequent watering since the soil will dry more quickly. Water thoroughly when the soil is dry to the touch, and mist the tree frequently to maintain high humidity. Because fertilizer is washed out with watering, fertilize once a month from early spring through late summer.

If the rootball of the tree becomes dense and water is not able to soak in, you can root prune. First prune the top back to compensate for the loss of roots. Then remove the plant from the container and prune the roots back also.

What do the terms espalier and cordon mean?

Espalier and cordon are two methods of training fruit trees that were developed in Europe. An espaliered tree has opposite pairs of branches trained outward from the main stem at right angles. A cordoned tree has the fruit-bearing spur shoots growing along the length of an

When and how should my fruit trees be pruned?

All fruit trees should be pruned. Unpruned trees will develop branches at bad angles, which can become weak and prone to breaking. The branches become crowded, reducing air circulation and light penetration, and the trees become progressively taller and wider, with the fruit borne mainly on the outside branches where there is sufficient light.

The ideal is to prune twice a year — once late in the dormant season before the buds swell and once during the summer. However, if you have a tree that has very tender buds or tends to bloom too early, wait until the buds begin to swell before doing that first pruning, since the trees will be more susceptible to damage from cold temperatures.

The late-winter pruning shapes the tree and encourages new growth. The summer pruning is mainly aimed at channeling the new growth in desired directions. Pruning mature trees from mid to late summer will help control the tree size (there is less stimulation of new growth) and will allow for better light penetration inside the tree. If you live where the winters are cold,

See also:
Pruning shrubs p85
Planting trees p109
Edible hedges p114
Unusual citrus p131
Biennial bearing of fruit trees p135

upright stem, which is trained vertically or at an angle of 45 degrees. Both training systems are space savers. They work best with dwarf trees, which require less pruning than standard-size trees.

Usually, although not always, espalier trees are trained against a wall or other support. Done well, a mature espalier-trained tree looks magnificent, and the method need not be restricted to fruit trees. Espaliered trees can be used to soften an empty wall or fence space or to make an edible border or hedge.

A cordon is a much simpler training system, useful in small gardens or where a large number of varieties are to be grown. The growth of the side branches is restricted, and only the fruit-bearing spurs are allowed to grow. In double and triple cordons, two or three stems are made to branch from the base of the tree and are then trained upward, parallel to each other.

In the cordon method of training fruit trees, *left*, the fruiting variety is usually grafted on a dwarfing rootstock and planted at an angle of 45 degrees. Prune laterals in summer to stimulate the growth of fruiting spurs; cut back the leader in spring only when the tree reaches the desired height.

An espaliered tree, *right*, has a central stem from which branches are trained horizontally in pairs about 18in apart. Any vertical shoots that grow from the branches must be cut back in summer to form fruiting spurs. Espaliers take up more space than cordons, so are less suitable for a really small site.

don't prune any later than mid-summer, so any new growth that is stimulated will have a chance to harden.

Generally, pruning a mature tree consists of removing dead or diseased wood, upright growth, watersprouts, and root suckers. The tree is pruned to maintain its desired shape, to thin out crowded areas, and renew fruiting wood. Specifics vary with the type of tree since growth and fruiting patterns differ.

There are two basic training shapes with possible intermediate forms you will want your trees to conform to. Which pruning and training system you choose depends on the space the tree has and the type and size of the tree. With a **central leader**, you will have a cone-shaped tree with a single, straight trunk and branches coming out of the trunk at an angle of about 60 degrees. There is good light penetration with this shape since the top branches are pruned closer to the trunk than the lower ones, but it takes some work to achieve it. Generally, dwarf trees are best trained to a central leader. Many, including apples, pears, plums, and cherries, tend to grow with one branch dominating anyway and are thus good for central leader training.

With an **open center**, you will have a vase-shaped tree, with several large main branches, which also allows good light penetration. This style is particularly good for trees like peaches and nectarines that don't

have a dominant branch and for vigorous trees, such as cherries, because it prevents them getting too tall.

As you prune you will make two kinds of cuts: **thinning** and **heading**. Thinning cuts remove all unwanted branches where they originate from the larger branch. Heading back is done to cut a branch back to a specific lateral branch or bud. Since thinning decreases the production of new shoots and heading encourages it, late-summer thinning cuts have a dwarfing effect, while dormant-season heading invigorates the tree.

Thinning cuts, *left*, remove branches from where they originate, while heading cuts, *right*, remove a portion of the branch back to a bud from which new growth will continue.

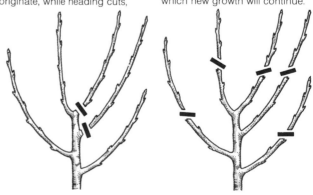

133

Why do my apples always have black blotches on them and little maggots inside?

Black blotches and little maggots pretty much sums up the appearance of the apples in many gardens every summer — these are the symptoms of two of the most common apple problems. The black blotches are the effects of scab disease, and the little maggots are the caterpillars of the codling moth. They are two different and distinct problems, requiring different treatments.

Scab is caused by a fungus that spends the winter months dormant, mainly on fallen leaves beneath the tree, although some fungal growth is also present in cankerous lesions on the twigs. Spores are produced on the leaves and in twig lesions in spring and are carried by rain splash and wind to the young foliage, which they infect to produce dark brown blotches.

More spores are formed there, and these, in turn, infect more leaves as well as the young fruits, which develop the characteristic crusty or scabby patches that make them unattractive to eat. The disease always tends to be worse when there is mild, wet weather around blossom time. Nothing can be done to cure the problem, but scab can be prevented to some extent.

The procedure usually recommended is to spray with an approved fungicide, as commercial growers do, in order to eradicate the fungus before it can infect the young leaves and fruit. The fungicide should be applied at regular intervals, according to the manufacturer's directions, from the time the buds burst until the petals fall. This can work well on small young trees, but is much more difficult on big trees, which are almost impossible to spray adequately.

Scab is a major disease in commercial apple crops and is generally treated by spraying, but the reason to do so is largely cosmetic. As a home gardener, the time and effort you will have to spend on fungicides to produce blemish-free apples for your own use is probably not worthwhile, especially with a large old tree, although you may want to spray a young tree to protect it from persistent attacks that could weaken it.

In any event, it is a good idea to take all the preventative measures you can. There are a number of apple varieties that are resistant to scab and you should consider planting these if you live in an area where the weather is particularly conducive to scab formation. Collect and burn or otherwise destroy (do not compost) leaves from beneath affected trees, and cut out and burn scabby twigs in winter.

What then of the codling moth caterpillars? These insects pass the winter in a pupal state, hiding in crevices in the tree's bark. In late spring, the adult moths emerge and the small, dingy females lay their eggs on leaves and young fruit. The resulting caterpillars burrow into the fruit, usually entering by the eye or close to the stalk so that the entry hole is undetectable. After

Why have the leaves on my peach tree curled up and turned red?

The cause is peach leaf curl, a disease that is also responsible for the disfigurement of the leaves on most ornamental almond trees. Peach varieties vary in susceptibility to this fungus, but none is absolutely immune.

The disease is always more severe in a season following a cold, wet spring, for this provides just the right conditions for the leaf curl fungus to thrive. The fungus survives the winter in cracks in the bark and on leaf buds; from there it emerges to infect the young leaves as they unfold.

This infection causes the characteristic puckering of the young leaves. Later, as the fungus grows within the leaf tissues, a white powdery bloom forms and a reddening develops. This powder is a mass of fungus spores, which are subsequently blown to the twigs, where they germinate in preparation for the winter once more.

To treat an infection, spray once with an approved fungicide any time from late fall, after the leaves have fallen, until the first buds begin to swell in the spring. Leaves that curl should be removed and destroyed since infected leaves can't be cured. It is possible to eradicate the problem from a fairly seriously diseased tree within three seasons if spraying is done faithfully.

The blistered and distorted leaves on many peach and almond trees are the result of infection by peach leaf curl fungus. Leaves develop a white powdery bloom, then redden before falling, and the growth of the trees, deprived of nourishment, is slowed.

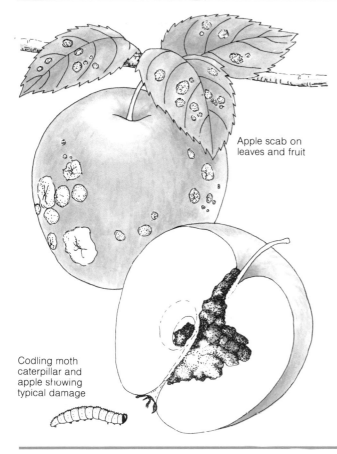

Apple scab on leaves and fruit

Codling moth caterpillar and apple showing typical damage

dining on the inner parts of your apples for a few weeks, the caterpillars re-emerge, leaving masses of dark excrement on the skin and inside the bars. They then crawl down to the bark and pupate until the following season.

How can you stop them? Insecticidal sprays can be effective if they are applied at the right times — beginning several days after peak moth flight. This solution is only as effective as your ability to spray the entire tree (difficult with large trees) and to time the sprays appropriately. (Check with your local Extension agent for types of sprays and timing.) Spraying is most effective on small trees.

There are a number of nonchemical controls you can try in any combination. These include growing a flowering ground cover, such as clover, buckweat, or mustard, to attract parasitic insects; scraping off loose bark where cocoons may be and collecting the droppings during the dormant season; wrapping burlap bands around the trees in early spring to attract the larvae underneath, and removing the burlap once a week in warm weather to find and kill the larvae; and destroying all infested fruit as it falls.

What are the black growths on the branches of my plum tree?

Black growths on a plum tree usually mean black knot, a common fungus disease of plums. The fungus spores germinate in the spring and are released in moderate to warm rainy weather. By late summer, knotty-looking black galls appear on infected branches. As the galls get larger, they cut off the supply of water and nutrients to the rest of the branch beyond the gall, causing wilting and death.

To control this fungus, prune and destroy all infected branches as soon as you notice the problem. Make the cuts at least 4 inches below the infected site. If the knots are on the main branch, cut away the diseased tissue down to healthy wood at least ½ inch beyond the infected site. You can also spray with an approved fungicide, in conjunction with pruning. Make the first fungicide application just before the buds break and apply twice more at 7-day to 10-day intervals.

To prevent an infection, try to remove any nearby wild plums and cherries that may harbor the disease. Plant new plum trees at least 600 feet away from any potential wild hosts.

Why do some fruit trees bear heavy crops one year and hardly any the next?

Biennial bearing is the process you are describing. Certain types of fruit trees — particularly apples and pears — and certain varieties are more prone to this than others, but it can happen with any fruit tree. It is more likely with a tree that is under stress from low fertility or low moisture. Biennial bearing results from poor flower initiation during a stressful, heavy crop year. It is difficult for a tree under stress to have enough energy for both a heavy crop and to develop fruit buds for the following year.

The way to prevent biennial bearing is to assure good fertility and moisture and to thin the flower buds, flowers, or small fruits prior to a heavy year. The general rule for thinning is to leave fruits about 6 to 8 inches apart and not bunched together in clumps. Anywhere from half to three-quarters of the flowers or small fruits can be removed by hand, or mechanically with a strong blast of water. Commercial orchardists sometimes thin with chemicals. There are pruning techniques that can reduce biennial bearing. Check with your Extension service fruit specialist for information.

What's the key to success with blueberries?

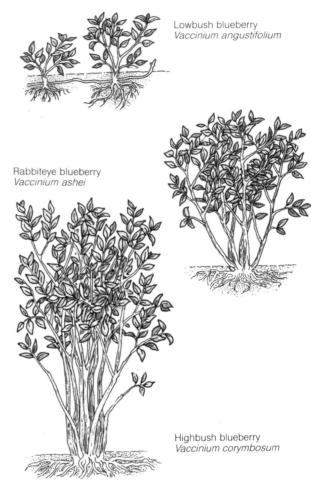

Lowbush blueberry
Vaccinium angustifolium

Rabbiteye blueberry
Vaccinium ashei

Highbush blueberry
Vaccinium corymbosum

The first step is choosing the right blueberry for your area. There are three different species of blueberries commonly grown. The highbush blueberry, *Vaccinium corymbosum*, hardy to zone 3, is the most common. Rabbiteye blueberry, *V. ashei*, hardy to zone 7, is more commonly grown in the South, where it is adapted to survive drought better. It also requires less fertilizer and less organic matter in the soil than highbush types. Although vulnerable to late spring frost, rabbiteye blueberries have less of a winter chill requirement than highbush or lowbush berries.

Lowbush blueberries, *V. angustifolium*, are very hardy and are usually found in the wild, but they have recently become more available to gardeners. Lowbush blueberries are spread by underground rhizomes, which allow them to stockpile carbohydrates, which act as a buffer in case the tops suffer from winterkill.

Varieties of both the highbush and the rabbiteye blueberries are adapted to a wide range of growing conditions and have differing disease resistances; there are early, midseason, and late fruiting varieties. With highbush blueberries, planting more than one variety will encourage cross-pollination and better, larger fruit. With rabbiteye and lowbush blueberries, planting two types for cross-pollination is even more important.

When you plant, select a permanent site where the bushes won't be disturbed. Plant in the spring or fall. Set the plants at least 6 feet apart in rows even further apart (plant lowbush blueberries 1 foot apart in rows 3 feet apart).

Blueberries have fine, slow-growing, shallow roots, so provide loose soil that is rich in organic matter to allow for easy root growth and moisture retention. They also require an acidic soil with a pH of 4.5 to 5.0. Since the roots are shallow, you will need to acidify only a small area of soil — and that is easily done by incorporating peat moss, leaf mold, sawdust, or, for a faster reaction, finely ground sulfur. These shallow roots also do best if covered with a heavy mulch to keep the soil moist and discourage competition from weeds. Select an acidic mulch such as pine sawdust, cottonseed meal, or shredded oak leaves.

As the plants grow, periodically test the soil to be sure it remains acidic. The plants will also need nitrogen; a slow-releasing decomposed organic fertilizer placed under the mulch in the spring should be enough. A lack of nitrogen will cause the leaves to turn red (as will insufficient water); too much nitrogen will cause vegetative growth at the expense of fruiting.

You won't need to prune for the first few years after planting, except to prune out flower buds in late winter before growth begins. This will prevent fruiting and help the plant to store up needed energy. Once the plant is well established, prune each year in late winter or you will get progressively smaller twigs and fruits.

It's helpful to understand how blueberries grow and flower in order to understand their pruning. As blueberries grow, the roots send up straight green canes whose tips die and turn brown during the fall and winter. The next year, these canes produce only lateral branches, since there are no tips. The lateral branches stop growing and produce flower buds, and later fruit, near the tips. Left unpruned, the canes will continue to branch and fruit, but after four or five years, smaller twiggy branches will develop and the amount and quality of buds will diminish. So regular pruning is necessary to remove the oldest canes.

To prune, remove all dead, injured, or diseased wood. Cut out the oldest canes (or about one-fifth of all canes). Do not trim the tips of the branches or you will get little or no fruit. To rejuvenate very old or overgrown bushes, severely prune the bush, right back to the soil line if necessary. You will probably get no berries the first year, but the plant will quickly recover after that.

See also:
Acid soil for blueberries p8
Pruning shrubs p85
Espalier and cordon fruit trees
pp132-3

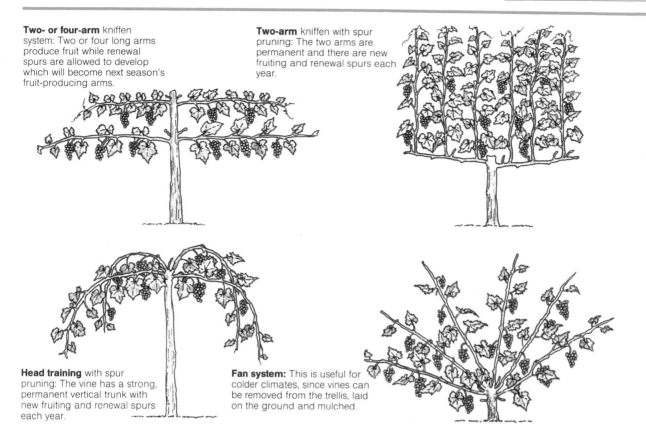

Two- or four-arm kniffen system: Two or four long arms produce fruit while renewal spurs are allowed to develop which will become next season's fruit-producing arms.

Two-arm kniffen with spur pruning: The two arms are permanent and there are new fruiting and renewal spurs each year.

Head training with spur pruning: The vine has a strong, permanent vertical trunk with new fruiting and renewal spurs each year.

Fan system: This is useful for colder climates, since vines can be removed from the trellis, laid on the ground and mulched.

Can you explain some of the methods for training grapes?

Grapes are trained to grow on a trellis to allow air movement and so that direct sunlight can reach the leaves and ripen the fruit. Which training system to use depends on the type of grape, the variety, convenience and, to some extent, your climate. With all systems, grapes must be pruned every year because once a cane has fruited, it won't fruit again. Fruits form only on buds that arise from the previous season's growth.

The four-arm kniffen system is most commonly used for training American grapes, while the two-arm kniffen system, which prevents excessive leaf shading, is commonly used for the vigorous muscadines grown in the South. European grapes are generally trained to have two permanent arms with spur pruning. Head pruning is used for European grapes grown in a small space. The fan system is sometimes recommended for grapes that require winter protection, since each cane grows near soil level and can be laid down and mulched easily.

Regardless of the training system you use, you should handle all young grape plants the same, aiming to produce a strong trunk and root system. When you set out the plants in the spring, cut the vine back to two or three buds, and stake the plants. Early in the first summer, pick out the strongest cane and allow that to grow, pinching out the other canes. As the one cane

grows, let several sideshoots develop where the horizontal supports will run.

The following winter or spring, prune back all canes, leaving three buds on each of two or four lateral spurs. The second summer, tie the side shoots to wires, remove the flower clusters (so the plant won't fruit yet) and remove the shoots from all buds. After the second summer, the plants will be ready for training. Prune at the end of the winter, while plants are still dormant.

For the **four-arm kniffen system**, choose four canes to be the arms and cut each one back to about ten buds, to produce fruit for that season. Choose four more canes for renewal spurs, which will produce next year's fruit. Cut these back to two buds. Remove all other canes.

For the **two-arm kniffen system**, proceed as for the four-arm system, but select only two arms.

For the **two-arm spur-pruning system**, choose two permanent arms. Each winter, cut back the strongest vertical shoots along the arms to two buds. These will become the fruiting spurs. Each bud left on the spurs will form a fruiting shoot next year.

For **head training**, allow a strong single trunk to grow attached to a sturdy 4-foot post. Allow five to seven branches to develop off the main trunk. Cut each branch back to two to three buds each winter.

For the **fan system**, train the vines so that each cane grows from the crown near soil level. Trim them back to 2 to 3 feet, lay them down, and cover with mulch for the winter. You can later prune to six healthy canes with several renewal spurs.

What is the best way to plant strawberries?

You can plant strawberries according to several different systems and each has its advantages. The matted row and hill systems are the two basic methods, with the spaced matted row an intermediate method that combines features of both.

With the **hill system**, plants are spaced 12 to 18 inches apart and the runners are removed. Compared to the matted row system, more plants are required so the expense is greater, and more labor is required to pinch off the runners, but the plants will be larger and healthier and the berries bigger.

You can allow some runners to develop to form big, healthy replacement plants. When grown this way, the plants can be treated like perennials, and the patch should be productive for six to seven years or more. This is the best method to use for growing everbearing varieties.

With the **matted row system**, you plant the strawberries 18 inches apart in rows 3 or more feet apart. The plants are allowed to set runners freely, with no intervention except to make sure the runners stay out of the pathways. Although there is little labor involved in this system, and it takes few plants to start, the individual berries tend to be smaller.

Also, after the second year, when you have many plants with a lot of berries, production drops as the plants get more and more crowded, and possibly diseased, and weeds invade. Generally, the plot should be tilled under and a new patch started with new plants after the second harvest. It is a good idea to have those new plants already growing so you don't miss a year of berries.

With the **spaced matted row system**, the plants are spaced as in the hill or matted row system and a limited number of runners are allowed to form around the mother plant. The advantages of this system fall midway between those of the two other systems of planting strawberries.

If the berry patch is healthy and the runners have produced strong daughter plants, you may want to maintain your matted or spaced row patch for another year or more, instead of tilling it in. After harvest, mow, scythe, or sickle the plants and thin out the old mother plants, leaving the daughter plants. With careful thinning and fertilizing, you can extend the life of the patch, but you will realize a smaller harvest from this renovated patch.

If your space is very limited, try growing strawberries in tubs, containers, or pyramids (cylinders of aluminum or similar material filled with soil and stacked on top of each other, with the plants spaced about a foot apart). Any container will work, provided the drainage is adequate. Use a porous, rich soil mixture. Remember that plants in containers need watering more frequently than plants in beds.

Whichever planting system you use be sure to choose healthy plants. Strawberries are very prone to virus diseases, but new virus-free strains have been developed and are readily available in most areas. These plants produce many more berries than the older, virus-infected plants.

The spaced matted row system is intermediate between the other two. A limited number of runners are set and are spaced around the plant.

In the matted row system, plants are spaced at least 18in apart in rows 3 or more ft apart. Plants are allowed to set runners freely.

In the hill system, plants are set close — only 12–18in apart — and kept from forming runners.

See also
Eradicating perennial weeds p58
Training grapes p137

Strawberries can produce abundant crops in soil-filled pots and planters. Small alpine strawberries are perfect for small containers.

The roots of a raspberry bush are perennial, but the canes are biennial, meaning they grow to their full height in one year, fruit the next year, and then die. So your pruning must take this into account.

Summer bearers send up canes in the spring that grow during the summer, initiate buds in the fall, and become the fruiting canes the following year; then they die. Prune these raspberries during the dormant season — late fall is a good time. Remove dead canes that have just fruited and any weak or damaged new canes. Then, with red, purple, and yellow varieties, cut the canes back to 4 or 5 feet. Leave the healthiest canes spaced 4 to 8 feet apart in a hedgerow or leave about six canes per hill. Black raspberries should also be summer topped; that is, 2 to 4 inches should be trimmed off the top of new canes when they are about 2 feet tall. This promotes strong lateral shoots that will bear heavily the next year.

Everbearers can be treated just as the summer bearers, but it is harder to distinguish the new canes from the old. The way to recognize the new canes (those that bore a fall crop) is that they will have lateral, or side, buds only at the tips of the canes, while the old canes will have these buds farther down. If you prefer a larger fall harvest at the expense of the summer crop, cut the canes down to within 2 inches of the ground before growth starts in the spring.

What do I need to know about growing raspberries?

Raspberries come in red, yellow, black and purple varieties. Some varieties are everbearing and some are summer bearers. Red and yellow raspberries multiply rapidly by suckering in all directions. They are a good choice for growing in 2-foot-wide hedgerows. Black raspberries do not sucker and propagate only by tip rooting. These can be limited to smaller hills. Purple raspberries can be similarly limited, although some will sucker and fill in the row.

Although raspberries are naturally adapted to cool climates, varieties have been developed for virtually all parts of the country. So buy a variety that is suitable for your area. To avoid disease problems, don't dig up plants from a friend; instead buy certified virus-free plants from a nursery.

The plants can tolerate light or heavy, but not wet, soils. They do best in rich, loose soil with plenty of organic matter and a pH of 5.5 to 6.8 — 6.0 is ideal. Before planting, eliminate all the perennial weeds from the site and mix manure or 10-10-10 into the soil.

The plants you buy will come bare-rooted or in pots. Soak bare-rooted plants in water for an hour before planting. Cut the canes back to 2 inches above the ground level to encourage new growth and balance the roots. Space the plants 2 to 3 feet apart in rows 6 to 7 feet apart.

You may want to set stakes or posts every 2 to 3 feet along the row and attach wire beginning 3 feet from the ground. Then you can train the canes to grow along these supports. Whether trellising is necessary depends in part on the variety and how you prune. Most varieties grow 5 to 6 feet tall or more and become laden with berries. It is often easier to manage the plants if they are trellised.

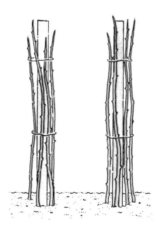

Where space is very limited, one raspberry plant can be set on either side of a sturdy post and up to nine strong canes tied to it.

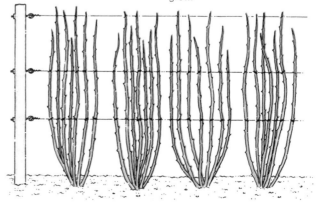

Economical use of space can also be made by growing raspberries in a single row along a fence. Space the plants about 18in apart and tie the canes in to the fence as they grow.

SEASON EXTENSION

Lengthening the growing season

What design features should I consider before I build a greenhouse?

Before building a greenhouse, consider what use you plan for the space. Are you looking for a place to start bedding plants and to shelter some plants from the first frosts? Or are you looking for a space that can be used to grow plants year-round? Do you want it to double as a sunspace for your own use? How much money can you spend on the project? Do you have a suitable site?

Although all greenhouses admit light, only the so-called solar greenhouses are designed to utilize the sun for most of their heating and lighting requirements. Solar greenhouses are capable of storing heat for use when the sun isn't shining, so they are less reliant on fossil fuels. This makes a solar greenhouse a good choice for a year-round structure that can be used to raise plants.

However, solar greenhouses can be expensive to build because the ideal construction includes two layers of glazing, extensive insulation above and below ground, a system for heat storage (water, rock, or earth in a passive system), and a solid, insulated north wall. You will probably want to install night insulation in the form of window blankets or shades to prevent heat loss. Solar greenhouses are often attached to an existing building, but they can be freestanding.

On the other hand, if you are not interested in raising plants year-round and are simply looking for a season extender for your garden plants, an inexpensive greenhouse, perhaps made of plastic and scrounged framing materials, may be the best choice. The structure can be freestanding or attached to your house. It can be provided with supplemental heat for the very coldest nights.

Freestanding greenhouses are tremendously flexible in terms of site location, size, and choice of materials. But with a freestanding structure you will have to walk across the yard to reach the greenhouse to check the condition of the plants, whereas attached structures are much more convenient. Attached structures are sheltered by the building they are attached to, so often they require less supplemental heat and can help to decrease winter heat loss from your home. Providing electricity and a water supply to an attached structure is likewise easier. But the site for an attached greenhouse may be limited by the slope of the land, the presence of shading trees, or the lack of a suitable south-facing wall for attaching the structure.

Greenhouses of various types are available as prefabricated units, often for the more elaborate type of structure, and they usually involve some assembling. Additionally, they may not be exactly what you want, and they offer little in the way of savings over building from scratch. Don't forget to check into the need for a local building permit before beginning construction.

See also:
Wood preservatives p10
Landscape planning p22

There are numerous
considerations when choosing a
greenhouse design. A wood and
glass greenhouse is much more
aesthetic and long lasting than
a poly-covered structure. The
plastic house, however, is much
cheaper to construct.

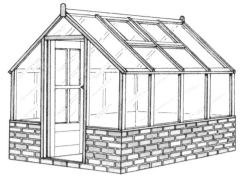

Wooden frame with a base of low brick walls

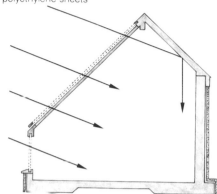

Metal framework covered with
polyethylene sheets

A "solar" greenhouse can be
attached to and integrated with
the house or can be a
freestanding type with a solid
north wall.

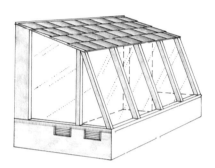

Attached greenhouse

Freestanding "solar" greenhouse

How do the various types of greenhouse glazings compare?

In a greenhouse, solar energy enters as light (shortwave radiation) and is absorbed by plants and surfaces and changed to heat (longwave radiation). The primary purpose of greenhouse glazing is to allow in the maximum amount of light and to decrease the amount of heat that is lost.

Most plastic glazings are transparent to both shortwave and longwave radiation, so they allow much heat loss; while glass, fiberglass, and acrylics are somewhat more opaque to longwave radiation, although there is still significant heat loss. The best resistance to heat loss is provided by layers of air, so multiple glazing with air space between the layers is often used.

Here are some pros and cons of some of the commonly used materials.

Double-walled acrylics and plastics Premade, strong, and lightweight, double-walled acrylics and plastics are relatively easy but expensive to install and are easily scratched. They have a 10-year to 20-year life span, depending on the brand.

Glass The advantage of glass is that it lasts indefinitely. But it is also heavy, sometimes difficult to work with, and it can create hot spots since it allows direct light transmission. Single-paned glass is easier to install than double-paned and allows greater light transmission, but it also allows more heat loss. It is used year-round mainly in warm climates and for greenhouses that are used simply as season extenders. Double-paned glass requires precise framing and sealing to be effective, but it is good for holding heat.

Polyethylene Very low-cost and easy to work with, polyethylene (generally used as double layers) has a short life expectancy (two to three years at most), is easily punctured, and allows significant heat losses. After two years, the light transmission is reduced enough to slow plant growth significantly. But it is a popular choice for large structures since it is so easy to install and inexpensive. Many commercial growers use a double layer inflated with a blower so there is less flapping and wear and reduced heat loss.

Single-layer fiberglass Various types are available, but in general, all of them are translucent, strong, lightweight, easy to install, and good for cutting into odd shapes. A disadvantage is that fiberglass loses its light transmission over time. The best grades are UV-treated with acrylic and can last 20 to 30 years; the cheaper grades deteriorate fast. Fiberglass can be coupled with polyethylene for better heat retention.

There are different and new materials on the market every day, which vary with respect to weatherability, durability, light and heat transmittance, life span, and costs. Check with suppliers to assess as many of these qualities as possible before deciding on glazing for your greenhouse.

I don't have a greenhouse, but I'd like to raise my own transplants. Can you advise me?

You don't need a greenhouse to start seedlings, as long as you can provide the appropriate conditions for growth. The vegetable crops that are easiest to raise as transplants include eggplants, peppers, cabbage, broccoli, and tomatoes. Melons, squashes, and cucumbers are sensitive to root disturbance, so where they do need an early start, they are best raised in individual containers.

Any container that will hold a few inches of soil and has drainage holes can be used for starting plants. Before using, sterilize the container by rinsing it in a solution of nine parts water to one part bleach. You can start plants in flats, and then transplant to individual cells, or thin the flats to space the plants farther apart once they are established. This is a critical step since overcrowded seedlings will not become healthy transplants. The growing medium should be lightweight, hold moisture well, have good aeration, drain well, and be free from disease (see Chapter 4).

While the seeds are germinating, keep the soil constantly moist and warm. As soon as the seedlings emerge, move them into the light. The quality and amount of light will greatly affect growth. Too short a duration of light or poor quality light will cause the plants to become tall and spindly, particularly if they are kept warm in relation to the light they receive.

If your plants are on a windowsill, turn them daily since they will grow toward the light. Aluminum reflectors around the plants will increase the light.

The best way to guarantee that your plants have sufficient light is to grow them under artifical lights. For seedlings, standard cool-white, 40-watt bulbs are adequate; the more expensive florescent grow lights provide a broader spectrum of light necessary for later flowering and fruiting. Place two bulbs for every 1 foot of width, 2 to 6 inches from the plants and leave them burning for 12 to 16 hours a day. Be sure to turn the lights off at night to enable the plants to utilize the products of photosynthesis.

Except when the seeds are germinating (when warmer temperatures are helpful and bottom heat is often recommended), it is best to keep your plants on the cool side (60 to 65 degrees F.). Growth will be slower and the plants will be sturdier. A 10 to 15 degree drop in temperature is particularly beneficial at night.

Improper watering can easily lead to unhealthy seedlings. Let the soil become dry to the touch, then water thoroughly, ideally from the bottom. Do not overwater or the plants will develop shallow, weak roots; overwatering can also lead to disease problems.

The plants will do best in an environment with 50 to 70 percent humidity. You can achieve this, if necessary, by misting the plants frequently or setting the containers on a bed of wet pebbles. Good air circulation, too, is important for circulating carbon dioxide and preventing diseases.

Fertilizing is not necessary until true leaves have formed (after the cotyledons or first two seed leaves). Then apply a liquid fertilizer every 7 to 10 days. Dilute the first few applications; using an over-strong application or applying too often will cause lush, weak growth that is susceptible to pests and diseases.

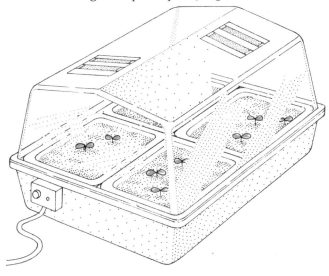

Since germinating seedlings require constant heat and moisture, an enclosed propagating box with a heating element provides an ideal atmosphere for germination. A less expensive means is to place the flats in a warm spot and cover them with a plastic sheet (that doesn't touch the soil), glass, plywood, or other covering until they germinate.

You can easily design a system for growing seedlings under lights. Here, the trays of plants are set on plywood supported by sawhorses, and the lights are suspended so that their height can be adjusted. Lights should hang 2–6in from the tops of the plants at all times.

See also:
Soil mix for seedlings p11
Disinfecting containers p42
Seed germination/hardening-off p44
Transplanting seedlings p48

Aphid control pp95, 96
Cold frames p144

What is the best way to control whiteflies in a greenhouse?

Like aphids, whiteflies are sap-sucking insects that cause similar damage by weakening plants and depositing sticky honeydew on which sooty mold fungi grow. They also cause yellow mottled leaves and general foliage discoloration. Although they occur in extremely large numbers, they are often not apparent until the foliage is disturbed; then the tiny, white insects erupt in a cloud. If you catch them early, you can control them with an approved soapy water spray, but be careful of mold and mildew problems caused by the moisture. Or you can trap them with yellow boards (to which they are attracted) covered with a sticky proprietary substance such as Tanglefoot.

You can control a severe infestation with an approved insecticide. The application must be repeated weekly in order to catch each fresh generation of adults as they hatch. Alternatively, you can introduce a beneficial insect, *Encarsia formosa*, a tiny parasitic wasp. It lays its eggs on the pupae of the whitefly, which

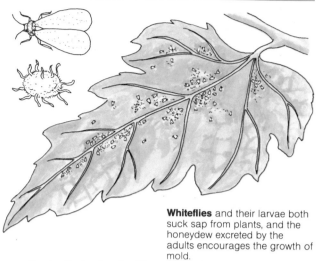

Whiteflies and their larvae both suck sap from plants, and the honeydew excreted by the adults encourages the growth of mold.

results in their death. If such biological controls are used, insecticides should not be used in the greenhouse. An unlikely sounding, but somewhat effective control suggested by some gardeners is to shake the plants to release the flies, then suck them up with a vacuum cleaner.

What measures can I take to decrease the chances of pest and disease outbreaks in my greenhouse?

While a greenhouse provides near ideal conditions for growing plants, it is also attractive to pests and diseases — without the natural balance and controls of the outdoors. The best way to prevent disease and pest problems is to practice good sanitation and to maintain your plants in a healthy state.

Good sanitation includes removing dead and fallen leaves and keeping weeds and fruits out of the greenhouse since they may be sites for pests, molds, and mildews. Remove old and unhealthy plants and don't try to save plants past their prime. Disinfect containers, and wash your hands and any tools used after working with diseased plants.

Provide good ventilation and air circulation and avoid overcrowding the seedlings. Proper watering is critical for healthy plants. Avoid watering on cloudy or rainy days when humidity is already high and avoid evening watering. Water thoroughly but only when the soil is dry to the touch. To avoid stressing your plants, fertilize on a regular schedule, but don't use too much or do it too often. Too much nitrogen, in particular, can lead to weak, susceptible growth. Here are some additional tips:

- [ ] Before bringing new plants into the greenhouse, check to make sure they aren't already infested.
- [ ] Be vigilant about looking for problems, particularly on the underside of leaves, which are easy to ignore. Any problem you catch early will be much easier to control.
- [ ] Don't touch the plants when they are wet — you could easily spread disease.
- [ ] Don't smoke in the greenhouse — you could spread tobacco mosaic virus to tomatoes, peppers, eggplants, and petunias.
- [ ] If you have permanent beds in the greenhouse, rotate the crops, just as you would outdoors. Don't overcrowd the plants.
- [ ] For bed plantings, choose disease-resistant varieties.

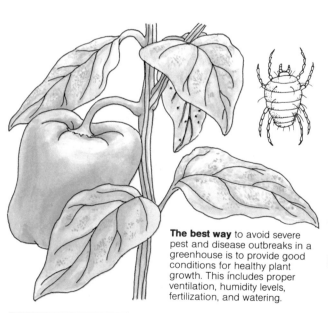

The best way to avoid severe pest and disease outbreaks in a greenhouse is to provide good conditions for healthy plant growth. This includes proper ventilation, humidity levels, fertilization, and watering.

What's the difference between a cold frame and a hot bed? How are they both used?

A cold frame is a mini-greenhouse. It is set outside and can be used to harden-off seedlings that have been growing indoors in containers. It can also be used to start seedlings when it is too cold to start them in the garden. Many cool-weather crops, such as lettuce, spinach, and radishes, can be sown directly into the soil inside the cold frame for fall, winter, and spring harvests, depending on your climate. It can also be used for forcing winter crops, again depending on your climate. When not in use during the summer, the top can be removed and it can be used as a nursery area.

A cold frame is basically a frame covered with glass, plastic, or fiberglass, which lets in light and traps heat. The construction of a cold frame can be quite simple — with hay bales for walls and an old storm window for the top. Or it can be quite sophisticated with insulation and automatic — even solar-powered — vent openings.

(All cold frames must have a way of venting, or opening the top, since they can easily overheat inside.) Ideally the top should slant toward the south (1 inch for every 1 foot of width) to provide the most light when the sun is low. The construction should be tight enough to keep out wind and cold; weather stripping around the top is often used. Sometimes additional insulation for the top, such as a thermal blanket, is needed on very cold nights. Some people recommend lining the back of the cold frame with plastic jugs filled with dark-colored water to absorb heat during the day and moderate night-time temperatures. They can be further insulated by banking soil around the sides and back. Remember to set the frame in a sheltered area away from cooling winds.

A hot bed is made along the same principles as a cold frame, but it provides extra heat — in the form of composting organic matter or electric lights or cables — to meet conditions in cooler weather than a cold frame can handle.

One way to make a hot bed is to dig a pit about 1 foot deep and partially fill it with a mixture of manure (preferably horse, sheep, goat, or chicken) and a carbon-containing material (hay, straw, leaves). Cover this with

How can I grow cool-season crops in the heat of summer?

Cool-season crops, such as peas, lettuce, and spinach, require cool temperatures (60 to 65 degrees F. is ideal) in order to develop properly and taste good. Hot weather will prevent pea blossoms from forming and retard the development of pods. Greens, such as spinach and lettuce, will lose water quickly in the heat and start to bolt (go to seed), which causes a chemical change that results in a bitter flavor.

There are a number of things you can do to extend the cool-season crop somewhat. First, be sure you are providing particularly rich soil and insuring a constant supply of water to the plants. Mulching will be a help in conserving water and keeping the soil cool.

A simple measure you can take is to provide some sort of shade for the plants. You can plant the cool crop in the shade of a tall crop, such as corn, or in a shaded section of the garden. You can also cover the plants with netting. Commercial shade netting is available in different densities, providing from 10 percent to 90 percent shading. Generally 10 percent to 30 percent shading is sufficient for cool-season crops, unless you live where the sun is especially hot and bright. You can support the netting with arched pvc pipe or wires. When the temperature falls, roll back the netting to allow the plants better light.

Another simple measure is to plant heat-resistant varieties. Many cool-season crops have varieties specifically bred to perform better in hot weather. Kagran

Summer Lettuce is a good example. Even with these heat-resistant varieties, it is still important to provide extra-rich soil and a constant supply of water.

In the end, though, you may find that the extra labor just isn't worth the effort of raising cool-season crops in unfavorable seasons, especially since your yields are most likely to be reduced. It makes more sense to raise plants that can take the heat. Numerous greens produce well during hot weather, including New Zealand spinach, Swiss chard, and collards. Save the cool crops for the spring, fall, or winter, when they will thrive without your intervention.

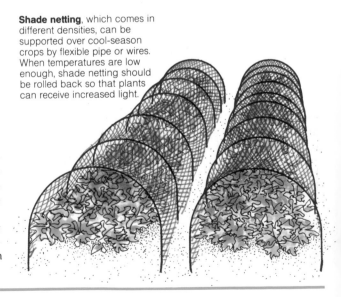

Shade netting, which comes in different densities, can be supported over cool-season crops by flexible pipe or wires. When temperatures are low enough, shade netting should be rolled back so that plants can receive increased light.

See also:
Hardiness zones/p18
Hardening-off p44
Mulches p122
Starting seedlings p142
Plant protection pp148–49

4 to 6 inches of soil to bring the mixture to ground level. Plant directly into the soil and cover the bed with a frame and glazing. As the organic matter decomposes, heat will be produced and trapped to warm the plants.

If wood is used for building the structure, you may want to treat it with a preservative. Copper napthenate types are considered safe to use around plants.

Whether you are using a hot bed or a cold frame, remember that you will need to pay close attention to the needs of your plants. As with a greenhouse, one of the primary considerations is to assure that it is properly vented, since temperatures can soar quickly in these structures. Except on extremely cold days, get into the habit of leaving the top ajar during the day. But remember that the more you vent, the more often you will have to water, since a closed frame will tend to trap moisture but an open one will release it into the atmosphere.

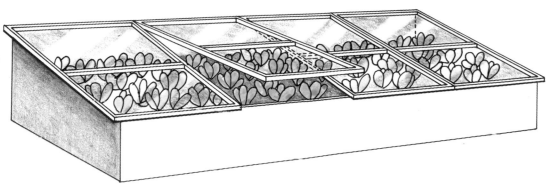

The basic design of cold frames and hot beds is similar, although hot beds incorporate a source of bottom heat, generally in the form of composting organic matter. The composting process releases heat which warms the bed and further extends the growing season.

Are there vegetable crops I can plant in the fall to get a head start in the spring?

Yes, although what you can plant depends on where you live, how much snow cover you receive, your soil type, the lowest winter temperatures, and so forth.

In the North, gardeners are always looking to extend the season since the growing season is so short. So planting what you can in the fall makes sense.

Garlic will start growing earlier in the spring and ultimately produce larger heads if it is planted in fall, allowed to grow 1 to 2 inches, then mulched with straw or hay for the winter. Spinach also winters over nicely if it is allowed to get several inches high before the severe weather sets in. The spinach should be well mulched or well covered by the snow. You can overwinter regular spinach or grow a special overwintering variety.

Some gardeners in the North report success with planting onions in the fall, although this is generally more successful in the South, where short-day onions are planted at this season. Although potatoes are rarely planted in the fall in the North, some people report success with planting them deeply and mulching heavily. This has been most successful when they have been planted in a light soil.

Many cool-season vegetables offer the possibility of overwintering and are worth experimenting with. These include corn salad (mâche), leaf lettuce, peas, dill, and parsley. Yield may be decreased, but the trade off is the pleasure of having extra-early crops.

Of course, there are also many crops that can winter over in a mature state for winter and early spring harvests. These include Brussels sprouts, parsnips, carrots, leeks, kale, and many others.

In warm climates, there are many more crops that are suitable for fall planting, and in several areas these vegetables will continue to grow throughout the winter. Short-day onions, broccoli, lettuce, peas, and celery are just a few of the many cool-season crops that are suitable for fall planting in the South.

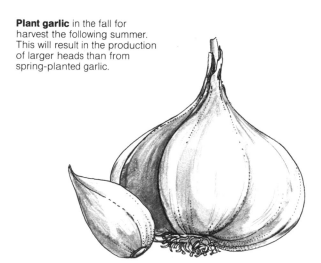

Plant garlic in the fall for harvest the following summer. This will result in the production of larger heads than from spring-planted garlic.

What conditions do I need for successfully storing root crops throughout the winter?

Traditionally root cellars have been used to store root crops. To maintain the quality of the vegetables and avoid desiccation and sprouting, the root cellar should be cool, moist, and dark. Temperatures of 32 to 40 degrees F. and relative humidity of about 90 percent are ideal.

But if you lack indoor space for a root cellar, there are several ways to store vegetables outside, provided the average winter temperature is below 30 degrees F. The simplest way to store many vegetables outside is to leave them in the garden, unharvested. When the ground starts to freeze in late fall, cover the row with an 18-inch layer of mulch. The mulch can be pulled away and the vegetables dug up as needed, except during periods of extreme cold. It is best to harvest all the vegetables before they resume growth in the spring and to use them immediately as they will not last after harvest.

You can also bury harvested root crops in containers in pits and mounds, which are filled and insulated with earth and/or straw. You may need to protect the root crops from rodents by lining with hardware cloth.

If you are planning to store your root crops in a root cellar or in a pit or mound, it helps to start with the best vegetables. Select varieties that are well suited to storage. For example, although all beets can be stored, Lutz Greenleaf and Long Season maintain their quality particularly well in storage. Vegetables will store best if they are harvested at the peak of maturity (neither underdeveloped nor past their prime) and when the weather is cold enough for good storage conditions, but before the ground freezes. As you harvest, set aside any damaged or bruised vegetables for immediate use.

It is best to harvest during dry weather since the vegetables will not be plump with water and there will be less soil clinging to them. It is not a good idea to leave them out to cure for a long period, as you would with onions or potatoes, but leaving them in the sun for a couple of hours so the dirt on the outside dries is recommended. Don't wash root crops before storing. Just trim off the tops, leaving 1 to 2 inches of stem to keep the juices in and diseases out.

Pack the vegetables in sawdust, sand, leaves or similar material to help maintain moisture. Layer the containers with packing material. In areas where temperatures may dip below freezing, pack extra insulation around the edges of the containers.

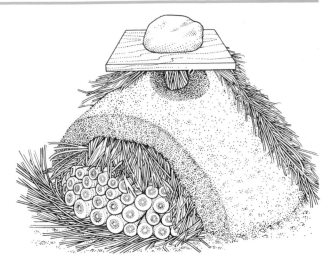

An outdoor storage mound insulated with straw and soil is a good method of storing root crops if you do not have a root cellar. This is only recommended in an area where winter temperatures average below 30°F.

Why are some vegetable plants more sensitive to frost than others? How can I protect them best?

When the dew freezes on the plants, you have a frost. When the air temperature drops so low that the water in the plant cells actually freezes (at temperatures lower than 32 degrees F., since dissolved sugars lower the freezing point), you have a hard, or killing, frost.

Whether a plant will survive a frost depends on its genetic make-up, as well as its physical conditioning and the environment before, during, and after the frost or freeze. Plants that have their origins in the tropics (tomatoes, melons, eggplants) are particularly sensitive and these should be harvested before the first frost. In the spring, tender transplants, set out before they have been hardened-off or too early in the season, are more likely to be frost damaged; in general, they will be more resistant if the temperature drops gradually.

Your plants are obviously more likely to suffer damage if they are not hardy in your zone. Also, overwatering and overfertilizing with nitrogen may result in plants that are overly tender.

To protect plants from frost, you can cover them with commercial garden coverings (see page 49) or even simple sheets or cartons. You will get best results if clothlike materials are laid on stakes rather than allowed to touch plants. Commercial growers often use irrigation or sprinkling to avoid frost damage since heat energy is released as water cools. If the water from the sprinklers remains liquid, the surrounding temperatures won't drop below freezing. Sometimes sprinkling the plants in the morning before the sun hits frosted plants, can reduce the potential damage.

See also:
Soil mixes for seedlings p15
Overwintering plants p18
Disinfecting containers p42
Starting seedlings p142

Cold frames p145
Plant protection pp148–49

 ## What types and varieties of vegetables will grow in a cool winter greenhouse?

During the winter, the limiting factors are reduced duration and intensity of light and cool night-time temperatures. Generally, leafy greens and root crops will mature under these conditions, but fruiting crops, such as tomatoes, will not.

Plants should be started in the fall in order to reach a good size before the low light and cool temperatures slow their growth. The varieties mentioned are also good for the limited space.

Beets Beets can be raised for both the greens and the root. Ruby Queen, Detroit Dark Red, and Golden Beet are recommended varieties.

Carrots Although carrots store easily, it's nice to have fresh, young carrots if you have the space. Try Tiny Sweet, Short-n-Sweet, and Golden Nugget.

Chinese greens Many different greens are particularly well adapted to growing in a greenhouse. Bok choy looks similar to Swiss chard but has smooth leaves. Shungiku (edible chrysanthemum) is a spicy green, good for salads.

Corn salad (mâche) A delicate, nutty-tasting green that tolerates extremes of temperature.

Lettuce Looseleaf and bibb types perform better than romaine and head types under these conditions.

Onions Onions raised for their tops are good for fresh eating and may have beneficial pest repellent properties. Bunching types are best; try Ishikuro, White Lisbon, and White Sweet Spanish.

Peas Peas grow well but they do take up a lot of space. Try Mighty Midget, Oregon Sugar Pod, and Dwarf White Sugar.

Radishes This is an easily grown crop that produces fast results if the right type is chosen. We recommend White Chinese and Chinese Rose.

Swiss chard This is a very productive plant for the greenhouse. Try Ruby, Lucullus, or Fordhook Giant.

Vitamin rich kale is a hardy cool-weather plant that will produce abundantly in a cool winter greenhouse.

 ## My indoor seedlings wilted and died suddenly. What happened?

It sounds like your seedlings were hit by damping-off, a fungus disease that affects young seedlings, often just as they are emerging. It is a very common problem, particularly in cloudy, wet weather, where the soil has very high levels of nitrogen, and where the seedlings are shaded. The fungi are more active under these conditions and the plants are more susceptible to attack.

Areas on the stem at the soil line may appear water soaked and discolored. If you should notice the problem early, remove the affected plants; you may be able to save the rest. To prevent it, follow good cultural practices. Don't water too often, don't fertilize before true leaves develop, use a sterile growing medium for starting seeds, sow seeds thinly for good air circulation, and make sure that there is good ventilation.

 ## Is there a good way to ripen green tomatoes that have been harvested before a frost?

Select developed green tomatoes without blemishes, bruises, or frost damage. To ripen some tomatoes quickly — within one to two weeks — store them at room temperature (60 to 70 degrees F.). To store tomatoes and allow them to ripen gradually, cover them with newspaper, keep them in the dark, and leave them at 55 degrees F. It is best if the air is moist, which prevents shriveling. The tomatoes will ripen in about four weeks with this method.

Another method is to pull the whole vine and hang it upside down in a basement or shed. The leaves speed the ripening and the tomatoes will ripen on the vine. In all cases, check the tomatoes often so that ripe or blemished tomatoes can be removed.

The best tomatoes for indoor ripening come from the youngest plants. You can even set out some later plants, after an early spring crop, so that you can harvest young green tomatoes for ripening well into the fall and winter.

147

Are row covers, tunnels, hot caps, and similar plant protectors worth investing in?

If you are looking to extend the season on either end, some sort of plant cover-up may be just the thing you need. Ranging from recycled plastic milk jugs to fabric row covers, these cover-ups provide protection from cold and frosts and enable you to set plants out in the spring before the last frost date or before the plants are fully hardened-off. Cold soil limits growth, but the heat-trapping action of these cover-ups warms the soil to encourage root growth. They also protect tender young plants from winds that can dry plants or break their stems. In the fall, these same cover-ups can protect the plants from frost and provide enough warmth to enable heat-loving plants like tomatoes to ripen their fruits.

Plant protectors come in two categories: individual protectors and row covers.

Plastic milk jugs These can be used to protect small young plants from frost and wind, although they don't provide much protection from cold temperatures. Remove the bottom of the jug and set the jug into the soil over the plant. You can vent excess heat in the day by unscrewing the top.

Hot tents Similar to plastic jugs, these conical, waxed paper coverings protect young plants from frost and winds but provide little protection from cold.

Wall O' Water This registered product is a water-filled plastic cylinder that is put in place around an individual plant. The water effectively stores daytime heat and releases it at night. Although Wall O' Water units are fairly expensive and take time to set up and often require staking to prevent them from toppling over in a wind, they can be quite effective in giving plants a good head start on the season and will last several years.

Tunnels A tunnel creates a mini-greenhouse over an entire row of plants. There are numerous types of tunnel you can buy or make from scrounged materials. Usually, a tunnel will consist of some type of hoop (made of pvc, plastic, wire, etc.), set at intervals over a bed or wide row. The hoops are covered with clear plastic. The tunnels can be made of a solid sheet of plastic, which can

Are there some vegetable plants that can be forced inside during the winter?

By forcing, we mean taking a plant that has stored energy in its roots and providing the right conditions to have the plant break dormancy and send up new shoots indoors. Two of the plants that are commonly forced to provide tender young vegetables when we need them the most are chicory and rhubarb.

Belgian endive and radicchio Both the green chicory, which is also known as Belgian endive or witloof chicory, and the red chicory, or radicchio, have been popular in Europe for many years and are becoming more so here.

To force chicory, sow the seeds outdoors in spring or early summer — or later in areas with mild winters. Before the ground freezes hard, dig up the plants. If the roots have frozen somewhat, they will sprout more easily. Trim the leaves back to about 1 inch. Plant the roots close together 10 inches deep in containers filled with 18 to 20 inches of soft soil or sand. Cover with damp newspapers and place the containers in a dark spot, with a temperature around 50 to 60 degrees F. Water once a week. The roots will send up new shoots in three to five weeks, and the new, tightly bunched growth will be sweet and mild. It is ready to harvest when the tips start to show on top.

Some varieties, such as the hybrid green Zoom, were bred just for forcing. Others, like the Red Verona, form good self-blanching heads outdoors but are also suitable

for indoor forcing.

Rhubarb Before it will sprout, rhubarb must experience a good freeze, so dig the roots as late as possible in the fall. The best are large, two-year-old or three-year-old roots. Dig the roots up with a ball of soil around them and remove the leaves. Leave them for six weeks in a bucket, where they will be protected from rain and snow but still exposed to the cold, since a cold treatment is necessary. After six weeks, bring the roots, still packed with garden soil, into a warm place (55 to 60 degrees F.). It doesn't matter whether there is light or darkness. Water to keep the soil moist. Within one month, the plant will have sent up stalks large enough to harvest. The harvest can continue for four to eight weeks.

Roots forced indoors cannot be replanted in the garden the following season.

Blanching and forcing the shoots of chicory (Belgian endive) removes the bitter taste and leaves a mild and delicate vegetable.

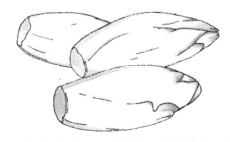

See also:
Hardiness zones/overwintering plants
p18
Hardy, half-hardy, tender plants
pp42–3 Hardening-off p44

Forcing bulbs p71
Unusual vegetables p122
Cold frames/overwintering fall crops
p145
Frost protection p147

be pulled up for ventilation, or the plastic may have ventilation slits in it (these tend to rip more easily). Ventilation is critical, since even on cool days, the temperature within the tunnel can get quite high. Tunnels will vary in how long they last. The plastic you use should be UV-treated so it doesn't break down quickly with exposure to the sun.

Reemay This relatively new registered polyester fabric allows light to pass through, but it traps the heat in. It is light enough to lay directly on the plants. All you have to do is weight the edges, leaving enough slack to allow the plants to push up the fabric as they grow. Since the material is porous, water will pass through, and the material will allow adequate air circulation. It comes in various widths.

Reemay is particularly good for protecting plants from pests (such as flea beetles) and can be left on all season. It keeps frost off the plants, but it may allow some damage as the plants are in direct contact with the fabric. It doesn't provide as much extra heat as the plastics, so it is not as good for night protection. Also, Reemay tends to break down quickly in bright sun and can become brittle when cold and frosted. Its life expectancy is one to several years.

When you have a row or plant cover in place, be sure to check soil moisture levels. Although most allow water in, they may not let in a sufficient amount. They also provide good conditions for weed growth, so you might want to use the row or plant cover in conjunction with mulch, which, if plastic, will also provide additional warmth for the soil.

Some of these protectors will keep out birds and can create an effective barrier to problematic insects, but remember that they will also keep out necessary pollinators for plants like melons and squash.

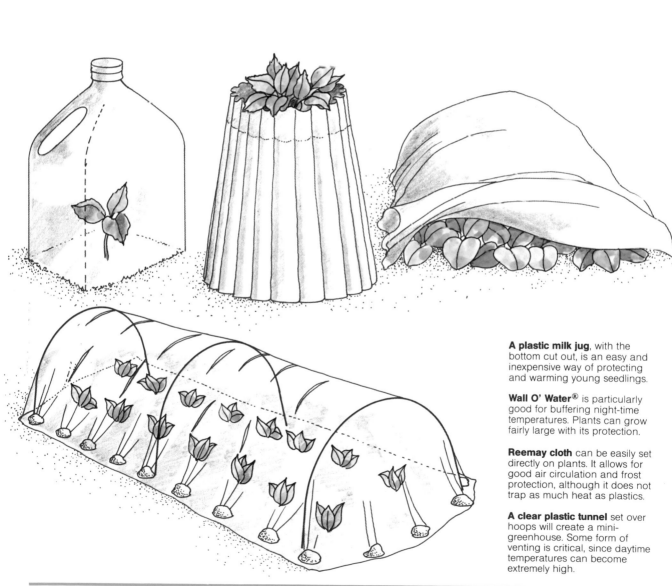

A plastic milk jug, with the bottom cut out, is an easy and inexpensive way of protecting and warming young seedlings.

Wall O' Water® is particularly good for buffering night-time temperatures. Plants can grow fairly large with its protection.

Reemay cloth can be easily set directly on plants. It allows for good air circulation and frost protection, although it does not trap as much heat as plastics.

A clear plastic tunnel set over hoops will create a mini-greenhouse. Some form of venting is critical, since daytime temperatures can become extremely high.

149

Resources

These listings include a sampling of companies and organizations that serve gardeners. For a current and more thorough sourcebook see *Gardening by Mail*, by Barbara J. Barton, available from Tusker Press, P.O. Box 597004, San Francisco, CA 94159. The book includes listings of companies offering seeds, nursery stock, tools, and supplies as well as listings of plant societies, trade associations, libraries, magazines, and books.

THE COOPERATIVE EXTENSION SERVICE

This is a government organization that provides farmers and home gardeners with a wealth of written information and advice. Since Extension offices are located in most counties of every state, they are useful for information on local gardening and are the best source of current information on appropriate pesticide use in your area. Most Extension offices also provide such services as soil testing and analysis, diagnosis of plant problems and plant identification. To contact your local Extension office, check under "Cooperative Extension", "Extension" or under the name of your county in the phonebook.

VEGETABLE AND FLOWER SEED CATALOGS

The following companies offer a good selection of varieties of common vegetable and herb seeds. Many also offer unusual herb seed, flower seed, special or imported varieties of vegetables, fruit trees, pest controls, soil amendments and garden equipment.

Burpee (W. Atlee) Co.
300 Park Avenue
Warminster, PA 18974
— Includes supplies, tools, bulbs, perennial plants

Comstock, Ferre & Co.
Box 125
Wethersfield, CT 06109
— Specializes in old varieties and new disease-resistant varieties

De Giorgi Co. Inc.
P.O. Box 413
Council Bluffs, IA 51502
— Includes many old and imported varieties

Harris Seeds
Moreton Farm
Rochester, NY 14624
— Includes supplies

Hastings
P.O. Box 4274
Atlanta, GA 30302
— Includes many Southern varieties

Johnny's Selected Seeds
P.O. Box 2580
Albion, Maine 04910
— Includes supplies. Specializes in varieties for short seasons.

Lagomarsino Seeds
5116 Folsom Blvd.
Sacramento, CA 95819
— Specializes in European vegetables, flowers.

Le Jardin du Gourmet
P.O. Box 44
West Danville, VT 05873
— Broad selection of European vegetables, herbs.

Lockhart Seeds
P.O. Box 1361
Stockton, CA 95201
— Specializes in seeds for central California.

Nichols Garden Nursery, Inc.
1190 No. Pacific Highway
Albany, OR 97321
— Specializes in varieties for the Northwest.

Park Seed Co.
P.O. Box 31
Greenwood, SC 29646
— Large variety of seeds, many for Southern climates.

Porter & Son
P.O. Box 104
Stephensville, TX 76401
— Wide selection of seeds for the South.

Seed Savers Exchange
P.O. Box 70
Decorah, IA 52101
— Yearly seed book lists seed available from member gardeners. They also sell a seed inventory list of commercial sources for many old varieties.

Stokes Seed Company
P.O. Box 548
Buffalo, NY 14240
— Large selection. Includes supplies.

NURSERIES/FRUIT

Most of the companies listed below offer plants (not seed) of small fruits, tree fruits and nut trees, unless otherwise indicated.

California Nursery Co.
P.O. Box 2278
Fremont, CA 94536
— Broad selection of fruit and nut trees for the West Coast.

Eastville Plantation
P.O. Box 337
Bogart, GA 30622
— Specializes in Southern varieties.

Edible Landscaping
Rt. 2, Box 343A
Afton, VA 22920
— Includes many unusual fruits.

Farmer Seed and Nursery
P.O. Box 129
Faribault, MN 55021
— Large selection of general nursery stock.

Dean Foster Nurseries
P.O. Box 127
Hartford, MI 49057
— Hardy fruits and nuts. Very large selection of small fruits.

Kelly Bros. Nursery
Dansville, NY 11437
— General nursery stock.

Nourse Farms
Box 485 RFD
South Deerfield, MA 01373
— Strawberries, raspberries, blackberries.

Henry Leuthardt Nurseries
Montauk Hwy., Box 666
East Moriches, NY 11940

Specializes in older
varieties, dwarfs,
espaliers.

Miller Nurseries
5060 West Lake Road
Canandaigua, NY 14424

Broad selection of fruits,
nuts, berries, ornamentals.

**N.Y. State Fruit Testing
Association**
Geneva, NY 14456

Features trial varieties.

Pacific Berry Works
P.O. Box 54
Bow, WA 98232

A selection of berries for
the West Coast.

Pacific Tree Farms
4301 Lynwood Drive
Chula Vista, CA 92010

Tropical and subtropical
fruits, nuts, ornamentals.

Peaceful Valley Farm Supply
11173 Peaceful Valley Road
Nevada City, CA 92010

Fruit and nut varieties for
the West Coast. Some
organically grown.

Raintree Nursery
391 Butts Road
Moreton, WA 98356

Fruit varieties for the
Northwest; edible land-
scaping information

Stark Brothers Nurseries
Louisiana, MO 63353

Fruits, nuts, ornamentals,
roses.

NURSERIES/ORNAMENTALS

Included in this listing are companies that offer
herbaceous perennials, bulbs, roses, shrubs and trees.

Antique Rose Emporium
Route 5, Box 143
Brenham, TX 77833

Old garden roses.

Bluestone Perennials
7211 Middle Ridge Road
Madison, OH 44057

Hardy perennials.

Busse Gardens
635 E. 7th Street
R 2, Box 13
Cokato, MN 55321

Hardy perennials.

**Clifford's Perennial
& Vine**
Rt. 2 Box 320
East Troy, WI 53120

Perennials

Dutch Gardens, Inc.
P.O. Box 400
Montvale, NJ 07645

Large selection of popular
hybrid Dutch bulbs.

Forestfarm
990 Tetherow Road
Williams, OR 97544

Western native plants,
herbaceous perennials,
trees, shrubs.

Foxborough Nursery
3611 Miller Road
Street, MD 21154

Dwarf and unusual conifers,
shrubs, trees

Heritage Rose Gardens
40350 Wilderness Road
Branscomb, CA 95417

Good selection of old roses.

Musser Forests, Inc.
Route 119 North
P.O. Box 340
Indiana, PA 15710–0340

Wide selection of trees,
shrubs, and ground covers.

Powell's Gardens
Old Highway 70
Route 2
Princeton, NC 27569

Large selection of
perennials, dwarf conifers,
shrubs.

Quality Dutch Bulbs
50 Lake Drive
P.O. Box 225
Hillsdale, NJ 07642

Broad selection of hybrid
bulbs.

River's Edge Farm
Rt. 4, Box 228A
Gloucester, VA 23061

Offers daffodils for
naturalizing

**Roses of Yesterday and
Today**
802 Brown's Valley Road
Watsonville
CA 95076–0398

Broad selection of old and
modern roses

Spring Hill Nurseries Co.
6523 No. Galena Rd.
Peoria, IL 61632

Wide selection of
perennials, ground covers,
flowering shrubs.

Tripple Brook Farm
37 Middle Road
Southampton, MA 01073

Northeastern native plants,
hardy bamboos, perennials,
flowering shrubs.

Wayside Gardens
Hodges, SC 29695

Large selection of ornamental
trees, shrubs, perennials,
roses, wildflowers.

White Flower Farm
Rte. 63
Litchfield, CT 06759–0050

Large selection of
perennials and shrubs.

The Wildflower Source
P.O.d Box 312
Fox Lake, IL 60020

Hardy native wildflowers.

WATER GARDENING SUPPLIERS

These companies offer a range of pool, pond and bog
plants, fish and supplies.

Lilypons Water Gardens
6885 Lilypons Road
P.O. Box 10
Lilypons, MD 21717–0010

Van Ness Water Gardens
2460 North Euclid
Upland, CA 91786

Paradise Water Gardens
14 May Street
Whiteman, MA 02382

GARDEN TOOLS AND SUPPLIES

These companies offer a range of hand tools, power equipment, soil amendments, fertilizers, pest controls and other gardening aids.

Clapper's
1125 Washington St.
West Newton, MA 02165
Tools, supplies, garden furniture.

Garden Way
102nd St. & 9th Ave.
Troy, NY 12180
Rototillers and other equipment.

Gardener's Supply Co.
128 Intervale Road
Burlington, VT 05401
Broad selection of tools, equipment, organic soil amendments and pest controls.

A.M. Leonard's
Piqua, OH 45356
Broad selection of tools and supplies for home and commercial gardeners.

Mellinger's, Inc.
2310 W. South Range Rd.
North Lima, OH 45356
Tools, supplies, biological pest controls

Necessary Trading Co.
Box 305
New Castle, VA 24127
Large selection of organic insect controls, tools, supplies.

Walter F. Nicke
P.O. Box 667
Hudson, NY 12534
Tools, gadgets, supplies — many imported.

Ringer Research
6860 Flying Cloud Dr.
Eden Prairie, MN 55344
Large selection of organic garden and lawn care products and supplies

Smith & Hawken
25 Corte Madera
Mill Valley, CA 94941
Large selection of garden tools and supplies. Many imported.

GREENHOUSES AND GREENHOUSE SUPPLIES

Four Seasons Greenhouses
425 Smith Street
Farmingdale, NY 11735

Greenhouse Specialities Co.
9849 Kimker Lane
St. Louis, MO 63127–1599

Gro-Tek
RFD 1, Box 518 A
South Berwick, ME 03908

Northern Greenhouse Sales
P.O. Box 42B
Neche, ND 58265

Pacific Coast Greenhouse Mfg. Co.
8360 Industrial Ave
Cotati, CA 94928

SOIL TESTING SERVICES

Before sending in a soil sample, ask the lab about types of testing available, costs and sampling instructions.

Cooperative Extension
Most local Extension offices and Land Grant Colleges provide basic soil testing services.

Biosystem Consultants
P.O. Box 43
Lorane, OR 97451

Peaceful Valley Farm Supply
11173 Peaceful Valley Rd.
Nevada City, CA 95959

Soil and Plant Laboratory
P.O. Box 1648
Bellevue, WA 98009

Woods End Laboratory
Orchard Hill Road,
RFD Box 128
Temple, ME 04984

LANDSCAPING PLANNING/GARDEN DESIGN

Laura D. Eisener Landscape Design
59 Maple Street
Waltham, MA 02154
Garden bulletins available on aspects of garden design

Sun Designs
P.O. Box 206
Delafield, WI 53018–0206
Information on garden structure designs.

Garden Design Magazine
American Society of
Landscape Architects
2733 Connecticut Ave. NW
Washington, D.C. 20009
Residential garden design periodical.

GARDENING ORGANIZATIONS

These organizations offer a range of publications, educational programs and opportunities for community involvement in the area of gardening and general horticulture. They are national organizations, many of which have local chapters. Contact national headquarters for information regarding publications and membership.

American Rose Society
Box 30,000
Shreveport, LA 71130

The Garden Club of America
598 Madison Avenue
New York, NY 10022

Men's Garden Clubs of America
5560 Merle Hay Road
Johnston, IA 50131

National Council of State Garden Clubs, Inc.
4401 Magnolia Avenue
St. Louis, MO 63110

National Gardening Association
180 Flynn Avenue
Burlington, Vermont 05401

MAGAZINES

"The Avant Gardener"
Horticultural Data
Processors
P.O. Box 489
New York, NY 10028

Summarizes news and new information on all phases of gardening.

"Flower & Garden"
Modern Handcraft, Inc.
4251 Pennsylvania Avenue
Kansas City, MO 64111

A general interest gardening magazine, with articles on all phases of home gardening.

"Garden"
The Garden Society
The New York Botanical
Garden
Bronx, NY 10458–5126

A general interest magazine covering gardening, botany, art, agriculture and history.

"Garden Design"
(See Landscape Planning)

Covers residential garden design.

"Horticulture"
Subscription Department
P.O. Box 2595
Boulder, CO 80323

A general interest magazine, devoted to all aspects of horticulture, focusing largely on ornamentals.

"National Gardening"
National Gardening Assoc.
180 Flynn Avenue
Burlington, VT 05401

A general interest magazine devoted primarily to fruit and vegetable gardening; seed sharing; horticultural news and public gardening program coverage.

**"Rodale's Organic
Gardening"**
Rodale Press, Inc.
33 East Minor Street
Emmaus, PA 18049

Devoted primarily to practical ideas and sources for organic fruit and vegetable growing.

"Pacific Horticulture"
Pacific Horticultural
Foundation
P.O. Box 485
Berkeley, CA 94701

A general interest magazine devoted to all aspects of Pacific Coast horticulture

"Plants & Gardens"
Brooklyn Botanical Garden
1000 Washington Avenue
Brooklyn, NY 11225

Each issue covers one specific gardening subject in depth.

"Texas Gardener"
P.O. Box 9005
Waco, TX 76714

A general interest magazine covering all phases of home gardening in that climate.

Index of questions

TREES AND HEDGES

VEGETABLES

FRUITS

SEASON EXTENSION

Index

Acknowledgments

AUTHOR'S ACKNOWLEDGMENTS
It gives me great pleasure to express appreciation to my friend and colleague Geoffrey Smith for so carefully reading the script and making a number of very valuable suggestions. I must dissociate him, nonetheless, from any errors of fact that may remain, and I certainly did not ask him to agree with all my opinions; especially those regarding *Rhus typhina*.

PUBLISHER'S ACKNOWLEDGMENTS
The publishers of *Gardener's Questions Answered* are especially grateful to Dr Brent Elliott and Barbara Collecott of the Royal Horticultural Society Lindley Library for their invaluable assistance.

ARTISTS
l = left, r = right, t = top, c = centre, b = bottom

Norman Bancroft Hunt: 1, 2bl, 4, 12, 13b, 18, 22–3, 24b, 28t, 20l, 44–5, 65, 76–8, 88–9, 90, 92–7, 113b, 119r, 120, 129, 132, 133t, 141c, 142r, 144–5, 149.

Jim Channell / Linden Artists: 42, 43, 48–51.

Jeanne Corville: 2br, 2tr, 38, 54–5, 59, 70, 72, 73b, 74–5, 98l, 102–3, 105r, 108, 110–13, 116, 117t, 134–5, 140, 143.

Karen Daws / John Craddock: 6, 33, 98r, 99, 104, 121, 123l, 124, 125t, b, 141t, 142l.

Tony Graham: 10c, 25, 29l, 66r, 67, 87r, 100, 103t, 133b, 146.

Carole Johnson: 2c, 21r, 34–5, 56–7, 64, 66l, 68–9, 79, 81–2, 84–5, 87b, 106–7, 109, 115, 130–1, 139.

Dee McLean: 19, 28b, 29r, 30.

Liz Pepperal: 20c, 26t, 31, 46–7, 52–3, 58l, 60–3, 71, 73t, 80, 86, 105l, 114, 117b, 118l, 123r, 125c, 126–7, 138, 147–8.

Jane Pickering: 2tl, 8r, 10l, 13c, 14t, 16–17, 24t, 26b, 27, 32, 39, 40–1, 83, 136–7.

Clive Spong: 8l, 14b.